SATISFACTION
GUARANTEED

ALSO BY SUSAN STRASSER

Never Done: A History of American Housework

SATISFACTION GUARANTEED

THE MAKING OF THE AMERICAN MASS MARKET

SUSAN STRASSER

PANTHEON BOOKS 🏛 NEW YORK

Library of Congress Cataloging-in-Publication Data

Strasser, Susan, 1948–
Satisfaction guaranteed : the making of the
American mass market / Strasser
p.   cm.
Bibliography: p.
ISBN 0-394-55292-X
1. Advertising—United States—Psychological
aspects—History.   2. Consumers—United States
—History.   3. Sales promotion—United States—
History.   4. Brand name products—United States
—History.
I. Title
HF5813.U6S79 1990 659.1′042′0973—dc20   89-42675

Book Design by Fearn Cutler
Manufactured in the United States of America
First Edition

For my father, with love and thanks

CONTENTS

IIIIㄷ〕IIIIIIIIIIIIㄷ〕IIIIIIIIIIIIㄷ〕IIII

ACKNOWLEDGMENTS

IIIIIIIIIC3IIIIIIIIIIIC3IIIIIIIIIIIC3IIIIIIIIIIIC3IIIIIIIIIIIC3IIIIIIII

I SPENT FIVE YEARS RESEARCHING AND DEVELOPING THE IDEAS IN this book under ideal and privileged conditions on both coasts. As a result, I have a long list of people to thank.

I was fortunate to receive enough financial and institutional support to spend two years working full-time on this project in Cambridge, Massachusetts. Money and indirect costs came from The Evergreen State College, the National Endowment for the Humanities through a program administered by the American Council of Learned Societies, the Bunting Institute at Radcliffe College, the Newcomen Society in North America, and the Harvard Graduate School of Business Administration. I am grateful to Joyce Antler, Jessie Bernard, Dolores Hayden, Otis Pease, Barbara Smith, and William R. Taylor, whose support of my work helped to make these grants possible.

In the "climate of expectations" at the Bunting Institute, I lived among more than forty creative women, with many of whom I am still sharing ideas. I am grateful to all of them for a Cinderella year, but especially to Teresa Bernardez, Ann Bookman, Kate Daniels, Jaimy Gordon, Marianne Hirsch, Margaret McKenna, Elaine Spatz-Rabinowitz, Gail Reimer, Jane Sharp, Valerie Smith, and Irene Vasquez. For help, intellectual stimulation, and friendship at the Harvard Business School, I owe thanks to Barbara Ankeny, Alfred Chandler, Patricia Durkin, William Lazonick, Patricia O'Brian, Edith Pripas, and Richard Tedlow. I am particularly grateful to John Quelch, who allowed me to constitute a mysterious presence in his consumer marketing course, and to Thomas K. McCraw, whose continuing support inspires me to work to deserve it.

Both before and after my time in Cambridge, I worked on ideas that framed my inquiry and that made their way into this book with and for many students and faculty colleagues at The Evergreen State College: John Aikin, Margo Boyer, Virginia Darney, Jack Gillis, Nancy Koppelman, Mark Levensky, Jean Mandeberg, Alan Nasser, Janet Nudelman, Jim Park, Matt Smith, Randy Tillery, the late Irwin Zuckerman, and other students in "Foundations of American Enterprise" and "1984." Melissa Roberts, my research assistant and stalwart supporter, deserves special mention. Thad Curtz displayed more than the usual level of collegial interest and contributed important insights. Dee Van Brunt gave genuine meaning to the phrase "administrative support."

No historian can produce or survive without considerable help from librarians and archivists. I am above all grateful to Ernestine Kimbro, Andrea Winship, and the interlibrary loan staff at Evergreen. Florence Lathrop at Baker Library, Cynthia Swank at J. Walter Thompson, and Ed Rider at Procter and Gamble made materials available to me that I could not have known about without them. Lucia Tsai provided research assistance at the Harvard libraries. And this would simply be some other book without the many illustrations from the Smithsonian Institution's Collection of Advertising History; my thanks to Vanessa Broussard, John Fleckner, and above all to Lorene Mayo, who seemed always willing to do me one more favor, always able to call upon her phenomenal knowledge of her collection to help me find something.

A number of people read and commented on entire drafts of the manuscript. Susan Porter Benson, Nancy Koppelman, Tom

McCraw, Roland Marchand, and Bethany Weidner corrected errors, contributed ideas large and small, and, as if their willingness to take the time to do it were not compliment enough, cheered me on.

Sara Bershtel read more than one entire draft. Her work, people kept telling me, was the kind editors don't do any more. I wouldn't know; it was the kind she did. Time and again, she demanded that every sentence be both comprehensible to her and true to my own sense of the book and of the facts. Despite the large number of sentences, she remained kind and cheerful to the end. I am very grateful. Thanks also to my agent, Mary Evans, and to the others at Pantheon on whose skills and care this book and I have depended, especially Fearn Cutler, Jeanne Morton, and Julia Bogardus.

As always, I got by with a lot of help from my friends during these years. Many people crossed and recrossed the boundaries between friendship and professional help and are listed above for specific contributions, but many others' love and support have made my work possible. Some of them have criticized pieces and stages of the manuscript, provided hospitality during research trips, lived with me, mopped my brow during the fevered times, helped read galleys, and otherwise made direct contributions to this book, but are not listed above. These include Laura Anker, Walter Harp, Madeleine Helbraun, Janet Hesslein, Max Holland, Lewis Hyde, Robyn Lipner, Tedd McCann, Lisa Marshall, Ginger Marshall, Loretta Neumann, Pamela Schick, Wendy Schofield, Laura Shapiro, Bill Shields, Stanley Sloss, Karen Smith, Pam Solo, Patsy Vigderman, and Larry Wolken. Finally, many but not all of the people on these pages were members of the hard-disk gang, all of whom contributed more than hardware and continue to sustain me.

SATISFACTION GUARANTEED

CHAPTER 1

IIIIC3IIIIIIIIIIC3IIIIIIIIIIIC3IIIII

AMERICAN
PIE

IN JANUARY OF 1912, THE PROCTER AND GAMBLE COMPANY OF CIN-
cinnati, Ohio, introduced Crisco, a solid vegetable shortening
that it described to the readers of the *Ladies' Home Journal* and
at least four other popular national magazines as "An Absolutely New Product, A Scientific Discovery Which will Affect
Every Kitchen in America." The unusually wordy ad, which had
much the same format as *Journal* editorial matter, explained that
two years previously, "a new and heretofore unknown food"
had been "discovered." Kept secret at first during company
testing, the product had then been provided to professional
cooks and domestic science teachers for further experimenta-
tion before its public debut. "The tests were successful," the
ad's first paragraph read, "and proved that the food was *ideal,*
something that the American housewife had always needed."

The rest of the advertisement concentrated on the product's
advantages, telling little more about the most elaborate and
expensive development process any consumer product had ever
been through. The experiments that produced Crisco had
begun in 1905, supported by capital from Procter and Gamble's
several successful brands of soap, including the well-known
Ivory. In part, the research was an attempt to generate a product

Crisco makes white cake equal to angel food in whiteness

An Absolutely New Product

Foods fried in Crisco are light and flaky

A Scientific Discovery Which will Affect Every Kitchen in America

TWO years ago, a new and heretofore unknown food was discovered. This discovery remained a secret while the food was submitted to every possible test. Then, within the last year, it was furnished to a large number of chefs and domestic science teachers to experiment with. The tests were successful and proved that the food was *ideal*, something that the American housewife had always needed.

The many advantages of this new food may seem unbelievable to women who never have had an opportunity to use it, but they are now known, proven facts in domestic science schools and in hotel kitchens, where cooking is a science or business.

This product is purely vegetable and is to be used in cooking wherever you now use animal fats, such as butter or lard. There is not a meal served in your home in the preparation of which Crisco, the new product for frying, for shortening and for general cooking, is not needed. It is impossible to give here *all* the advantages of Crisco, but the ones which come closest to home are outlined.

This Seems Impossible Until You Do it Yourself

YOU can fry fish in Crisco, and the Crisco will not absorb the fish odor! You then can use the same Crisco for frying potatoes without imparting to them the slightest fish flavor. Heretofore, you may have hesitated to fry fish because it meant the wasting of so much lard. With Crisco, not a drop need be thrown away; it can be used and re-used, which makes it very economical. Will you not make this fish and potato test and learn for yourself that it is possible to fry food after food in the same Crisco without imparting to one food the flavor of another?

Dry Frying — A Radical Change

THERE is another unusual feature of Crisco which makes a radical change in frying. You have noticed that the quicker you fry, the better results you secure. All cook-books say "Heat your fat smoking hot." Lard smokes and burns at 400 degrees, and any temperature above this point is not practical, owing to the discoloration and the quantity of smoke given off. You can heat Crisco very much hotter than lard (455°) and it will not burn nor smoke. To realize fully the advantages of this high frying point of Crisco, cook potatoes in it.

Cut the slices a quarter of an inch in thickness; soak them in cold water; then thoroughly dry them in a cloth.

Heat the Crisco very hot and put in just a few potatoes at a time.

Do not put in too many at once, or there will cool the Crisco and you will lose the benefit of its high frying point.

Crisco fries so quickly that a crust forms instantly and prevents absorption, thus the full flavor is retained and the potatoes are more healthful than when soaked with grease. The outside is a rich, golden brown and the inside is light and mealy, like a baked potato. No black specks spoil your food, and no "frying odor" permeates your dining-room and kitchen. When you use Crisco for frying, the improvement is so marked that you can see the difference at once.

Have You Hesitated to Eat Pastry?

FROM a standpoint of health, the discovery of Crisco is of great value. Pie has been called the great American dessert, and many have eaten it *in spite of the fact that they believed it to be indigestible.* Crisco makes foods more digestible. Doctors are the strongest advocates that Crisco has. Many physicians personally are recommending it to their patients, because the vegetable ingredients, of which it is made, are more readily assimilated than are animal fats. They know that Crisco has great nutritive value, and since its discovery you can eat freely foods that heretofore you could not digest.

A New Standard

UNTIL Crisco was discovered, butter was the standard for good cake-making. Crisco gives a richer, finer flavored cake than can be made with butter. Butter is nearly *one-fifth* water, while Crisco contains no moisture, but is *all* shortening. Cake made with Crisco may be kept longer without loss of its original fine flavor and soft texture. Both table and cooking butter vary in flavor and richness during the different seasons. Crisco never varies. There is but one quality — the best. This unfailing richness, this absolute uniformity enable you to make your cake delicious with regularity. Your results in cake-making do not vary in the exasperating way they have done heretofore, so you never waste foods because they do not "turn out" well. You get actually better results than with butter, *at about half the cost.* Crisco makes as fine and wholesome a cake as rich cream, with an equally delicate and delicious flavor.

Butter Nearly One-fifth Water

Every Woman is Interested in This

FROM the viewpoint of economy, Crisco, the new product for cooking, excels. Foods fried in Crisco absorb less, consequently there is more Crisco left. In deep frying, it is apparent how little Crisco is used — how much of it is left, as one woman said, so little Crisco was absorbed that it seemed to her as though she had just as much when she finished as when she started to fry. This is another reason why Crisco is so economical.

Crisco also keeps excellently. It does not become strong. It is so clean and pure in origin and manufacture that it stays sweet and fresh. Crisco is never sold in bulk, but is put up in immaculate packages, perfectly protected from dust and store odors. No hands touch it, no unsanitary paddles nor wooden boats. You are sure that every package of Crisco is wholesome. Dip out a spoonful and look at it. You will like its very appearance, for it is a pure cream white, with a fresh, pleasant aroma. It is crisp and flaky, just the proper consistency to make it ideal for creaming in cake or for working into pie crust.

Lard Two-thirds Gone

Crisco Two-thirds Left

THESE are strong statements, but they are facts which you can prove for yourself. Give your grocer an order for a package today. It requires no experimenting — you use it where you now use butter or lard, and in just the same way. Make the fish and potato test; try it for "dry" frying; try Crisco pastry, Crisco white cake, best of all try Crisco biscuits, and you will become a Crisco enthusiast and realize why this discovery will affect every family in America.

On request, we shall mail a fully illustrated booklet, showing many other advantages of Crisco, the new, and heretofore unknown, strictly vegetable product for frying, for shortening and for general cooking. Address Dept. D.

Sold by grocers at 25c the package except in the Far West

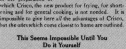

Fry Fish, then Potatoes in the same Crisco. The Potatoes will not Taste of the Fish.

For Cooking CRISCO — Use wherever you would use Butter or Lard

Crisco—Better than butter for cooking

Crisco is being placed in the grocery stores as rapidly as possible. If your own grocer does not yet keep it, you probably will find it in one of the other stores in your neighborhood; if not, we will send you by mail or express, charges prepaid, a full sized package for 25c. If you order from us, write plainly your name and address, and also let us have the name of your grocer. Not more than one package will be sent direct from us to any one customer. THE PROCTER & GAMBLE CO., Dept. D, Cincinnati, Ohio.

The first Crisco advertisement, from the *Ladies' Home Journal*, 1912.

that would assure P & G its supply of cottonseed oil, which it was already using to make soap. Although the company owned and operated several cottonseed-crushing mills and had contracted for the total output of others, the market as a whole was influenced by four corporations. The American Cottonseed Oil Company and the Southern Cottonseed Oil Company dominated the selling; Armour and Company and the N. K. Fairbank Company, both of which manufactured cooking fats compounded with lard, dominated the buying. By creating and marketing new products that used large quantities of cottonseed oil, Procter and Gamble could achieve not only financial growth but a more powerful position in purchasing its raw materials. For five years, under top-secret conditions, the laboratories worked to solve the technical difficulties of producing an all-vegetable solid fat in commercial quantities. In 1910, they achieved a patentable product.

Created in the laboratory and advertised as a replacement for the animal fats customarily rendered as part of the slaughtering process, Crisco may be understood as an artifact of a culture in the making, a culture founded on new technologies and structured by new personal habits and new economic forms. Many historians have described the forty or so years on either side of the turn of the twentieth century as a period of major change, a new stage of economic development. During this time, the United States completed the transition from an agricultural to an industrial society, while modern organizational systems and advanced technologies for production and distribution transformed industry itself. Countless new products—some of them packaged versions of goods people had used for centuries, others completely new—may be understood as material representations of that transition and its effects on American daily life.

Since colonial times, wealthy urbanites had eaten from ceramics made in English factories, and more typical Americans had bought certain manufactured products during much of the nineteenth century. Machine-made textiles had overtaken homespun in economic importance before the Civil War, and most households owned cast-iron stoves by 1880. But most people still grew some of their food or bought it from the grower, and almost everybody still wore some homemade clothing.

During the next thirty years, Americans everywhere and of all classes began to eat, drink, clean with, wear, and sit on products made in factories. Toothpaste, corn flakes, chewing gum, safety razors, and cameras—things nobody had ever made at home or in small crafts shops—provided the material basis for new habits and the physical expression of a genuine break from earlier times. While the population almost doubled between 1880 and 1910, American industry produced seven times as much pig iron, nine times as much paper, fourteen times as much cotton-seed oil, and nearly four times as many railroad freight cars to transport all the new goods made from these basic materials. Without land for gardens or time for handcrafts, even poor urban workers joined an expanding market for manufactured goods. The many people who still lived far from stores shopped from the Sears and Montgomery Ward catalogues, which pictured nearly every kind of manufactured product America had to offer.

Many of these goods came from new kinds of factories, organized on the principles of "continuous-process" or "flow" production. Decades before Henry Ford and his men applied continuous-process principles to the 1913 Model T in the first assembly line, companies packed meat, brewed beer, and canned vegetables using conveyer systems, rollers, and gravity slides that sent materials through the production process automatically, in a continuous stream. The idea had been used in flour milling for over a century. During the 1880s, inventors developed new machinery that made flow production possible in the manufacture of soap, cigarettes, matches, breakfast cereals, canned goods, and many other products. As a result, factories could process massive batches of raw materials.

New techniques for national marketing emerged in tandem with the mass-produced products they promoted. People who had never heard of toothpaste had to be told that they needed

This automatic can-making process, 1885, an example of flow production, was organized by Edwin Norton, who was later instrumental in both the American Can Company and the Continental Can Company.

———————————————————————|||〔〕|||———————————————————————

it; the very ideas of chewing gum and flashlights had to be introduced to a population accustomed to goods made at home or by craftspeople. The companies that made them, like all marketers, promoted their own products, Crisco or Colgate's. Like all marketers in new product categories, they also had to sell the category, packaged cereal or safety razors. And as the creators of the first national market for manufactured consumer products, these companies faced a further task. A population accustomed to homemade products and unbranded merchandise had to be converted into a national market for standardized, advertised, brand-named goods in general.

This process had been under way for three decades when Procter and Gamble introduced Crisco in 1912. The new shortening appeared near the end of a major transition in American marketing, and in its fundamental principles its marketing campaign more closely resembles a modern one than it does Procter and Gamble's earliest attempts to sell Ivory soap. The Ivory-selling efforts were hardly a "campaign." The product itself had been created not by years of development but by accident: the first floating soap came from a vat that was stirred too long. Similarly, the marketing procedure lacked the careful design that would characterize the company's later endeavors. For ten years after its first Ivory advertisement in 1881, the company made only sporadic use of its slogans, "99$^{44}/_{100}$% Pure" and "It Floats"; it advertised Ivory in a variety of periodicals, sponsored poetry contests, and offered prints suitable for framing, without a developed plan or a definable set of marketing principles. Harley Procter, the son of one of the company's founders, was committed to advertising, but had to contend with other, more reluctant partners. Ivory was a remarkable success, however, providing a model for other P & G products and for other national marketers. From the 1880s onward, American companies "discovered" products and experimented with national marketing strategies that would turn those products into profits as quickly as possible. They examined each other's successes and failures and, in consort with an emerging advertising profession, began to articulate principles and design marketing programs.

As Procter and Gamble turned from product development to creating a coordinated marketing strategy that would develop the market for Crisco, it could rely not only upon its own experience but on the collective practice of national marketers. The company had particular lessons to learn from an important competitor, the N. K. Fairbank Company. Makers of the highly successful Fairy soap and Gold Dust washing powder, Fairbank had recently failed with Cottolene, a shortening made of cottonseed oil mixed with animal fat that it had advertised widely for a number of years. Perhaps a public still conscious of the controversy over conditions in food factories that had stirred Progressive reformers and culminated in the 1906 Pure Food and Drug Act found it even harder to believe that a soap company could produce safe food; perhaps cooks were satisfied with lard, butter, and such ethnic preferences as olive oil and chicken fat. Procter and Gamble executives could not know the precise

TRY COTTOLENE

Manufactured by
N.K. Fairbank & Co. CHICAGO
ILL

ST LOUIS.   NEW YORK.   BOSTON.   MONTREAL.

A Cottolene trade card. Small lithographs like this were packed in with products or distributed by retailers before the turn of the century. Cottolene, manufactured by an important Procter and Gamble competitor, had failed despite wide publicity, a few years before Crisco's introduction.

causes of the Cottolene failure, but they understood that their new product would not sell itself.

At the end of April 1911, the company's executive committee met in William Procter's office to vote on the name and the label design. They approved a package incorporating the company's moon-and-stars logo and substituted "Crisco" for "Krispo," a name they had adopted the month before, but on which a Chicago cracker manufacturer had a prior claim. They then turned the product over to Stanley Resor, who had left Procter and Collier, the company's own advertising agency, to establish a Cincinnati office for J. Walter Thompson. Resor assigned copywriting responsibility to Helen Lansdowne, the woman he was later to marry and with whom he would acquire both financial and administrative control of this major New York advertising firm; Lansdowne would become the first woman in the Advertising Hall of Fame. Procter and Gamble was so concerned about marketing Crisco that the board of directors for the first time opened its meetings to a woman. Five times during 1911, Lansdowne took the train from New York to Cincinnati to represent the agency and "answer questions from the woman's point of view."

Product testing continued, now outside the company laboratories. University-based food researchers received samples for testing and recipe development; the company later quoted these scientists and home economists, testifying to Crisco's purity and goodness. The product made its first public appearance at a summer party for P & G employees. Like the Cincinnati clubwomen who soon began attending "Crisco teas," the workers carried home full-sized (one-and-a-half-pound) samples of the product. In October, Cincinnati's Burnet House Hotel and Queen City Club adopted the shortening; they were eventually followed by Chesapeake and Ohio Railway dining cars and New York City's Lüchow's Restaurant. During these tests, the company continued to refine the product, altering the formula in response to complaints that it went rancid.

Meanwhile, Resor and Lansdowne tested seven or eight different sales-promotion plans simultaneously. In one city, they tried newspaper advertising; in another, nothing but streetcar ads or outdoor posters or store demonstrations. In some cities, house-to-house canvassers sold the product; in others, salesmen courted retailers in conjunction with a house-to-house campaign. A specially hired staff worked on a more general analysis of the shortening market, investigating the competition and the uses of various products.

In December of 1911, a month before the first national advertising, the company sent packages containing three to six full-sized cans to every grocer in the United States, with a letter describing the forthcoming campaign. "We want you to have

Crisco in stock, so that you can supply the first demand this advertising will create among your customers," one such letter read. "Sell the six cans, and then order what further supply you need from your jobber." "Crisco is being placed in the grocery stores as rapidly as possible," the January magazine ad told the grocers' customers. "If your own grocer does not yet keep it, you probably will find it in one of the other stores in your neighborhood." For the first few months, shoppers who failed to obtain Crisco through the stores could buy a package (but only one) direct from Procter and Gamble, for twenty-five cents and the name of the offending grocer. By the end of 1915, the company could report in a *Saturday Evening Post* advertisement that "through the length and breadth of the country, in big stores and little, Crisco is now a staple."

During those first four years, the company promoted Crisco extensively and continuously, not only advertising in national magazines but enlisting grocer support. Cooperating storekeepers wrote letters to their charge customers, enclosing booklets about the shortening and offering to add Crisco to the delivery order. "Just let us send you a small package today on our recommendation," a Dallas form letter read. "Then see if it doesn't change completely your ideas of fried foods." A Rochester, New York merchant sent his letter on a printed folder supplied by the company, picturing a black cook displaying a plateful of biscuits. "We have seldom had anything that has met with such immediate success," he wrote.

For several years, six Crisco demonstrators toured cities throughout the country from September through June, conducting week-long cooking schools. The schools were paid for by Procter and Gamble, arranged for by a P & G advance man, and cosponsored by local newspapers, which lent their names to the schools—the "*Herald* Cooking School"—and their columns to the new product. A pseudonymous writer for the Fort Smith, Arkansas *Southwest American,* for example, was much taken by demonstrator Mrs. Kate B. Vaughn, "a perfect dear" and a "woman's woman" who served her audience peas, lamb chops, potato nests, white cake, marshmallow pudding, and baking-powder biscuits. "Mrs. Vaughn used a new shortening for these biscuits and told why she used it," the writer declared, "all of which caused me to stop in at my grocer's and purchase a can of the stuff, which I tried with great success last night."

In its 1913 prospectus for newspaper publishers, the company asserted that the demonstrators downplayed product promotion. Although they did discuss Crisco, their lectures covered other topics as well. "For, if women believed the lecture was there merely to promote or advertise a trademarked article, they would not be so apt to come a second time," the company told the publishers. "The audience may or may not, however, believe that the manufacturer of Crisco remunerates the lecturer in some way for the endorsement she gives the product." Given that the endorsement involved handing out full-sized samples and Crisco recipe pamphlets, only the credulous would believe otherwise.

These pamphlets, illustrated with pictures of the demonstrators, published the results of a continuous process of recipe development that also enabled Procter and Gamble to furnish cookbooks through the mail. By June 1912, consumers could write for *Tested Crisco Recipes,* a free paperback with a hundred recipes and "the interesting story of Crisco's discovery and manufacture." Late in 1913, a new book appeared: *The Story of Crisco,* in a complimentary version with 250 recipes, and in a cloth-bound "quality edition" available for five 2-cent stamps. The latter, *A Calendar of Dinners,* suggesting 365 menus with 615 recipes, went through at least twenty-six editions by 1925. These books supplemented the company's other cooking instructions. Recipes appeared in Crisco advertising as early as April 1912, and an eight-page, circle-shaped recipe booklet was packed inside the lid of every can.

Other packaging innovations aimed the product at particular markets. Soon after a special ten-pound container was created for their compact dining-car kitchens, twenty-two railroads adopted Crisco. Another special package, advertised in the Yid-

Cover, *The Story of Crisco*, 1913. Procter and Gamble offered this free booklet through the mail.

dish media and sold in Jewish neighborhoods, bore the seals of Rabbi Lifsitz of Cincinnati and Rabbi Margolies of New York, who pronounced the contents kosher. Margolies, according to *The Story of Crisco,* "said that the Hebrew Race had been waiting 4,000 years for Crisco." By enabling immigrant cooks to bake American pie without lard, Crisco joined the forces of Americanization, a movement that enlisted many home economists and social workers who hoped to transform foreigners through their eating habits.

At the end of the first year of Crisco marketing, J. George Frederick, former editor of the widely read advertising industry weekly *Printers' Ink,* wrote that the campaign had established a new standard for modern marketing. In a *Printers' Ink* article entitled "Efficient Planning Before Advertising," he described the testing procedures, infusing his prose with the popular jargon of efficiency and scientific management. "Instead of filling the earth and the sky and all that therein is with flashes of publicity and grand hurrah," he maintained, Procter and Gamble "has in a final and authoritative manner indicated the maximum efficiency method of marketing and finding distribution for a new product."

The methods were not quite final; over the next seventy-five years, marketers developed more sophisticated techniques that employed technologies and systems undreamed of in 1912. Nonetheless, both the Crisco publicity and the campaign planning look strikingly modern. Today's marketers employ many of the same general planning principles and promotional techniques, although they apply them to television commercials and rely on computer-analyzed statistics. The testing and refining of the product formula, label, and marketing strategy continue, for Crisco and for other successful consumer products. The kosher packages and the dining-car marketing provide evidence of what is now called market segmentation and product positioning, with special packages, product formulas, and marketing campaigns aimed at particular groups of potential buyers. Late-twentieth-century consumers still receive free samples and read recipe suggestions in magazine advertising. And although little record remains of the Crisco teas, they probably sounded much like the focus groups that contemporary marketers convene.

Now as at the turn of the century, cans of Crisco and other everyday objects function as artifacts of culture: they represent and are embedded in networks and systems of human relationships. Even the most common mass-produced goods can take on meaning as souvenirs, gifts, or purchases made in somebody's company. Less obviously, household objects embody both the relationships and routines of private daily life and the social relationships of production and distribution. Though both will wash, a chunk of soap handmade from wood ashes and animal fat, used or sold directly by its maker, is an artifact distinct from a bar of Dial or Dove, labeled with its Universal Product Code and sold at the supermarket. Chemically dissimilar and made with tools and processes from separate eras, the two soaps incorporate quantitatively different amounts of human labor in qualitatively different forms: the handmade soap produced for use, the factory-made produced for wages. The uniformity of the modern soap hides the human involvement in its production. Its distribution depends on telephones, computers, refined fossil fuels, and the people who make those technologies possible. Cost accounting, antitrust law, stock-market fluctuations, and the whole panoply of contemporary financial procedures and government policies regulate both production and distribution of every bar.

New ways of relating to the objects of everyday life—the material culture of American society—developed along with this physical and economic landscape. During the decades around the turn of the century, branded, standardized products came to represent and embody the new networks and systems of production and distribution, the social relationships that brought people the things they used. Household routines involved making fewer things and purchasing more; consumption became a major part of the work of the household. Formerly *customers,* purchasing the objects of daily life from familiar craftspeople and storekeepers, Americans became *consumers.* They bought and used mass-produced goods as participants in a national market composed of masses of people associating with big, centrally organized, national-level companies. As they came to depend on complex goods from distant sources, they came to understand less about how things were made, how they worked, how they could be fixed.

This combination of private and public change amounted to nothing less than a major cultural shift that entailed new kinds of needs. Human needs, as the twentieth-century study of anthropology has established, are cultural constructs. They have their sources in—and affect—customs, ideas, attitudes, social organization, religion, environment, economic organization, material resources: in short, the elements of culture. Some people need yams and breadfruit, others Post Toasties and Kellogg's corn flakes. In the culture emerging at the turn of the

––––––––––––––––––––––––––––––|||€)|||––––––––––––––––––––––––––––––

Lazenby's Mercantile Store, Monroeville, Alabama, 1915. At stores like this, Americans found and bought the new merchandise made possible by mass production.

twentieth century, a culture increasingly organized around the mass production and marketing of consumer goods, new needs surfaced in tandem with new products and with the new ways of life that characterized urban industrial society.

The corporations that made and distributed mass-produced goods did not necessarily set out to create needs, nor did they do so in any straightforward way. Procter and Gamble made Crisco in order to sell it. The company employed home economists to develop recipes, but did not in fact care what consumers did with the product as long as they bought it. Its goal, in Thorstein Veblen's words, was the "quantity-production of customers," the making of consumer markets. Sometimes manufacturers produced needs among children for products that parents bought. Those with goods in established product categories put most of their marketing effort into producing a demand for a particular brand, not a need for the product itself.

The process that makes people into consumers amalgamates changing ideas, habits, technology, demographic trends, and many other facets of culture, few of which are controlled even by the most powerful marketers, who concentrate their efforts on perceiving and taking advantage of those changes. In marketing Crisco, Procter and Gamble courted women in Vermont and Arkansas whose mothers had churned and rendered their own fats; buying shortening for the first time, these women were making decisions about whether to buy lard from Armour or Swift, butter from some more local concern, or Crisco from P & G. But the product could be incorporated into a culture even without a direct appeal from the company. Marketing experts presumably never addressed the Yup'ik and Inupiaq women of Alaska, who adopted Crisco to use in a berry confection called, in Yup'ik, *akutaq,* formerly made from caribou fat or seal oil. On the other hand, cultural factors could also outweigh marketing efforts. Despite their size and the size of their advertising budgets, manufacturers' manipulative power was limited by ethnic, regional, and personal preferences.

Cultural shifts happen piecemeal, with new developments interacting in complex ways and exhibiting contradictions and incongruities that frustrate the historian's effort to tell a clear story of cause and effect or even to provide accurate generalizations. People create those shifts by living their lives, making decisions that they may consider trivial or wholly personal but that have critical effects in the aggregate. Housewives and storekeepers may not perceive changes in production and distribution even as they help to make them. Over the course of a long transition, they might recognize new practices and routines only in retrospect. As pioneer business historian Ralph Hower once wrote of nineteenth-century retailing, "Although men tended to cling to what seemed to be the normal practice at the moment, that 'normal' never stayed the same for long."

The foundation for the rapid transformation that accompanied mass production after 1880 had been laid throughout such a long period of change. Beginning before 1820 with the textiles of the industrial revolution, new products had come sooner to the growing cities than to the countryside, while in both rural and urban environments, wealthy people enjoyed more benefits from economic growth than did the poor. Business cycles brought depressions about every twenty years, each graver than the one before as more people depended on wages and manufactured products, and each slowing some new trends and generating others. Despite this uneven development, the general tendencies were apparent; analysts of household life began to comment on the transition from production to consumption around the time of the Civil War. As production moved out of households and artisans' shops and as the United States extended its territory to the west, an ever-expanding market for manufactured goods was not only an economic abstraction. At the crossroads general store and at Macy's, clerks and customers traded in an environment of constant change. New products from new companies—indeed, new kinds of products from new kinds of companies—found their way into those stores, and into people's homes and daily routines.

Still, some generalizations are possible about the "normal practice" for distributing manufactured goods through most of the nineteenth century. Regional manufacturers went into business, established relationships with commission merchants or other wholesalers who disposed of their entire product, and regulated their businesses according to the demands of those middlemen. Most goods were sold as unbranded commodities, and the wholesalers wielded the power in the system, buying from the producer who offered white soap or tenpenny nails at the best price. Wholesalers dominated distribution. Often large firms with branch offices and warehouses in many cities, they controlled retailers' credit and held substantial power in regional financial circles. They took the major responsibility for extending the commercial system into frontier communities, sending salesmen into new territories by rail and stagecoach to drum up business for the new manufactured products. Wholesalers, in other words, controlled marketing in both of its senses: they did the physical work of distribution, and they took responsibility for product promotion.

The manufacturers who adopted the conveyor belts and gravity slides of flow production, however, needed to dispose of their huge outputs. Because mechanization demanded large amounts of capital, they sought predictability and control; they could not afford large overstocks and they wanted to free themselves from dependence on the wholesalers. They took their cue from a few industries, such as book publishing and patent medicines, where manufacturers courted customers directly, placing advertisements in magazines, selling by mail, or offering commissions to salesmen who went from house to house and put on public displays, the fabled medicine shows. Copyright and patent holders held monopolies on their products, and the largest and most successful flow producers imitated their strategy with brands. If retailers and wholesalers could purchase Uneeda Biscuits or Ivory soap only from the National Biscuit Company or Procter and Gamble, they would have to pay the manufacturers' prices.

Some of the mass producers had specific concerns that prompted them to take over part or all of the wholesalers' functions, establishing sales and delivery forces to deliver the products to retailers, or selling equipment in manufacturer-owned retail stores. Swift and the National Biscuit Company had to find ways to handle massive quantities of perishable goods. Singer, McCormick, and Remington had to provide instruction and repair services for tens and then hundreds of thousands of individual seamstresses, farmers, and typists. These corporations could not depend on the existing distribution system, assigning their products to various types of middlemen who might deliver stale crackers or fail to train salespeople.

Other successful new flow producers—companies like Procter and Gamble, the American Tobacco Company, and Libby, McNeill, and Libby—assumed less of the burden of distribution. Some established warehouses, but in general they entrusted the physical handling to wholesalers. Still, wholesalers' traveling salesmen might boost competitors' goods and encourage retailers to do the same. Because their massive outputs demanded dependable markets, these manufacturers began to promote their own products. Furthermore, because boxes of corn flakes and bars of soap cost so little, manufacturers could not afford to influence the market by changing prices: a penny off on a five-cent product amounted to 20 percent. They therefore took great interest in new promotional techniques.

These large companies integrated production and distribution into modern centralized organizations, but the transition to mass production and mass distribution was neither centralized nor smooth. It involved fundamental systemic conflicts. Mass merchandisers—department stores, mail-order houses, and chain stores—were establishing their own integrated organizations. Some became gigantic firms that dwarfed all but the largest manufacturers; they bought goods in quantities that permitted them to influence markets, challenging manufacturer power. Large wholesalers bought unbranded goods and even the factories that made them, labeled the merchandise, and promoted it to retailers; these privately labeled goods usually sold for lower prices to the consumer and provided better profits for the storekeeper. Besides these challenges, the large integrated manufacturers had to confront their dependency on tens of thousands of small retailers, integral members of their communities who were often ignorant of modern business methods.

The manufacturers' branding strategy required cooperation in the store, the scene of the act that most concerned them: the purchase itself. Advertising might implant a brand name in people's minds, but people actually bought things by requesting them from the proprietors and clerks who retrieved goods from the walls of shelving behind the counters at general stores, groceries, drug stores, and other retail shops. Before 1912, not even the chain stores had self-service. Disaffected retailers could sabotage manufacturers' expensive marketing campaigns by refusing to carry a product or by recommending a substitute when a customer asked for a particular brand.

Indeed, the Crisco campaign nearly faltered because of the prospect of such refusals, brought on by the terms originally offered to the trade. The affair began when O. P. K. Hjermstad, proprietor of a general store in Chippewa Falls, Wisconsin, wrote to Procter and Gamble, thanking the company for his six free cans of Crisco but declining to carry it because the product offered him inadequate profit. "It is time for the retail grocer to wake up and protest against the unfair treatment accorded to him by so many of the national advertisers of the day who want to make of him a mere automaton for the vending of their wares, with little or no compensation for services rendered," the merchant concluded his letter; "the customer simply puts the money in the slot and the manufacturer gets it all." He sent a copy to Paul Findlay, a leading wholesale grocer and business writer, who took the retailers' case to the company. Findlay demonstrated that the Crisco terms precluded any profit, even for the grocer who sold the shortening for the suggested price of twenty-five cents, and he convinced the company that it should reduce the grocers' price by fifty cents per case.

The Hjermstad story demonstrates the ultimate dependence of large manufacturers upon small retailers. Although the first Crisco advertisement had advised consumers to seek the product at other stores if their own grocer did not carry it, customers held strong loyalties to the people with whom they did business, which might surpass their interest in nationally advertised prod-

"*Here it is*"

Through the length and breadth of the country, in big stores and little, Crisco is now a staple.

Storekeepers everywhere are selling it, not merely to meet the demand, but because they are enthusiastic over its many merits.

The use of Crisco in their own homes has shown them that in economy, digestibility and convenience Crisco *is* what they tell their customers—"the ideal cooking fat".

CRISCO
For Frying—For Shortening
For Cake Making

Crisco is rapidly taking the place of butter and lard for cooking.

It is more convenient, more digestible and more appetizing than lard. It is more economical than butter.

It is made in a specially designed building lined with tile and flooded with sunshine.

If you want to know more about Crisco and the conditions under which it is prepared, send for the "Calendar of Dinners". This cloth-bound, gold-stamped book contains, besides the story of Crisco, a different dinner menu for every day of the year and 615 recipes tested by the well-known cooking authority, Marion Harris Neil. Address your request to The Procter & Gamble Co., Dept. K-12, Cincinnati, O., enclosing *five 2-cent stamps.* A paper-bound edition, without the "Calendar of Dinners" but with 250 recipes, will be sent free on request.

This Crisco ad, from the *Saturday Evening Post,* 1915, illustrates the personal relationships characteristic of early-twentieth-century retailing "in big stores and little."

ucts that they had not yet tried. The company soon dropped that advice, concentrating instead on the efforts to court the trade that had begun with the grocers' samples. A campaign in the trade press announced the new terms, and within the year merchants had been enlisted as active Crisco promoters in the form-letter campaign.

The big manufacturers courted merchants through personal relationships, hiring salesmen to mobilize retailers in support of marketing efforts. In a fully developed marketing campaign, store displays—placards and pyramids of packages, artfully arranged in the window, on the counter, or on an upper shelf—reminded customers what to ask for. Manufacturers' salesmen constructed these displays, performed demonstrations in stores, and brought print advertising to the merchants' attention. They competed with each other for display space, much as manufacturers and their salespeople now compete for supermarket shelf space. Their job linked campaigns aimed at the people who might literally consume products, the potential cigarette smokers and breakfast eaters, with the promotional efforts directed at the druggists, grocers, and other small retailers who sold them.

The salesmen's job depended on the transportation and communication systems that were central to the cultural shift and as essential to mass production as raw materials and factory machinery. Market-building required systems that could move large quantities of raw materials, finished goods, energy, and information over long distances. Railroads were still expanding at the turn of the century; in 1915, about half of the track mileage was less than twenty-five years old. The telegraph system was substantially renewed in 1909, when the American Telephone and Telegraph Company bought a controlling interest in Western Union and began a program of shining up dingy telegraph offices and marketing new services. Telephone subscribers could order telegrams over the phone, and the company began to employ operators and equipment during formerly quiet times by offering inexpensive "night letters." Now a com-

By 1919, when this photograph was taken in Stockton, California, many manufacturers' salesmen like Jell-O's Tom Reardon drove company automobiles.

pany's sales manager could sit in his office and communicate quickly with the sales force in the field.

Shorter-range communication and transportation served to develop local markets. Telephones and streetcars extended the range of city dwellers, no longer limited to face-to-face communication within walking distance. On electric streetcars, first installed in Richmond, Virginia, in 1888, people commuted to work from newly built suburbs that followed the tracks; they could even ride from town to town on the interurban lines that sped through woods and fields. No longer confined to neighborhood shopping, urbanites rode the streetcar to shop at downtown stores. Small-town merchants coordinated their sales and special events, and pooled their resources to pay carfares for passengers from rural areas and from other towns. Even without leaving their houses, well-to-do shoppers could patronize distant stores, calling merchants on the phone to have groceries, dry goods, and drugs delivered. Used primarily for local calling, phones in or connected to the Bell system numbered over 1.5 million by 1902, and over 6 million by 1910, doubling again to over 12 million during the decade after that.

Less tangible than telephones and trains but equally important to the market-making process for the new goods was the legal framework for the corporation. In the early years of the nineteenth century, states had awarded corporate charters that granted limited privileges to groups building canals, turnpikes, colleges, and other undertakings for the public good. Beginning with the founders of the New England textile industry, nineteenth-century manufacturers took advantage of the opportunities this legal form provided for concentrating wealth, creating interlocking directorates, and limiting the involvement of absentee owners. Above all, the corporate form offered protection: limited liability.

By the end of the nineteenth century, the corporation was "the basic instrument of private collective action," in the words of historian Peter Hall. Two fundamental legal changes during the late 1880s and the 1890s gave it even more potential. First, a series of Supreme Court cases beginning in 1886 granted the corporation the legal rights of a person, without a person's legal accountability. A corporation could be fined but could not be sent to jail; the protection of its officers was one of its primary reasons for existence. Secondly, the Court, along with the states, extended protection to new kinds of corporate assets. It redefined the nature of property to include not only physical objects but such intangibles as earning power, goodwill, and access to markets. New Jersey and Delaware passed laws permitting corporations to own real estate in other states and stock in other corporations. By the turn of the century, the corporate form was flexible enough to permit both owners and managers to pursue a variety of strategies. The new laws made the limited-purpose charter a thing of the past, promoted the separation of management from ownership, and encouraged the growth of genuinely national enterprises.

Turn-of-the-century Americans met these corporations as

customers of small groceries and variety stores, large drug
chains, huge mail-order firms, city department stores, country
general stores, and many other kinds of retail operations. Some
of these still offered the face-to-face personal relationships traditional to retailing; in others, customers became consumers,
experiencing personally the cultural trend that would characterize twentieth-century buying. As participants in the branded
mass market, consumers entered mutually dependent but un-
equal relationships with large corporations. Old-fashioned commodity relations had been embedded in human relationships:
customers bargained over prices and quality with storekeepers,
who bargained with wholesalers, who did so with manufacturers.
The new commodity relations, entailing self-service buying of
branded products with marked prices, masked the underlying
relationships. From the manufacturers' standpoint, the wide-
spread distribution of industrial products offered the potential
of a new peace to a society sharply divided by class and alerted
to the misdeeds of big businesses by the generation of Progressive reformers. Everybody could join the "class" of consumers
in the marketplace, a new arena for individuals' relationships
with corporations that promised salvation from the strife of the
turn-of-the-century workplace.

The history of people's relations to manufactured products is
an intimate business. Any attempt to analyze how people get and
use things brings up personal subjects—lessons shoppers
learned from their parents, sentimental attachments to particular objects and particular brands, relationships with the people
they go shopping with and for. From the start, consumer marketing operated in the intersection between this private world
and the more public one of corporate production and distribution. As toothpaste users and wearers of ready-made clothes,
people shopped for goods to use privately, literally entering the
public marketplace for most of what they bought. The makers
of those goods, often companies with publicly traded stock,
large payrolls, and factories creating long-lasting environmental

impacts, investigated and attempted to affect private habits in hopes of market success.

The first Crisco advertisement called the product "something that the American housewife had always needed," but Procter and Gamble did not gear production to the needs of consumers. Initiating product development because of a supply consideration in the cottonseed-oil market, this company and others attempted to design consumer demand to meet the needs of production and company growth. Throughout the twentieth century, advertisers have claimed that they discover wants and needs rather than creating them, that markets exist somewhere "out there" waiting to be tapped. Some advertising specialists have been more candid, however, at least with each other. "It is all very well to get the sales of things that people want to buy," a speaker told the Nashville Ad Club in 1916, "but that is too small in volume. We must make people want many other things, in order to get a big increase in business."

In creating the techniques to make people want things, marketers developed principles that belied neoclassical economic theory. According to that theory, price—determined in the marketplace by supply and demand—functions as an information feedback system, telling producers how much of their product to make. When prices go up, the rational manufacturing firm (which can theoretically regulate supply but not demand) will increase output; when they go down, it will cut back on production. In actual practice, manufacturers operated on the new principle that demand could be created by the manufacturer. They initiated market research in order to procure direct market information that might make planning possible before production. Market investigation supported market creation: Resor and Lansdowne analyzed the market for Crisco as part of the process of making one. Furthermore, manufacturers attempted to set prices directly, not only to their own wholesaler customers but also to retailers and consumers; price became, in modern jargon, an element of the "marketing mix," an attribute of the product. With heavy investments in the machinery of mass production and in massive quantities of raw materials, no manufacturer could afford to be the passive factor of neoclassical economics or the relatively weak link in an old-fashioned chain dominated by large wholesale merchants.

The rational consumer of neoclassical theory balances personal concerns about price and quality and chooses among competing producers. Here, too, the new marketing repudiated the neoclassical doctrine. As real income rose and cheaper manufactured products proliferated, people could afford to make decisions about their purchases on considerations other than price. By advertising branded products, manufacturers explicitly intended to eliminate price competition and to eclipse price sensitivity: the consumer who would accept no substitutes for Ivory soap or Steinway pianos would be unwilling to settle for another product just because it was cheaper.

The new goods and the new marketing clashed with elements of an older system that remained powerful for some time. The conflict generated a complex and shifting struggle among the various groups that made up the constantly changing market, as they both cooperated and undercut each other in their attempts to gain some control over the marketing process. On the one hand, the power that brands gave manufacturers was constrained by consumers' close relationships with local merchants and retailers' connections with wholesalers. On the other, to promote strong brand identification, manufacturing corporations established reputations and relationships with consumers as surely as the corner grocer did through personal contact and personality. The triumph of these new relationships during the forty years or so around the turn of the century created the basis for contemporary consumer culture. Since that time, they have flourished at the boundaries between public and private life, the theoretical boundaries of the marketplace and the literal ones of the supermarket parking lot where the products of corporate decision-making are transformed into intimate objects that people use daily.

CHAPTER 2

|||||⊂]||||||||||||⊂]||||||||||||⊂]||||

THE
NAME
ON
THE LABEL

"IT IS WONDERFUL TO NOTE THE VOLUME OF PACKAGE TRADING IN food products, groceries, and patent medicines," wrote Artemas Ward, a leading copywriter and editor of both grocery and advertising trade magazines, in 1900. "Sugar, molasses, vinegar, flour, cheese, dried apples—a hundred and one things once regarded as staples to be sold only in bulk now come within the package field. Alcohol, ammonia, bay rum, come sealed and labeled. Nobody ever thinks of buying liquors or wines except in bottles, showing where they come from, and who is responsible for their condition and character. The same thing is true of tobacco and cigars, of shoe polish, of baking soda, of stove blacking, of pins and needles, of sewing silk and cotton thread and hairpins. There has been a revolution in the methods of American trade within the past twenty years."

In fact, the revolution had only just begun. Most Americans in 1900 still bought sugar and vinegar from barrels and vats at small groceries or at general stores that also sold unlabeled packets of pins and tenpenny nails in bulk. Yet branded, packaged products inaugurated an approach to marketing that Ward's contemporaries tried out in all kinds of industries, that was buttressed by new laws and legal precedents, and that by the end of the twentieth century held sway in companies selling hamburgers, books, and health care as well as at Procter and Gamble and Heinz. That approach changed customers and storekeepers into consumers and dealers, operating in a market not defined by their millions of personal interactions but bounded by the initiatives of large corporations.

Since the early years of Singer sewing machines and McCormick reapers in the 1850s, successful businesses had stamped and painted their companies' names onto their products and established direct relationships with the people who used them. Those firms, creating markets for expensive machines that required servicing and instruction, initiated such techniques as installment buying, the trade-in allowance, and the yearly model change. They controlled distribution by doing it themselves, hiring salespeople who demonstrated the equipment to farmers and seamstresses, and establishing authorized dealerships in cities and towns.

Like Singer and McCormick, the makers of chewing gum, tobacco, packaged foods, paint, and soap products adopted a strategy that established relationships with end users based on techniques designed to create markets for branded goods. Some of those companies experimented with authorized dealerships; the American Tobacco Company even set up a chain of retail outlets, the United Cigar Stores. Most, however, distributed through independent hardware, drug, and grocery stores. Branding offered manufacturers a new kind of control when supported by effective advertising, by altering the balance of power in the traditional chain from manufacturer to wholesaler to retailer to customer. No longer were customers to rely on the grocer's opinion about the best soap; no longer could wholesalers choose among various manufacturers who might fulfill their orders. People asked for Ivory, which could only be obtained from Procter and Gamble. For manufacturers, the branding strategy proved to be successful for growth, and a satisfactory response to some of the Progressive reformers' attacks on manufacturers' abuses. By marking their products, manufacturers took responsibility for them, and therefore presumably for the conditions under which they were produced.

Like so many other changes in daily life during the second half of the nineteenth century, those linked with packaged products depended in part on new technology, as inventors and entrepreneurs applied themselves to packaging materials and processes. The first paper-bag-making machine was patented in 1852 by Francis Wolle, who was to form the Union Paper Bag Machine Company, which eventually owned or controlled 90 percent of the paper-bag business in the United States. In the late 1860s, a patent was granted for the now familiar square-bottomed bag. Throughout the next decade, British and American printers

By the early 1880s, machine-made paper bags were in general use. Many manufacturers supplied retailers with bags printed with advertising, but enterprising merchants like Robert McCaughern ordered their own.

devised techniques for printing on metals, and manufacturers applied those processes to a variety of decorated tins. By the early 1880s, the folding cardboard cartons that would eventually contain Uneeda Biscuits and Kellogg's Toasted Corn Flakes could be produced by machines. The first "automatic-line" canning factory brought the continuous-process concept to canning in 1883, with machinery that could make cans at the rate of about 3,000 per hour. The resulting interest in packaging continued to spur development after the turn of the century: fully automatic bottle making after 1903, aluminum foil after 1910, and cellophane, first manufactured in France in 1913.

Manufacturing companies that chose to invest in the new machinery and purchase the new packaging materials found themselves literally making a new kind of product. Branded goods like Uneeda Biscuits and Quaker Oats used machines and materials not required for bulk production: paper, glue, and printing ink, and machinery for folding, filling, and sealing cartons and cans. To the extent that they guarded food products from insects and protected all kinds of goods from deterioration, packages gave manufacturers greater control over product quality and provided a selling point for consumers concerned about sanitation. Labeled packages showed "where they come from, and who is responsible for their condition and character," in Artemas Ward's terms, and they could be differentiated from their competition in advertisements that displayed their pictures. Clever packaging—like the Colgate Ribbon Dental Cream tube that molded toothpaste so it "Comes Out a Ribbon, Lies Flat on the Brush"—could give a product unusual qualities that might be construed as advantages. An early advertising textbook made the point clear. A label or carton, it stated firmly, was not an advertising medium but "an integral part of the commodity itself." Colgate and Quaker Oats sold products consisting of the container and its contents, not goods packed in containers. Such companies urged their salesmen to introduce new sizes and packaging materials with almost as much fanfare as wholly new products.

This advertisement for the most popular turn-of-the-century brand of tooth-brush sold the packaging as much as the brush. From *Collier's*, 1905.

"Boy With Wheelbarrow," a 1901 National Biscuit poster, lithographed in four colors by the Forbes Lithograph Manufacturing Company of Boston. It measured 9 by 14 feet, divided into sixteen sheets, each 28 by 42 inches.

No company exploited its packaging as a selling point as relentlessly as the National Biscuit Company, which urged consumers to forswear the cracker barrel in favor of the company's In-Er-Seal package. This carton, created by National Biscuit's lawyer on his kitchen table, interleaved cardboard and waxed paper. It was introduced with the Uneeda Biscuit on December 27, 1898, patented in March 1899, and given the name "In-Er-Seal" in 1900. By 1908, the company packaged forty-four products in this carton, including ZuZu ginger cookies, Nabisco Sugar Wafers, and Social Tea Biscuits. The company had spent more on advertising than any other in the country except for American Tobacco and Royal Baking Powder, and most of those ads featured the packaging and the boy whose yellow slicker, like the In-Er-Seal, protected him from moisture.

In modern marketing terms, the emphasis on packaging in the National Biscuit advertising served as "product education." The company was promoting not simply its own products but the product category: packaged crackers and cookies. This was necessary in part because some customers were suspicious or fearful of packaged food. Cans and boxes concealed colors and odors and prevented shoppers from tasting food before they bought it. Six years after the 1906 federal Food and Drug Act, a grocer's magazine claimed that "many people are afraid of canned goods because of sensational stories which are repeatedly printed about them." The article recommended that grocers increase packaged-food trade by holding store demonstrations, which would allow tasting, allay fear, and offer an opportunity for consumers to learn new ways of eating and cooking. "The difficulty with the sale of a good many new things is the housewife doesn't know how to prepare them," this article asserted.

Companies usually abandon product education and concentrate on pushing their own brands once the category is established and competitors have challenged the leader's share of the market. In National Biscuit's case, this took decades; the category was not well established until after World War I. The many regional bakeries that had been consolidated into National Biscuit made literally thousands of kinds of cookies and crackers. In 1908, they produced dozens of biscuits for bulk distribution in addition to the forty-four packaged varieties. As late as 1923, the National Biscuit Company still did 75 percent of its business in bulk. The cracker barrel had been supplanted, not by the In-Er-Seal package, but by new bulk packaging: covered glass-front tins that permitted display of the merchandise. With the important exception of Uneeda, its first packaged product, Nabisco did not concentrate on advertising its brands.

Still, the symbols of the National Biscuit advertising—the boy in the slicker, the circle-and-cross trademark, and the word "Uneeda"—made a major contribution to the concept of the brand as late-twentieth-century consumers understand it. That concept was still relatively new at the turn of the century. For most of the nineteenth century, manufacturers generally sold their entire output to middlemen, who would distribute it to the trade for sale to households. Unlike traditional craftspeople, who often knew their customers and, following the practices of artists and of crafts guilds, marked their goods with their names or with special symbols, these manufacturers left their goods

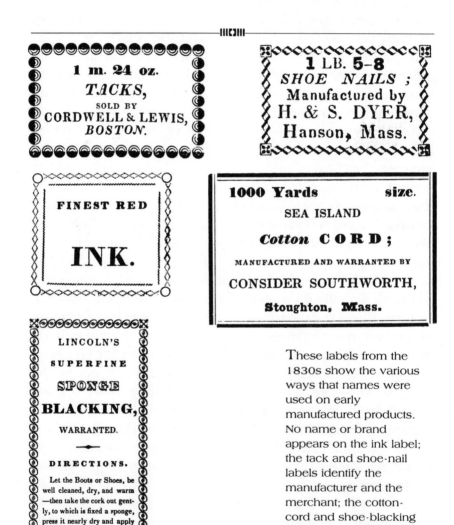

These labels from the 1830s show the various ways that names were used on early manufactured products. No name or brand appears on the ink label; the tack and shoe-nail labels identify the manufacturer and the merchant; the cotton-cord and shoe-blacking labels use brand names, with and without manufacturer identification.

unmarked. If the merchandise bore a label, it as often displayed the name of the wholesaler or the retailer as that of the manufacturer. Some labels carried a name that did not identify either the maker or the seller, although it might be that of a person or place somehow connected with the product.

To the late-twentieth-century consumer, the concept of the brand seems self-explanatory, almost natural. Like the rancher's mark on a straying steer, both manufacturers' brands and the less expensive "house" brands (also called "private labels") serve to identify a source: branded labels name and identify the manufacturer or distributor who can be held accountable for the goods. As a result of that accountability, the brand stands for the consumer's expectation of product quality. As late as 1884, however, when A. Schilling & Company, San Francisco tea merchants, published a book of advice for traveling salesmen promoting tea imported from Japan in its Perfection cans, the branding concept was not defined in this modern sense. Some famous brands had already been launched—Procter and Gamble was advertising Ivory, for example—yet the Schilling "special brand system" suggests that Americans did not necessarily connect the symbolism and information on product labels with their expectations about the products.

Schilling used brand names, but neither its own name nor those of the retailers who sold its tea appeared on the labels. The company gave each merchant sole use of a brand—perhaps named "Treasure" or "Mayflower"—in his town; larger orders qualified him for brand control in a county or state. Merchants who ordered twenty-five chests or more (each containing 120 pounds of tea) were eligible to sell cans bearing multicolored labels lithographed in Europe; each chest included twenty pieces of advertising matter—"napkins, mats, small fans, lamp shades, fancy cards, etc." Those who bought less got labels printed in Japan from woodcuts, and no advertising matter. Schilling might sell more than one brand to different merchants in the same town; townspeople might find Treasure tea at one store and Mayflower at another. The firm stressed that it would not grant the exclusive right to sell tea in Perfection cans.

Schilling celebrated its cans for the protection they offered from dirt and air, and for the absence of lead, then commonly used to line tea chests. In contrast to National Biscuit twenty years later, however, the company downplayed the conceptual importance of the packaging. *"The can is simply a box or chest,"* Schilling emphasized, no more an indication of quality than a flour sack, a soap box, or a cigar box. Any grade of tea might come in a can. "It is ridiculous to suppose that a merchant buying a tea for which he paid 55 cents in the Perfection Tea Can, should be thought to have the same class of tea, and be expected to sell it at the same price, as another merchant who paid only 35 cents for his, simply because it is packed in the same kind of package," the company asserted. "An idea like this at once defeats the very object of the special brand system, which is to enable merchants to put their own price upon their tea, just as they do when they get it in bulk chests."

Unlike most packaged-goods companies at the turn of the century, which suggested retail prices and campaigned to be allowed to set them legally, Schilling explicitly offered store-keepers freedom in price-setting. In order to protect the merchant customer's right to charge whatever he wanted, the company urged salesmen to "so arrange matters that nothing on the label shall give the consumer, or the salesmen for competing houses, the slightest hint of the value of the tea within the can." Several qualities of tea—to be labeled with terms like "Extra Choice," "High Class," "Superior," and "Fancy"—might be sold under any one brand, but these referred only to relative quality within that one brand. The company told salesmen to prevent competing merchants with different brands from employing the same terms, so that the quality of Mayflower Fancy could not be compared with that of Treasure Superior. Thus in the 1880s Schilling used its brands not to identify itself to the consumer but to convince retailers that tea bought from this company would not have to confront competition in price or quality. "The label has nothing to do with the character of the tea," the company emphasized, in direct opposition to the concept of branding that would develop during the next two decades.

A series of labels for canned corn reveals many features of that development process. The earliest label (A) was used on corn packed in Maine by Nathan Winslow and his junior partner (perhaps his nephew), John Winslow Jones, and distributed to agents in New York, San Francisco, and Australia. Because tin cans, first used commercially in 1839, found their primary market in mining and exploring expeditions and military campaigns until the 1880s, packers were obliged to find distant outlets. On this label, the Winslow company identified itself, advertised its other products, and gave distributors' addresses, but used no brand name, headlining instead the contents—"Green Corn!" The directions urged the "consumer" (in a literal use of the term) to season to taste, suggested two modes of preparation (one of which would not dirty a pan—convenient on an expedition), explained to those unfamiliar with canned goods or not in possession of a can opener how to get to the food, and offered a recipe suggestion.

When John Winslow Jones succeeded Nathan, he retained both the Winslow name and much of the descriptive label language. His new label recommended that purchasers "look well

A

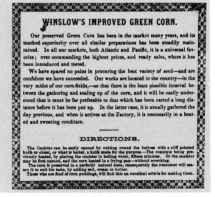

J. WINSLOW JONES' IMPROVED GREEN CORN.

Our preserved Green Corn has been in the market many years, and its marked superiority over all similar preparations has been steadily maintained. In all our markets, both Atlantic and Pacific, it is a universal favorite, ever commanding the highest prices and ready sales where it has been introduced and tested.

We have spared no pains in procuring the best variety of seed—and are confident we have succeeded. Our works are located in the country —in the midst of our cornfields—so that there is the least possible interval between the gathering and sealing up of the corn, and, it will be easily understood, it must be far preferable to that which has been carted a long distance before it is put up. In the latter case it is usually gathered the day previous, and when it arrives at the Factory it is necessarily in a heated and sweating condition.

DIRECTIONS.

OPEN CAN ON THE BOTTOM. Warm in Stew Pan with Butter half the size of an egg, half a cup Milk, tea-spoonful Salt; season with Pepper. SERVE HOT.

The practice is too prevalent, particularly at Hotels and Restaurants, of serving up Sugar Corn in warm water, which makes a perfectly tasteless and unpalatable dish, when the corn itself is really of the finest quality.

GLOBE
TRADE
JWJ
MARK
BRAND.

WINSLOW'S
GREEN CORN.
WORLD RENOWNED.
PREPARED BY
JOHN WINSLOW JONES,
Successor to
NATHAN WINSLOW & CO.
PORTLAND, MAINE.
ALSO, MEATS, FISH, AND VEGETABLES.

Owing to the immense demand for Hermetically Sealed Goods, large amounts of Worthless articles are offered for sale, which render it very important for purchasers to look well to the BRAND they purchase.

B

GREEN SUGAR CORN

OXFORD PACKING Co PORTLAND ME.

DIRECTIONS FOR PREPARING
THE USUAL MODE - THOROUGHLY WARM (NOT COOK) WITH THE ADDITION OF A PIECE OF BUTTER THE SIZE OF A HENS EGG AND A GILL OF WATER OR MILK. SEASON TO TASTE
· · · SUCCOTASH · · ·
TAKE ONE CAN OF SHELLED BEANS AND TWO CANS OF CORN AND PUT IN A SAUCEPAN WITH HALF A POUND OF BUTTER THOROUGHLY WARM AND SEASON TO TASTE. A LITTLE CREAM OR BROTH MAY BE ADDED IF DESIRED. SOME PEOPLE PREFER SALT PORK IN PLACE OF BUTTER.

PACKED AT DIXFIELD, OXFORD CO. MAINE

C

WHITE DIAMOND BRAND
MAINE CORN

WHITE DIAMOND BRAND
J. S. SILVERS & BRO.
CRANBURY,
NEW JERSEY.

D

to the BRANDS they purchase," (B) and offered them two names
to go by: "Winslow's Green Corn" and "Globe Brand," the
latter identified by a "trademarked" image that the company
may or may not have registered. New directions assumed more
familiarity with cans and can openers, furnished a recipe with
precise measurements, and warned against a common but unpalatable mode of preparation.

The remaining labels all show a new emphasis on design in
part made possible by turn-of-the-century printing techniques.
Such updated methods did not necessarily imply a correspond-
ing modernity in the use of the brand concept, as the unbranded
Green Sugar Corn label from the Oxford Packing Company (C)
suggests. In typical labels produced for private brands (D), the
printing process was arranged so that a brand like White Diamond could be used for more than one client. The label read
"Packed for," not "Packed by"; the name of the wholesaler or
retailer was then filled in.

Another label (E) identified corn distributed by Thurber,
Whyland, and Company, one of America's largest wholesalers,
which offered a full line of privately labeled canned vegetables.
Thurber, Whyland printed labels both with and without its own
Windham brand, in a uniform style, with information in three of
the many languages used by the urban retailers who bought this

E

F

company's goods. Its promise of "pure and wholesome" food echoes language used by the political movement that produced state legislation and, in 1906, the federal Pure Food and Drug Act.

Burnham and Morrill's label for its Paris Sugar Corn (F) made a more explicit promise of purity and exemplifies the modern use of the brand to identify the manufacturer. This company entered the corn it packed in Paris, Maine, in a small exposition in Paris, France, as well as in the Philadelphia Centennial and the World's Columbian Exposition, the famous Chicago World's Fair of 1893. The medals displayed on the label were intended to persuade new consumers to try the goods, while the repetition of the brand name "Paris" might give them something to remember that would bring them back as old customers.

Manufacturers like Burnham and Morrill intended their brands and the trademarks that gave them legal status to help consumers differentiate their products from competing ones, and thereby to create demand. Ideally, the product itself could be differentiated—by flavor, by efficacy, or by some other attribute. People would come to the store knowing they preferred, or wanted to try, the floating soap or the toothpaste that came out flat on the brush. Often, however, the differences were minor or nonexistent; then shoppers who could remember a trademark or the look of a package might still ask for a brand by name.

As the branding concept developed, the leading corporations devised different tactics for using it. Libby, Swift, and Armour all used their company name to brand the many products they made. Some—like Armour sandpaper and Armour bacon—were quite unrelated in consumers' minds, but together they were intended to support and differentiate the overall brand image. Procter and Gamble used a different strategy, giving its products such separate brands as P & G Naphtha, Ivory, and Star, three names for soaps that competed with each other. Similarly, tobacco, tea, and coffee companies branded many blends of various flavors and qualities and attempted to differentiate their brands from each other as well as from those of competing firms. In either case, branding committed the company to producing standardized products—or, in the many industries still dependent on rudimentary technologies or agricultural exigencies, to attempting to do so. Consumers' expectations of consistency would help create goodwill, the favorable consideration of customers that derived from a company's reputation and, by the 1890s, an intangible but legally salable form of property.

Goodwill had a longstanding history in the law regarding retail trade. Legal precedents for the concept were established in England around 1600, and the term was first used in 1743. A 1769 case explicitly held it not to be property: goodwill, the court claimed, could not be sold because a potential purchaser had no power to keep it. It emanated from customers, who could choose to patronize another business and who themselves could not be purchased. United States Supreme Court Justice Joseph Story, who wrote the most authoritative and formative legal opinions and texts of his day, described goodwill in 1841 as a business establishment's "advantage or benefit . . . beyond the mere value of the capital stock, funds, or property employed therein, in consequence of the general public patronage and encouragement which it receives from constant or habitual customers, on account of its local position, or common celebrity, or reputation."

This "advantage or benefit" had monetary value in common

practice: retailers selling their businesses charged more than the value of the stock and fixtures. Legal thinkers debated goodwill's legal status as property throughout the last three decades of the century, along with that of other intangible forms. In the *Slaughter House* cases of 1872 and 1884, a majority of the United States Supreme Court reiterated the common-law concept that limited legal property to physical things. The minority opinion began to hold sway in the lower courts during the ensuing years. Finally, in a series of cases beginning with the 1890 *Minnesota Rate* case, the Supreme Court held that property encompassed not only physical things but expected earning power, sale value, and the liberty of access to markets. This crucial redefinition made goodwill into legal property and revised the legal status of stocks, bonds, and credit, thus facilitating the development of the corporate form.

Throughout this period, the courts reversed themselves several times over the property rights relating to trademarks, the legal symbols of goodwill, which also had long-established rights in common law. The confusion stemmed in part from the changing definition of property, in part from a conflict between property issues and questions of public protection from fraud, and in part from successive revisions of trademark legislation. Although the United States Constitution specifically referred to patents and copyrights, it made no provision for trademarks. Responding to cases in the civil courts and to a growing international interest in trademarks, Congress passed the first American trademark act in 1870. In the first year, 121 marks were registered.

Manufacturers began not only to mark their goods and promote their own marks but to organize societies to foster trademarking in general. The first such organization and the most famous foreign trademark society, the Union des Fabricants, was founded in Paris in 1872. Five years later, organizational efforts began for what became the United States Trade-Mark Association, which adopted a constitution and bylaws in December of 1878. Its early officers included Edward Clark, the president and marketing genius of the Singer Manufacturing Company, Bowles Colgate of the soap family, and Eberhard Faber, whose name may still be read on pencils.

Less than a year after the USTMA first met, the Supreme Court held the 1870 and 1876 trademark statutes unconstitutional. The organization immediately instituted lobbying efforts for what became the trademark acts of 1881 and 1882. It collected information from manufacturers, seeking to determine the extent of trademarking, in order to combat opponents' arguments that trademarks were unnecessary to commerce. Few goods bore trademarks, these adversaries claimed, and most existing marks labeled spirits, tobacco, and patent medicines, the latter already protected under patent law. The association continued its public relations efforts long after the laws were passed, exhibiting at fairs including the 1893 Columbian Exposition, where it received a medal for its display of trademark literature.

In 1898, President McKinley named Francis Forbes, then president of the USTMA, to head a commission charged with revising the patent and trademark statutes. The report, incorporating two proposed bills, was submitted two years later, and Congress finally passed legislation in 1905. The new act established trademark registration as prima facie evidence of ownership, which meant that those who registered their marks would be favored in court. It allowed for registration of all marks that had been in use for ten years or more, and provided for the destruction of infringing labels and packages as well as for the recovery of damages for infringement. It prevented goods from entering the United States bearing infringing trademarks, and gave jurisdiction to federal courts regardless of the citizenship of the parties involved. This time, ten thousand new marks were registered within a year of the act.

Unlike patents and copyrights, trademarks did not expire. The mark had to be new, not in common use to designate similar articles; it had to be exclusive, not used by two or more persons or corporations; and it had to be attached to the product in some

Companies printed their trademarks on all of their advertising materials, but also used them in circumstances that might not directly relate to promotion, like this 1907 Wrigley letterhead.

——

way—printed, stamped, or pasted on the article itself, or on a wrapper, bottle, label, or tag. Under the 1905 law, later amended, a trademark could not consist of words that described the product, or of proper names of people or places, all of which might reasonably be used by other manufacturers. The law permitted the use of a company name only if it was presented in some distinctive manner, such as unusual lettering.

Stamped onto sides of beef, crackers, and bedposts, prominent in advertisements, and emblazoned on company letterheads, trademarks built corporate images outside direct selling transactions. The Standard plumbing-fixture company even altered its typewriters so that "Standard" could be typed with the trademark's Gothic lettering. Some successful marks transcended their makers and came to define the product category, to the distress of the companies whose goodwill they represented. "The word 'Pianola' is not a term applicable to Piano-players in general, but the specific name of the instrument manufactured and sold by The Aeolian Company," readers of the advertising pages in *McClure's Magazine* learned in 1905. "There is no Kodak but the Eastman Kodak," that company had

Manufacturers stamped trademarks directly onto their products, and infringing competitors imitated them there as well as on the packages. These
biscuits were used as evidence in a case tried in the Circuit Court of Indiana
from 1905 through 1907.

asserted in a small box in the corner of an advertisement seven
years earlier. In 1899, Eastman took full-page ads to explain
further: " 'Kodak' is a Trade Name applied by us to cameras and
other goods of our manufacture. We originated and registered
the word 'Kodak.' The trade-mark is our exclusive property." By
1905, the year of the new trademark law, the firm had found a
snappier slogan: "If it isn't an Eastman, It isn't a Kodak."

Like the Xerox Corporation later in the century, the makers
of Pianola and Kodak wanted to protect their marks because
trademarks and the goodwill they represented had become valuable business assets. In 1911, when the Supreme Court dis-
solved and reorganized the American Tobacco Company, its
trademarks were estimated to be worth $45 million out of $227
million in total assets. The president of the National Biscuit
Company appraised "Uneeda" at more than $1 million per let-
ter, while a Coca-Cola officer valued his firm's trademark at $5
million. Edward S. Rogers, a Chicago lawyer who published one
of many advice books on trademark law, stressed the arbitrary
nature of such figures. He quoted auditors and other executives
from major national manufacturing firms, many of whom were

Packages of Uneeda and Iwanta biscuits, used as evidence in an 1899 case, one of many brought by National Biscuit against its imitators.

nearly as frank as the one who ended a financial statement with the words, "We realize that this plan is entirely arbitrary." Still, Rogers referred his readers to two accounting textbooks that offered discussions on valuing such intangible assets.

Successful trademarks were widely imitated, and the most celebrated manufacturers spent considerable time and money in court pursuing the imitators. "This case is too plain to waste many words over it," Judge Lacombe of the United States Circuit Court in New York's Southern District declared in the action brought by the National Biscuit Company against the makers of Iwanta Biscuits. The defendant claimed to have put "considerable thought" into selecting a name that would differentiate his goods "so that there could be no possibility of mistake." He failed to convince the judge, who considered it curious that so many manufacturers "seem to find their inventive faculties so singularly unresponsive to their efforts to differentiate." Lacombe ruled for Nabisco. Local bakers all over America infringed on the company's trademarks; by 1915, National Biscuit could publish results of thirteen successful suits, and other manufacturers had abandoned 882 imitative marks without being brought to court.

Often the larger companies won because they could afford to

———————————————— ⅢⅭⅢ ————————————————

Exhibits from *Coca-Cola Company v. Williamsburgh Stopper Company, et al.,* a case that lasted for a decade in the federal courts.

litigate for years or even decades. In a case that went from 1912 to 1922, Coca-Cola successfully sued the makers of Espo-Cola. "Esposito may use the word 'Cola' and may use the word 'Espo,' but when he expresses either or both of those words in a style of script commercially unheard of except for advertising purposes, I am persuaded that he goes too far," wrote the judge. Yet despite the generally greater resources of the national advertisers, their cases were occasionally unsuccessful. Coca-Cola filed suit for infringement against Citro-Cola on the basis of name, bottle size and shape, label design, and a pamphlet that described the product as a preparation "for making the popular drink of the day at a minimum cost." "Perfect in color, smell, taste and in every respect," Citro-Cola told druggists. " 'A word to the wise.' " In 1909, the court ruled that the names and bottle designs shared features in common use at drug stores and soda fountains for beverages and syrups. And, although the pamphlet might be suggestive of imitation, it was not necessarily an incentive for soda-fountain operators to substitute Citro-Cola when patrons asked for the beverage that was yet to be dubbed the "Real Thing."

Companies that could afford to do so invested heavily to avoid innocent infringement. In April 1913, R. J. Reynolds's law firm initiated inquiries about the status of a number of names that had been proposed for the company's new cigarettes. In July, Reynolds paid Salvatore Ragona of New York City $300 for the rights to the name "Red Kamel," its goodwill, the die, and 5,000 cigarettes. In October and November, the company launched two new brands, Camels and Red Kamels, the latter an elegant, cork-tipped cigarette retailing at twice the price of Camels. Early in December, the lawyers discovered a Philadelphia firm that claimed also to have bought the Red Kamel brand. Although Ragona disputed this claim, R. J. Reynolds paid another $3,000 to buy the title a second time, acquiring also 200,000 cigarettes, 15,000 boxes, and 5,000 cartons. The company manufactured Red Kamels until 1936, but the brand never took off. In any case, Reynolds's major concern was to protect the name

"Camels," the product that established marketing practices for the modern cigarette industry.

During the years after the 1905 law, litigation about trademark infringement and unfair competition became central to an understanding of trademarks as a legal field. In 1912, a firm of patent attorneys with offices in New York and Washington published the first of a series of booklets explaining trademarks to businessmen. The pamphlet had doubled in size by 1915, with nearly forty new pages, all containing excerpts from case law about infringement and unfair competition that made for considerably more difficult reading than the original pages, which offered advice to manufacturers on picking trademarks and described good ones. Most patent-law firms and many advertising agencies, business magazines, and independent publishers offered such advice. The matter of an effective symbol went well beyond the law, according to Glen Buck, the Chicago advertising agent who had designed famous trademarks for Ford, Van Houten's Cocoa, and others. The question "What constitutes a good trademark?" Buck maintained, should be answered with another: "What makes a great play—or poem—or picture—or building—or dinner?"

The trademark, Buck wrote in 1916, "is being served to us with the salad at conference dinners; discussed where directors gather; torn into shreds by the analyzing class publications; profoundly expounded by wrinkled-browed lawyers." It was born "in the earliest dawn of civilization," he pointed out, "but it has been only since the development of advertising to its present hopeful state that it has become a subject for conversation in thundering subway trains. . . . The trademark is in the atmosphere." Indeed, the economy and the culture had adopted trademarking as surely as any individual manufacturer. In 1912, Congressman Philip P. Campbell of Kansas even introduced a bill in Congress making goods in interstate and foreign commerce illegal "without printing, embossing, or stenciling the name and address of the manufacturer upon such article or commodity."

"The bill is along the same lines as the pure food law," the congressman maintained, designed to combat "dishonest and unscrupulous manufacturers, and . . . convict-made and sweat-shop goods." Trademarks made their makers accountable, and thus offered manufacturers ammunition against Progressive reformers, who called attention to unsanitary practices in food factories both before and after the 1906 Pure Food and Drug Act. Swift and Company explained this reasoning to stockholders. "Dressed and cured meats and provisions are sold under Swift & Co.'s own name," the firm wrote in its 1910 Year Book, one of the first published annual reports. "Fresh meats bear the number of the abattoir where dressed; cured meats and provisions are either skin-branded, box-branded, tagged or labeled. These brands make Swift & Co. doubly responsible to the public; they keep them on the alert to maintain [both] self-imposed and Governmental high standards."

Whether or not the public believed that manufacturers' brands signified high quality, people learned the most advertised brand names. In 1917, when an article on the subject appeared in the first volume of the *Journal of Applied Psychology,* every one of three hundred men interviewed could think of at least one brand of fountain pen, watch, and soap, and although they named thirty-six brands of soft drinks, nearly two-thirds mentioned a single brand. By the early 1920s, studies showed that people asked for brands at stores, and that brands dominated sales in many industries. Ninety percent of Chicago grocers interviewed in 1920 said that more than three-quarters of their customers requested baked beans by brand name, and Campbell's soup was the best-seller in 145 out of 147 stores.

Branding was certainly not by itself a sure-fire strategy. Many—if not most—branded products failed, and even such extraordinarily popular and widely advertised brands as Sapolio household cleaner and Egg-O-See cereal died, early examples of what marketers now call the "product life-cycle." Yet successful brands were central to marketing schemes that built powerful companies. Nearly all the brands mentioned by a majority of the 1,024 subjects studied by two New York University researchers in 1920–21 are still familiar: Kodak cameras, Singer sewing machines, Campbell's soup, Postum, Old Dutch Cleanser, Wrigley's chewing gum, Colgate toothpaste, Welch's grape juice, and Arrow collars—made by Cluett, Peabody, and Company, which continued to use the trademark on shirts after separate collars went out of fashion.

Branding was part of a strategy that created demand even if production capacity was insufficient to fill the orders. W. K. Kellogg's first national advertising, in the July 1906 *Ladies' Home Journal,* admitted that as of May 10, with its mills working around the clock six days a week, it had a backlog of orders for nearly half a million packages. The sales manager for the American Sugar Refining Company acknowledged that his firm could only fill about two-thirds of each order with Domino Package Sugars. Yet he continued to urge his salesmen to promote Domino in packages rather than sugar in bulk. "Remember that you are DOMINO salesmen first!" he ended the circular letter that revealed the shortage. Both companies assured customers that they were working as hard as possible to increase production capacity. For weaker firms with stronger competition, such assurances sometimes failed to work. ITS TOO LATE NOW CANCEL, Philadelphia's Strawbridge and Clothier wired the makers of Munsingwear union suits in 1888. LETTER RECD WONT KEEP PEOPLE WARM SHIP AT ONCE, read another telegram, from Indiana.

The Kellogg and Domino marketing programs, creating demand regardless of supply, exemplify a fundamental transformation in manufacturers' attempts to coordinate supply and demand. The production-driven marketing necessitated by the massive outputs of flow production increasingly gave way to marketing-driven production, with decisions about output based on sales records and sales plans, and with sales offices responsible for coordinating the flow of goods through the production process. By 1910, the Sherwin-Williams Company used daily and weekly sales reports as a basis for deciding on output. "I will say that our sales campaigns are, of course, largely affected by the producing capacity of our factories," wrote Adrian Joyce, the general manager of the company, "but during the

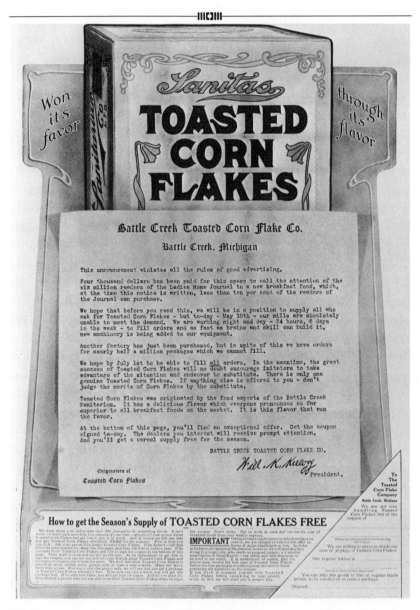

The first Kellogg national advertising appeared in the July 1906 *Ladies' Home Journal.* It was written with the assistance of Arch W. Shaw, an original Kellogg stockholder, a member of the first board of directors, and the editor of *System,* a prominent business magazine.

past few years our sales organization has kept ahead of the factory output all the time. In other words, we have been crowding our factories to the limit in order to take care of orders from the sales department."

The companies that could best achieve smooth coordination between expanding output and new orders were those that did their own marketing. This practice was inaugurated—in Singer's case as early as the 1850s—by companies with specific marketing problems, many introducing new products that required demonstration, instruction, and after-sales service, with no channels of distribution already established. They were followed during the 1880s and 1890s by manufacturers who built capital-intensive factories, using continuous-process machinery and methods to produce great quantities of low-priced goods like cigarettes, breakfast cereals, and matches. To create, expand, and maintain the markets for their large volumes of goods, these manufacturers assumed control over their marketing networks and methods. Such companies grew to dominate not only their own industries but industry itself, building immense factories and marketing around the world, integrating production and distribution within their organizational systems.

Even some companies in the differently organized clothing and furniture industries successfully branded and marketed their own products before World War I. Producing goods in relatively small factories and limiting themselves to domestic markets, they never made the lists of the largest industrials, but they did build prosperous businesses that lasted for many decades. Makers of nonfashion clothing in standard sizes— socks, underwear, and work clothes—could market their goods as packaged products, selling Munsingwear and Levi's in the same general stores that carried Quaker Oats and Diamond matches. Products that required more sales effort went to specialized small clothing, furniture, and shoe stores that served as the primary outlets for Arrow shirts, Hoosier kitchen cabinets, Bissell carpet sweepers, and Buster Brown shoes.

Not all manufacturing companies adopted the branding strategy. Another way of disposing of outputs was more traditional: making goods for private labeling. As they had for many decades and as they do today, wholesalers at the turn of the century sold products under their own brands, and many wholesalers offered their retailer customers a line of goods to be marked with the retailers' names. "Look out for corn flake pit-falls," the Kellogg Toasted Corn Flake Company warned in a 1910 advertisement. "As a last resort a few small unknown manufacturers of Corn Flakes, *who couldn't succeed with their own brands,* are packing private brands. . . . Some salesmen claim that they are packed by Kellogg, and some only go so far as to say that they are 'just as good as Kellogg's.' *Neither statement is true.* Kellogg packs in his own packages only." Heinz, Van Camp, and some other large advertisers likewise refused to manufacture private brands.

When Kellogg named names in its magazine for grocers in 1912, it accused not a "small unknown manufacturer" but the Quaker Oats Company, which packed Montgomery Ward's Sunset corn flakes. "We know it to be a fact because we can see from our windows right across the street from the Quaker corn flake factory the Sunset packages going through the mill," Kellogg wrote in response to a trade-paper request for proof. "If the manufacturer's name were on the label, no such proof would be required," the company pointed out, accusing the mail-order house also of providing a market for prison-made goods, and publicizing the Campbell bill that required all goods to bear trademarks.

Companies that produced private brands defended their practices. "We manufacture nothing but private brands, but we refuse to be classed as 'business pirates,' " wrote V. B. Brown, the advertising manager for the Wabash Baking Powder Company. "The real 'pirates' are found camping on the trails of the regular brands," he insisted, pointing to the Coca-Cola trademark imitators. Private-brand manufacturers protected their markets by providing high-quality goods at lower prices for the consumer and higher margins for the retailer, wrote Brown. "What interests every manufacturer," he maintained, "is not the *publicity* of his particular brand, but a *market* for the sale of his goods."

Yet branding did not merely offer a market. It offered a predictable and controllable market: protection against competition, against industry price fluctuations, and even against the effects of business cycles. During the 1880s, with bulk prices plummeting in their industries, the makers of Duryea and Kingsford starch and Quaker oatmeal preserved and even advanced their profits. Manufacturers producing branded fine writing papers maintained their prices after the Panic of 1893 better than makers of staple paper products such as newsprint and wrapping paper. By 1909, some admen argued that a million dollars' worth of advertising could not destroy Ivory soap—in essence, that Procter and Gamble had made itself invulnerable to competition. Even the advertising manager for Woodbury's soap took this position, commenting that Ivory "is about 99 45-100 per cent imbedded in the broad American mind . . . at the expense of much time, some money and a few brains."

Ivory was perhaps the most spectacularly successful example of the branding strategy. Packaging, labeling, advertising, and selling through retail outlets owned by others offered manufacturers a way to take control of a product's marketing and distribution without setting up their own stores or establishing house-to-house sales forces to create business relationships with households. In industry after industry, leading firms consciously chose this strategy, promoted just as consciously by advertising industry organizations and trade journals. Yet the strategy entailed inherent systemic tensions. Large national organizations introduced the enormous quantities of goods manufactured by the new methods of mass production into a fragmented distribution system. Regional wholesale firms and many small local storekeepers formed that system, which was based on familiar relationships and the personal interactions of credit and bargaining. Branding and advertising were transforming those relationships, but manufacturers had to work with them and within the limitations they imposed.

CHAPTER 3

THE
CHAIN
OF
DISTRIBUTION

IN 1909, AFTER THIRTY YEARS OF PRODUCING PRIVATE-LABEL PROD-
ucts, the Scott Paper Company began to manufacture and market its own brands. Initial promotional efforts included small
advertisements in many national magazines, samples, and "a
little booklet in the form of a novelette" inserted in every package of toilet paper, describing the sanitary properties of other
Scott products. The conversion enabled Scott to solve a major
production problem by reducing its line from the three hundred
different articles it had been making for various wholesalers to
just five products with its own label. "Each year the jobbers'
claims grew more insistent," explained sales manager Arthur H.
Scott three years later. "Price concessions, more elaborate labels and packages, special styles were demanded. . . . If we did
not accede to their demands they would buy elsewhere."

Scott not only stopped manufacturing for wholesalers but
chose not to sell through them. The company divided the country into thirty selling regions, each with a sales and distribution
headquarters; the salesmen came together at the factory for an
annual convention to refresh their training with the new advertising plans and sales arguments. The high cost of such a sales
force, Scott maintained, was offset by its principal advantage:

promotion by a salesman devoted to Scottissue and Sanitissue, "not, like the jobber's salesman, spreading his interest thin over a multitude of things." If a business thus organized were to grow so big that distribution became more trouble than it was worth, he claimed, "the jobbers will welcome the line with open arms. A big, going business, with the retailers in their territories demanding the goods, is worth paying attention to, and no jobber worthy of the name is going to cut off his nose to spite his face."

Arthur Scott's company succeeded with a strategy that brought it up against huge, well-organized wholesaling firms and required it to deal directly with thousands of small retail businesses, many quite precarious. In the nineteenth-century economy, a system of regional manufacturing, regional sales, and regional credit had pivoted on wholesalers, who dominated trade in the drug, hardware, grocery, and dry-goods businesses. Even at the end of the century, wholesalers were well financed and better established than most companies manufacturing consumer products. They held responsibility for the physical handling of goods, organizing complex systems for distributing many different products to many different retailers, who ordered in small quantities. Often large, highly rationalized, and powerful firms with branch offices in many cities, they controlled retailers' credit and held substantial power in regional financial circles.

Early in the nineteenth century, the primary middlemen had been commission agents, firms that handled distribution for a fee without purchasing the goods from the manufacturers. The term "jobber," originally applied to merchants who broke down lots of imported goods and distributed them to retailers, was by 1870 used interchangeably with "wholesaler" to refer to a new kind of middleman that had become dominant. This "full-line, full-service wholesaler" owned the goods he sold, an assortment (or "full line") that he offered through traveling salesmen who, in most lines, showed retailers samples. The growing manufacturers preferred the new wholesalers to commission agents. Because they bought goods outright, the manufacturers no longer

Traveling men are up in arms against railroads limiting dimensions of trunks as baggage.

This cartoon, reprinted from a hardware trade journal in a 1911 traveling
salesman's magazine, discusses a perennial problem between wholesalers
and the railroads, whose baggage limits restricted salesmen's efforts to
show goods by sample.

had to wait for payment until the goods were sold to retailers,
and could invest their money in new production facilities instead
of tying it up in stock. The full-line, full-service jobbers, in other
words, relieved manufacturers of the financial responsibility for
distribution.

Wholesaling establishments grew with the railroads. Omaha,
for example, was linked to the transcontinental Union Pacific
in 1872 with a bridge across the Missouri River. During the
next twenty years, while prominent citizens organized financial
support for railroad development, some of the city's best-
established retail firms added wholesale departments or abandoned their retailing for exclusive wholesaling, and jobbing
firms from other cities moved to Omaha and opened branch
houses there. Omaha wholesaling grew sixfold from 1875 to
1890, with 306 wholesale houses competing with firms in Chicago, St. Louis, Kansas City, and San Francisco for retailer business as far away as Idaho, Oregon, and Washington.

By bringing manufactured products to frontier communities in such places, wholesalers took the major responsibility in opening up territory for manufactured goods; to the extent that there was a national market before national marketing, it was created through sales, not advertising. Wholesalers' traveling salesmen crisscrossed America on trains and rode horses and stagecoaches into remote places to drum up business. Salesmen operating out of Denver for Marshall Field's substantial whole-sale business even took bobsleds through open country to reach towns off the railroads.

These "drummers" gave regional wholesalers the capacity to offer personalized service to their far-flung retailer customers. In small cities with good hotels, drummers unpacked their trunks and sample cases in special sample rooms where local merchants could see the goods without having to travel to Chi-

---

||||⊃|||

Wholesalers' "drummers" serviced remote establishments like this general store in Bev-erly, Washington, photographed by Asahel Curtis in 1910.

Traveling salesman in the field, from *Tales of the Road,* a 1905 book of salesmen's reminiscences first published in the *Saturday Evening Post.*

cago or New York. They handled loss and damage claims in the field and undertook credit checks and collections. Traveling salesmen were expected to take their credit duties as seriously as their sales, although as one writer in a salesmen's magazine noted, the good salesman was a "poor collector" because the two kinds of work suited different kinds of people.

Free from their bosses and from conventional family life, drummers were reputed to spend their evenings drinking, gambling, and flirting. Even sympathetic accounts reinforced this image. "As long as he was a pioneer, covering new territory, opening up new business, he was allowed to do pretty much as he pleased, provided he delivered the goods," one writer reminisced in the *Commercial Travelers' Magazine* in 1910. "Many a good man went down the road of booze or cards or girls," this reminiscence continued, describing the old-time drummer as a "live wire." "The latest slang, the latest song, the latest joke, and often the latest dance, were among his specialties." As the missionary work of the drummer gave way to the more regularized functions of holding and servicing established trade, wholesalers organized trained, supervised, salaried sales forces and attempted to recruit sober, married men.

Drummers served the small independent stores that dominated American retail trade. Other kinds of retailers existed. In 1880, people bought goods from department stores and urban street carts, from country peddlers, and from stalls at public markets. A few patronized new establishments that would prove

Traveling salesmen's own jokes, like this cartoon from a 1911 salesmen's magazine, more often concerned hotels and trains than farmers' daughters.

ARTHUR WOODMAN

COULDN'T BE ANY WORSE.

"What's the best hotel here?"
"The Palace."
"Have you ever stopped there?"
"No. But I have stopped at all the others."

to be the seeds of major retailing innovations: Frank W. Woolworth opened his first successful branch that year; the Great
Atlantic and Pacific Tea Company, decades ahead of other
chains, operated a hundred Eastern stores; and since 1872,
Montgomery Ward of Chicago had been shipping parasols and
harnesses to the farmers who ordered from its catalogue. Most
retail purchases of manufactured goods, however, were made at
the general merchandise stores that served small towns and
rural areas, where groceries, hardware, drugs, shoes, and dry
goods were sold in the same crowded room, and at the urban
stores that specialized in one or another of these lines.

 Small stores could be started with little capital, by people with
little experience. A 1905 Massachusetts census showed that the
forty-five stores in Nantucket County operated with an average
capital investment of $2,333; Filene's, Jordan Marsh, and other

---

In towns large enough to support more than one store, small businesses specialized in
groceries, drugs, hardware, and other lines. Throughout the United States, they operated
along Main Streets like this one in Hammond, New York, 1908.

big-city stores raised the Suffolk County averages, obscuring the predominance of small businesses in Boston's ethnic neighborhoods. In Johnstown, Pennsylvania, at the turn of the century, east central European immigrants ran tiny stores capitalized at under $500. Many such merchants failed, went to work in the mills, and returned to shopkeeping if they managed to reaccumulate savings—a pattern common enough to challenge conventional notions that small-business ownership represented a linear upward mobility.

Operated by their owners with help from spouses and children and perhaps a few hired clerks, such small, financially precarious businesses held a central place in American retail trade well into the twentieth century. As late as 1923, over two-thirds of American retail business was done at these "mom-and-pop" stores. The character of each depended on the personality and

---

Husbands and wives so commonly worked together as partners in small business enterprises that these came to be known as "mom-and-pop" stores. This one was photographed about 1909.

temperament of the proprietor, or more often, of the family that worked together tending the business. Since small retailers' families often lived behind or above their stores, women could function as full partners, pausing to stir the soup or tend to small children in the interstices of business. As the children grew, they went to work for their parents, clerking, keeping stock, or serving customers from delivery wagons.

―――――――――――――――――――――-|||⟨⟩|||-―――――――――――――――――――――

Small merchants were important forces in immigrant communities, serving as translators, bankers, and brokers for jobs and housing. Stores like Hoffman's Kosher Grocery in Seattle, here shown in 1919, enabled communities to maintain traditional ethnic food practices.

Serving townspeople who had no way to carry groceries home from the store, delivery-wagon drivers also looked out for the old and the sick. Employees of Charles W. Smiley, a grocer in East Stroudsburg, Pennsylvania, are shown here about 1914.

Small stores and their proprietors constituted important forces in their communities. In immigrant working-class neighborhoods, as one historian writes of Poles in New Jersey, shopkeepers "wrote and translated letters, extended credit and advice, held money, brokered jobs, found housing, arranged steamship tickets, and served as general 'agent' for their inexperienced countrymen and countrywomen." Rural storekeepers performed many of the same services. Retail stores served as gathering places and centers of gossip, often brought by delivery-wagon drivers, who also kept their eyes out for the aged and infirm. Successful storekeepers offered employment to younger members of the community, in a variety of skilled and unskilled tasks.

Above all, stores offered credit, the keystone of the customer-retailer relationship. Credit enabled workers' families to subsist from paycheck to paycheck and farmers to subsist from harvest to harvest. Grocers in Homestead, Pennsylvania, settled ac-

Small stores functioned as gathering places and centers of gossip; with the advent of telephones, they brought together even those who could not be physically present. This is Bertha Boisseau, Renton, Washington's first telephone operator, at her post in Boisseau's Confectionery.

counts every two weeks, on the Carnegie Steel Company's "pay Friday." In Ada, Minnesota, buying on credit peaked during the preharvest months of July and August. Some Ada stores rendered farmers' bills only once a year, while people living in town customarily settled accounts monthly.

Small retailers who managed to thrive made it possible for whole communities to survive bad crop years and layoffs; their support of a strike could make the difference between success and failure. "Grocers knew their customers personally, and therefore granted credit freely to the trustworthy," social worker Margaret Byington reported about Carnegie's partial shutdown of the Homestead steel mills following the Panic of 1907. "They felt that the confidence thus created would help their trade when better times came. Grocers . . . taxed their credit to the utmost, saying that they would trust their regular customers as long as the wholesalers would trust them."

Credit might produce bitterness and suspicion rather than trust. Storekeepers heard endless tales of financial distress, and told their own, about deadbeat customers whose unpaid accounts threatened the financial stability of marginal businesses. Likewise, customers complained about their creditors. Steelworkers' wives in Homestead claimed that grocers charged more for goods purchased on credit. A Slovak immigrant recalled Fetchik's market in Bridgeport, Connecticut: "In the other stores I could get stuff for eat much cheaper and in Fetchik I have to pay almost double. . . . They rob plenty of money from the people in all these years. Once you have a book in that store you have to pay all your life."

Despite such resentments, people of limited means used credit universally. In Ada's eight leading stores, credit purchases in 1912 ranged from about 40 to 60 percent of total sales. Credit was a way of life everywhere and in all kinds of stores, but especially for grocers and their customers. Only 10½ percent of the nonchain groceries reporting to the Harvard Bureau of Business Research in 1918 sold strictly for cash. Sixty-two percent of the stores that granted credit did two-thirds or more of their business "on the book." Another Bridgeport immigrant commented that grocery credit persisted in the Hungarian community as late as 1940: "That's the way they started when they first came here. They didn't have so much money, so that's the way they had to buy. They got used to it, so they still buy by the book."

Retailers' financial survival depended on granting credit judiciously. "Credit is Lending," the *Grocers' Review* warned in a 1904 headline. Merchants who would demand security, interest, and a fixed time for payment if customers asked to borrow money simply handed out goods on credit. "Goods and money are the same thing," the article stated firmly. "Whenever credit is extended to a customer it is the actual equivalent of lending that customer so much money." Another article in the same issue, reprinted from a stationers' magazine, warned small shop-

An account from Centre
Harbor, New Hampshire.
Judging from his
purchases, Mr. Simonds
lived in town.

keepers not to give their friends credit concessions, for business
should not be conducted on the basis of friendship. "If they are
true friends they will not ask you to do business for nothing, for
few men are in business for their friends' sakes."

At least in part because of credit problems, small businesses
commonly failed. More than a quarter of the retail stores started
in Poughkeepsie, New York, between 1874 and 1933 closed
within a year, and only about half lasted longer than three years.
Two-thirds of Oshkosh, Wisconsin retail businesses established
between 1890 and 1912 folded within that time. The authors of
the Poughkeepsie study suggested that the mortality rate was
even higher in larger cities. Wholesalers and manufacturers
dealing directly with retailers had to take such failures for
granted. "Always give us a full report of any change in firm

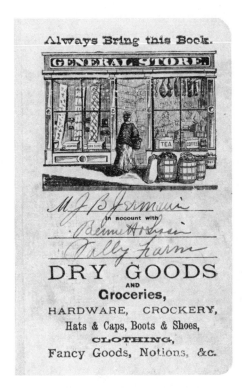

Always Bring this Book.

GENERAL STORE

M. J. B. Jerman
in account with
Bennet Hansen
Tilly Farm

DRY GOODS
AND
Groceries,
HARDWARE, CROCKERY,
Hats & Caps, Boots & Shoes,
CLOTHING,
Fancy Goods, Notions, &c.

Many grocers kept track of customers' credit in small books like this one, which customers were required to bring with them to the store. Buying on credit therefore was called buying "on the book."

names and give us the name of the successor who bought the store," the Iten Biscuit Company told its salesmen in 1916. Such a change was not to be treated as a new account; the market did not grow and the salesman got no credit for his labors in establishing a relationship with the new proprietor.

Even stores that stayed in business did so precariously. "It is safe to say that for many years there have not been more than one or two stores that have really made any money," reported the Ada, Minnesota survey. Retailers in that village lived, not on the current profits of their stores, but on the same savings and investments that had enabled them to go into business in the first place.

Observers believed that financial instability followed from inexperienced people's attempts to enter retail trade. " 'Anybody can keep store' is the slogan," wrote Columbia University marketing professor Paul Nystrom in 1915, commenting on his tabulation of the previous occupations of Oshkosh retailers. "It seems a matter for small wonder, then, that so few are able to succeed." Nine years later, Harvard's Melvin Copeland commented, "With a continual influx of men from other occupations into retail trade . . . this business, with few exceptions, heretofore has been largely an unskilled occupation." In 1921, a federal agent investigating the New York grocery trade on charges of profiteering described most violations as due to inadequate business training rather than intent to defraud the public. "When I get ready to write my book entitled 'Grocers I Have Met,' neither the hero nor the villain will be pictured as riding in limousines, wintering at Palm Beach or summering at Newport," the agent commented. "The average retail grocer in New York and elsewhere is glad to make a living—and let it go at that. . . . [He] is so busy lugging boxes, barrels and crates around that his actual finances are a profound mystery to him."

Finances would always be mysterious, critics contended, to the many retailers who failed to keep good books. Introducing a simplified accounting system that the Federal Trade Commission published in 1916, the commission's chairman asserted that "the majority of retail merchants do not know accurately the cost of conducting their business." The Harvard Bureau of Business Research concurred. "A surprisingly large proportion of the retail grocers of the country," it reported in 1919, "do not keep accounts that are even approximately accurate." Many merchants kept haphazard records or none at all; few recorded cash transactions; most knew nothing about taking inventory, figuring margins, defining stock turn, or calculating numerical measures of their business. "What's the use?" asked one druggist of investigators who wondered why he did not keep books or figure his costs. "I have no one to account to but myself." Druggists were said to be especially negligent because they considered themselves professionals, more interested in health care than in commerce. Yet even after the 1913 federal income tax, the vast majority of retailers really did not have anybody to account to, since hardly any earned more than the $4,000 exemption for married people.

Haphazard store accounts might not even get rectified by bank statements, because many small merchants did not use banks, although for decades they were advised to do so by writers on retail trade. "Every dealer should keep a bank account," counseled an 1883 handbook. "The money is safer, not so carelessly expended, and the checks by which it is paid out stand as vouchers and receipts." In 1912, a grocers' magazine provided the most elementary explanation of the advantages of banks (safe vaults) and bankers (useful information). "Depend upon it," the author wrote, "bankers always know what is going on in a community in a financial way." The 1920 edition of *Success in Retailing,* published by the Butler Brothers wholesaling firm for its variety-store customers, advised: "Have a bank account, even though it be a small one. This is the most convenient method of paying bills and a very effective means of keeping track of your money."

In some transactions, there was no money to keep track of. "Country dealers are often obliged to take eggs, butter, etc., as pay for sugar, starch and soap," the 1883 grocers' handbook admitted, although it advised against doing so. Barter persisted commonly in country districts for at least another half-century. In 1919, 87 percent of the general-merchandise stores reporting to the Harvard study received farm produce from their customers, especially eggs and butter; they paid farmers in cash, merchandise, or credit, or with special tokens that could be used as payment for merchandise in the future.

Barter was a special case of bargaining, which small merchants continued to do, despite the fixed prices established in large stores where customers did business with hired clerks rather than with proprietors. Decades after Marshall Field's and Macy's adopted the one-price principle, the word "bargain" continued to function as a verb describing a price-setting process that engaged buyers and sellers at least theoretically as equals, not as a noun characterizing a low price set by the seller. One Italian American recalled his grandmother's interactions with the immigrant merchants in her New York neighborhood. Entering a store, she would "ignore the proprietor . . . and peruse the shop's merchandise with the most casual, haphazard manner she could affect. . . . After a while, my grandmother would begin to ask the prices of items she fingered suspiciously, indicating that they were obviously inferior. In response to his replies, she would immediately unhand the item in question, her every facial and bodily nuance saying it was repulsive in quality and its price a moral outrage. After these unhurried preliminaries, bargaining would begin in earnest . . . starting at outlandish extremes, she and the merchant would bark out final prices."

Most retailers used secret price marks composed of letters, which facilitated bargaining by reminding the merchant of his own buying price. A 1911 *Business Man's Encyclopedia* called such marks "universal" and taught storekeepers how to create them. Each digit was coded; an item bought for forty-seven cents would be marked DB according to the following scheme:

1 2 3 4 5 6 7 8 9 0
V A N D E R B I L T

"In a similar way 'MAKEPROFIT,' 'CALEBSMITH,' or 'CHELMSFORD,' could be used," the book explained. *Hardware Store Business Methods* (1901), a collection of articles reprinted from the trade journal *Iron Age*, offered both a similar alphabetic system and a code that resembled neither letters nor numbers.

Retailers bargained not only with their customers but with wholesalers' drummers. Another *Iron Age* article advised that merchants keep records of price quotations, because they were "too numerous to trust to memory." Merchants who knew competitive quotations could place orders at once upon hearing a good price, avoiding the expense and delay of soliciting more quotations only to find that the best price was already at hand. "More than this, it can be used as one of the buyer's most powerful levers in obtaining good prices from traveling salesmen." The article went on to offer instructions on bargaining, explaining that salesmen represented their firms and had "authority to quote the lowest prices and terms necessary to secure trade."

"Salesmen seldom name their best price first," the article explained, "so never appear anxious to buy. They are generally more anxious to sell than the buyer is to order, and will not lose a sale until they have reached their limit." If a salesman quoted a price that did compare favorably with other quotations, the merchant should "solicit further concessions, if not in price, then in discounts, length of time, freights, etc." A 1911 textbook on salesmanship taught bargaining from the salesman's side. "The Tactics of Selling," a lesson packed with military imagery, described "a battle of wits": "All through, from beginning to end, the salesman must be a tactician, arranging beforehand his plan of campaign, leaving nothing to chance; and yet in the battle he must think of nothing else but the victory." The best tacticians, of course, won charmingly, leaving storekeepers looking forward to their return.

"Converse freely with these periodic visitors," the *Iron Age* advised. "They have seen much and in their line can tell much that will prove both interesting and valuable to the buyer. Owing to the proverbial veracity of their craft, it is well at times to take their statements with more or less salt. But treat them well; show an interest in their welfare, and they will see that yours does not suffer." Good relationships with salesmen could be translated into good relationships with the wholesale houses they represented, essential to business survival. Retailers were dependent on these larger merchants not only for obtaining goods but for obtaining credit. In essence, jobbers served as bankers to small merchants.

As creditors, the wholesalers had a vested interest in retailing success that could work to the storekeepers' benefit or detriment. They could withhold credit and goods if store operations did not conform to their standards, and even salesmen who had no other credit duties were called upon to make reports on the general ambience of the stores they visited and the likely creditworthiness of their proprietors. On the other hand, wholesalers

WHY DO THEY DO IT? SEARCH ME!
By Sumner Fauley

The village merchant prefers to read the news to his friends, who assemble to discuss the happenings of the day, rather than to use the commercial traveler with a little courtesy.   Did it ever happen to you?

Good relationships between salesmen and storekeepers faced many ob-stacles, detailed in a series of cartoons for the *Sample Case,* a salesmen's magazine, in 1919. Here the merchant favors his clientele over the occasional visitor.

⫶⫶⫶

could and did use credit to invest in promising prospective retailers. Marshall Field, a man personally interested in the de-velopment of the West, frequently joined his credit man, Harlow Higinbotham, at meetings with such new customers. After some investigation, the historian of the company writes, "the young man would be told to go ahead—open up a store and Field's would finance him in part or give him long-term credit. A typical arrangement was that, if the merchant was to have a $20,000 stock, Field gave him perhaps $5,000 to $10,000 credit. Even this seemingly small help usually meant that nearly everything that the merchant handled thereafter would be purchased from Marshall Field and Co., Wholesale."

The merchandise would be branded with the Field private label or with the particular brands that Marshall Field's carried. The company negotiated exclusive contracts as sole agents for the West or for the whole United States on items ranging from the basic Clark's O.N.T. thread to the luxurious Alexandre brand kid gloves manufactured by Fortin Fils and Deschamps of Paris; it sold these goods not only in its famous Chicago store but through its much larger wholesale department. Field's managed its own manufacturing facilities as early as 1870, primarily producing ready-to-wear clothing, but also towels, napkins, and umbrellas that it sold in both its wholesale and retail divisions. In 1900, Marshall Field's lace factory made $9,000 in profits, its underwear factory $14,600, and its suspender factory $5,400. After Marshall Field died in 1906, the company created a manufacturing division that came to be known as the "Fieldcrest Mills," administering cotton mills and other factories, primarily in the South.

Marshall Field's was unusual in its size and its growth, but many other jobbers bought some manufacturing facilities outright and operated retail divisions. Such large retail-wholesale operations, like the emerging chain-store systems and the two Chicago mail-order houses, Sears and Montgomery Ward, adapted flow principles to distribution, organizing systems that could move large quantities of goods. Other large retailers followed their lead, buying in quantity, doing their own wholesaling, and in some cases manufacturing. One leading drug wholesaler bought a manufacturing firm and created a nationally advertised product, Steero bouillon cubes, which it sold to other jobbers and to retail grocers, delicatessens, and candy-store soda fountains.

The old lines between jobber, manufacturer, and retailer were blurring. By the early 1880s, the editor of a New York grocery journal described this confusion as a serious threat to manufacturers. "We recall the time here in this city when the jobbers and manufacturers were two entirely distinct classes; when the former were content to sell the goods of the manufacturers; and when the idea of a jobbing house making or putting up its own soap and starch and baking powders and blue and cigars and canned goods and the thousand and one things usually sold to the trade had not entered the fertile brain of would-be monopolists in the grocery line." By the end of the century, writers routinely described the situation in the distribution system as "chaos." Even the distinctions between trades were getting confused: the divisions between groceries, dry goods, and drugs were not as clear as they had been earlier.

The confusion was exacerbated by manufacturers, who increasingly handled their own marketing. The branding strategy did not itself dictate channels of distribution. Manufacturing firms had to choose among numerous ways to get the goods to households, to the hundreds of thousands of small stores that might carry them, or to middlemen who would do the physical work of distribution.

Some companies established retail operations, selling through the mail, using door-to-door salesmen, or setting up stores and hiring managers and clerks. Singer, with the longest history of manufacturer's retailing, built a worldwide network that ran 8,000 stores and employed 40,000 house-to-house salespeople by the early 1920s. Aluminum cookware and vacuum cleaners were also widely sold door-to-door. Companies in many fields began as mail-order businesses. Such direct relationships between manufacturer and consumer, however, required companies to put much of their expansion capital—indeed, much of their income—into the sales effort. During the three years that the Ingersoll company sold its watches by mail, for example, it estimated that it spent ninety-eight cents for every dollar it took in. Ingersoll turned instead to selling through a variety of retail outlets—jewelers, drug stores, general stores, department stores, hardware stores, and railroad station concessionaires. Most national marketers did their actual distribution through such independent retailers, though they might send advertising matter through the mails or deposit samples on doorsteps. They established contacts with consumers through their advertisements, their promotional schemes, and their company images, not direct business contacts with households as customers.

In certain industries, manufacturers granted independent retailers the right to operate as authorized dealerships, also called "exclusive agencies." Munsingwear sold its underwear directly to a network of merchants who were prepared to handle the large number of individual items in a line consisting of many styles in seventy fabrics and in sizes for men, women, and children. In shoes, building supplies, furniture, clothing, and, ultimately, automobiles—industries where purchases were infrequent—people might go out of their way to get products they had seen advertised. Manufacturers in those industries sacrificed universal distribution for the better service they could get from their authorized dealer networks.

Some manufacturers did their own wholesaling. Heinz, which chose this method from the start, built an immense organization to distribute its "57 Varieties." By 1922, it maintained fifty-eight branch offices and warehouses and seventy foreign agencies. The American sales force employed over a thousand men, working out of branch offices that carried the retail accounts. Other manufacturers maintained accounts with both wholesalers and retailers. Ingersoll, for example, distributed two-thirds of its output through wholesalers after moving away from mail order, but also sold watches directly to 20,000 retailers.

Most manufacturers did use wholesalers for the physical work of distribution, though they might hire a few salesmen or use the mails to establish and sustain their own connections with storekeepers, devising promotions to induce merchants to order from their regular wholesalers. Warehouses and large sales forces were very expensive, and maintaining accounts with thousands or even hundreds of thousands of small shopkeepers presented an administrative burden beyond the capacity of most manufacturers. On the other hand, depending entirely on wholesalers was risky. They might push competitors' products or their own private brands, and they could not be relied upon to persuade retailers to carry new products or to display brands in store windows. Hotpoint began in California, and in its early years did its own shipping and warehousing and sent salesmen to stores in that state. When it went national, the company turned to middlemen for distribution, but solicited and maintained a dealer network through direct-mail dealer advertising. The Wrigley company wrote to 17,000 retailers when it introduced Spearmint to the New York metropolitan area, enclosing a coupon for a free box, redeemable at the wholesaler's.

Probably the most cogent analysis of the changing relationships between wholesalers, manufacturers, and retailers came from Arch W. Shaw, editor of *System* and *Factory* magazines, publisher of many well-regarded business books, founder and financial angel of the Harvard Bureau of Business Research, and a Kellogg board member and original stockholder. In "Problems in Market Distribution," a 1912 article that became one of the seminal works of marketing thought, Shaw described the five functions of middlemen. They assumed the financial risks of credit losses and of the actual loss of goods damaged or destroyed in shipment or in warehouse fires and floods; they transported the merchandise; they financed distribution; they sold the goods, promoting them and providing information about them; and they performed the physical functions involved in assembling, assorting, and reshipping.

Shaw pointed beyond the chaos that resulted from manufacturing and retailing firms performing some of these functions to other important new institutions that specialized as "functional middlemen." In most industries, insurance companies had assumed much of the risk, and banks took care of much of the finance. Another crucial development had lessened manufacturers' financial dependence on middlemen. "The application of the corporate form to industrial organization," Shaw wrote, "has made it possible to draw together larger bodies of operating capital and hence to place the producer in a stronger financial position." Even the stock market, in other words, had assumed a traditional middleman function.

The transportation function had been taken over by direct-transportation companies, a field then dominated by four large firms—Adams Express, American Express, United States Express, and Wells, Fargo—two of which later moved into finance. These companies did not offer service to millions of people in rural areas, although after rural free delivery was instituted in 1896, moonlighting postmen often carried packages from train depots to postal patrons on their routes. As Shaw pointed out, the federal government would become a functional middleman with the institution of parcel post, a subject hotly debated in trade circles at the time he wrote because of the great benefit it would confer on the mail-order businesses. Congress passed the parcel-post legislation in August 1912, the same month his article appeared.

Jobbers still performed the function of assembling, assorting, and reshipping merchandise, and their traveling salesmen still promoted goods and provided information about them, but Shaw's analysis clarified their recent eclipse. Earnest Elmo Calkins, who with his partner, Ralph Holden, is said to have designed the first advertising campaign, had described the situation as early as 1905 in a bluntly titled *Printers' Ink* article, "Eliminating the Jobber." Calkins explicitly pointed to national advertising, which encroached on the jobber's selling function and put manufacturers in a commanding position in the distribution system. "To the manufacturer who advertises," he wrote, "it makes no difference what jobber or what commission man buys his goods. All of them will have to buy them in the end."

Like Scott Paper and Heinz, some national marketers did eliminate jobbers from their distribution schemes. By 1913, other companies including Spalding, Sherwin-Williams, Gillette, Colgate, and Victor Talking Machines sold directly to retailers. Procter and Gamble first attempted to bypass jobbers in New York City that year, expanding its sales force from a dozen

to more than seventy-five after the biggest wholesalers had refused to carry Ivory and Crisco on the company's terms. Over
the next few years, the jobbers returned to handling the company's goods, but the incident provided experience for P & G's
move to its own distribution system in 1920.

For some firms like the National Biscuit Company, assuming
the wholesalers' transportation and assembling functions offered better control over perishable products. The more universal reason for eliminating the jobber, however, involved the
selling function. "The jobber has no particular interest in praising the goods," Schilling explained to its salesmen as early as
1884, advising them to forgo jobbers' large orders. With no
loyalty to manufacturers or their products, jobbers could not be
expected to make special efforts, especially when introducing
new kinds of products that required explanation or demonstration. Nor could manufacturers expect wholesalers to push products that competed with their own private brands.

Even so, the administrative burdens of handling distribution
and the costs of establishing a sales force were sufficient to deter
some very large companies, especially ones that faced little competition. The Diamond Match Company, which controlled 90
percent of the match industry, sold through jobbers and promoted that strategy. An assistant sales manager told *Printers' Ink*
that he could not see "the wisdom of adopting a policy which
would lose for him the services of 70,000 jobbers' salesmen."
Those salesmen handled orders for hundreds of thousands of
retailers, with whom distributing manufacturers had to establish
accounts, an awesome clerical load. Managing those accounts
required them to train salesmen as credit raters and collectors,
and to tie up capital in retailers' credit. Given the inefficiency of
doing business with shopkeepers who could not even keep
books, manufacturers might well prefer to avoid the financial
and administrative burdens of dealing with retail trade and to
confine their own business to more reliable customers, the
larger, better-managed wholesaling firms.

Despite the many articles in the trade press about "eliminating the jobber," then, the distribution system continued to depend on these middlemen. In 1918, a decisive majority of the retailers studied by the Harvard Bureau of Business Research relied on wholesale grocers for all of their flour, sugar, salt, baking powder, soda, cocoa, dried fruit, nuts, soap, canned goods, condiments, tobacco, and breakfast foods. Cracker and bread baking and coffee and tea processing were the only food-manufacturing industries where direct distribution had prevailed. Many national marketers used wholesalers but also established national sales forces that promoted goods and provided information, dressed retailers' windows, held store demonstrations, and rallied retail support for marketing campaigns. These "salesmen" took orders that they turned over to the storekeepers' regular wholesalers.

Despite these orders, the largest wholesalers openly resisted national brands, pushing the private labels on which they made higher profits, and recommending that retailers push them as well because they, too, would make more money. As creditors to small stores, the wholesalers had cause for concern. Like Crisco under its original trade terms, many of the national brands offered retailers less margin than their costs of doing business. Whereas most observers agreed that retailers needed margins of about 18 to 20 percent to make any profit at all, Uneeda Biscuit, Pet condensed milk, and Cream of Wheat paid 16⅔ percent, Royal baking powder 12½ percent, and Pillsbury's flour, even bought by the barrel, between 6 and 11 percent. Crisco was originally set at 16⅔ percent; after the price was reduced, grocers could make 22 percent on the product.

This question of margins was explored in a purported dialogue between two immigrant grocers that appeared in the July 1903 edition of the *Anco Special*, a "journal" that the giant Austin, Nichols wholesaling firm published for its customers. "Don't sell 'em," responded grocer number 2 to his friend's complaint that he lost money on "proprietary articles" like Quaker Oats and Uneeda Biscuit. "Goodness knows I don't *want* to sell 'em, but what am I to do when people ask for 'em every day?" replied grocer number 1. "Give 'em something else," responded number 2, suggesting Nichols's Crushed Oats. The dialogue provided a retailer-financed plan for introducing the Austin, Nichols product through full-sized free samples to customers who requested Quaker Oats. It also gave lessons in substitution, furnishing merchants with the words they needed in a model sales talk ("I'm sorry, madam, I'm out of it at present . . .").

The "substitution evil," as it was called in the advertising trade press, depended in part on consumers' trusting relationships with merchants. "The influence of the retailer in intimate touch with the consumers is far greater and more effective than that of a distant manufacturer whose appeal is by means of the printed word alone," a writer pointed out in *System*. Most customers did not even tell retailers directly what they wanted; a research study indicated that only seventeen out of a hundred buyers of advertised goods said "I want so-and-so." Eighty-three asked a question, "Have you so-and-so?" Whether the answer was "Yes, but . . ." or "No, but . . . ," retailers could easily use it as a lead to suggest an alternative, and a good salesman could even substitute for a product that had achieved brand loyalty. "Try this instead of that, Mrs. Brown; it's just as good," the article quoted a grocer's quiet response to a woman's regular soap order. "Mrs. Brown looked at him curiously for a moment as if surprised at the suggestion, met his firm, assuring glance, then answered 'All right.' The dealer did not argue or say anything detrimental to one soap or in favor of the other."

Retailers' direct contact with consumers, this article maintained, made them into "the power that concludes sales." For all the power of the manufacturers, they depended on the two-way relationships created by that contact. Consumers purchased goods in stores, which belonged to retailers; manufacturers had to rely on alliances with the people who sold their products. Manufacturing businesses might be larger and more efficiently managed, but manufacturing executives would do well, as one wrote, to "drop that attitude of class distinction—treat [the retailer] as a man, with just as much of a right to a share of the world's plunder as we have." Manufacturers who established

Substitution warnings were common in advertising. This page from an
1888 Fleischmann's yeast calendar combines the substitution message
with sentimental imagery.

good relationships with storekeepers could exploit their strategic position by getting them to recommend products, to give the
manufacturers window space, and to open their stores to
demonstrators. Those who did not risked having their advertising programs undermined by substitution or by retailers' failure
or refusal to stock a product. Most manufacturers therefore
devoted substantial resources to courting retailers through

salesmen, through the trade press, and through the mails.

Some, however, went on the offensive. The makers of Hires root beer threatened soda-fountain operators who gave customers substitutes without even telling them. In a full-page ad in the *Soda Fountain,* Hires listed the names of bottling companies and drug stores the company had sued for representing other beverages as Hires. "SUBSTITUTION," the headline read. "Does it Pay? Well, *does* It?" The company revealed that it had organized a substitution department that employed both inspectors and lawyers. "It is *expensive* and *unpleasant,* for *us* and *for the substitutors,* but we have no choice but to fight for our rights and our customers and from now on we mean to do it."

A grocer's magazine defended substitution, using another soap example, a merchant who recommended a less expensive soap of "No. 1 quality." "Some persons will say, 'That was substitution.' If so, substitution was only another word for salesmanship," the article argued. This grocer gave his customer better value for her money, while making more money for himself. "Such management illustrates the fact that there is a distinct dividing line between mere store-keeping, or 'tending store,' and being a real merchant, one whose ability to sell whatever is for his own interest and the interest of his customers is the first consideration." Some retailers substituted without regard for quality and without apology. N. C. Jensen, a Chicago grocer interviewed for a 1922 marketing survey, sold more Monarch baked beans than any other brand, although he personally rated them last in quality, behind Heinz, Snider's, Campbell's, and Van Camp's. "Mr. J says that he makes fifteen cents more per case on Monarch beans than on any other brand and for that reason he has pushed them very hard," reported the investigator.

Consumer advertising warned customers about such behavior. "BEWARE OF IMITATIONS," cautioned an ad for Sapolio, a gritty scouring soap that was for many decades one of America's best-known cleaning products. "Grocers often substitute cheaper goods for Sapolio, to make a better profit. Send back such articles, and insist upon having just what you ordered." "If substitutes are offered," Gillette suggested, "refuse them and write us at once for our booklet and free trial offer." Many advertisers taught consumers to look for trademarks in order to avoid substitutes. "CAUTION," the Standard Sanitary Manufacturing Company alerted *McClure's* readers in 1905. "Every piece of 'Standard' Ware bears our guarantee 'Standard' 'Green and Gold' label, and has our trade-mark 'Standard' cast on the outside. Unless the label and trade-mark are on the fixture, it is not 'Standard' Ware. Refuse substitutes—they are all inferior and will cost you more in the end." Like the letters sent from the company's business office, the advertisement printed the word "Standard" in its trademarked lettering every time it appeared.

In industries like sanitary fixtures, which made products not purchased frequently, manufacturers avoided substitution by establishing authorized dealerships. But the universal distribution sought by producers in the grocery, drug, and hardware trades required making every retailer into an authorized distributor. Manufacturers therefore aimed to cut down on salesmanship as the grocer's magazine defined it, and to turn storekeepers into "dealers" of their products, whose job was to distribute.

Still, the retailer was far from becoming, in the words of the Wisconsin storekeeper who fought the Crisco trade terms, "a mere automaton for the vending of their wares." On a systemic level, the enormous output made possible by the new processes of mass production was being introduced into an unwieldy and old-fashioned distribution system, dominated by still-powerful regional wholesalers who supplied credit and goods to a multitude of small shopkeepers, many with unstable businesses. Merchants did not develop into dealers as fast as manufacturers wanted them to; distribution continued to rest on the personal relationships that they formed with wholesalers' salesmen and with customers in the communities they served. Likewise, their customers still shopped by asking merchants and clerks to hand them the goods, and were just beginning to develop into consumers.

The consumer role demanded trust in manufacturers and belief in the words on their labels. For all their statements of support for retailers, manufacturers had to win consumer trust away from the storekeeper in order to build that level of confidence. One advertising company claimed in 1913 that this had already been accomplished in New York. In small towns, the ad explained, grocers and customers related with "friendly intimacy and the 'what do you recommend' attitude . . . the grocer is sometimes your neighbor and often your trusted friend of years' standing." In New York, on the other hand, "he is usually regarded as an institution that tries to make all the profit he can out of your trade. In New York City people put their trust in the manufacturer."

The advertisement exaggerated. Many New Yorkers patronized ethnic merchants who resembled the small-town grocer. And many had come to the city from smaller towns and from the countryside, both in America and in Europe. Like small-town Americans, these people had been raised on goods produced at home and by people they knew, or at least personally recommended by trusted advisers. In New York as elsewhere, manufacturers had to build trust on many levels: confidence in their companies, in their products, and in the market, and belief in the new ways of life that the new goods of mass production symbolized and created.

CHAPTER 4

NEW PRODUCTS, NEW HABITS

ANTHROPOLOGIST MARY DOUGLAS AND ECONOMIST BARON ISHER-wood, attempting to define consumption in a way that could apply to any human culture, maintain that "consumption starts where market ends. What happens to material objects once they have left the retail outlet and reached the hands of the final purchasers is part of the consumption process." Seen this way, the creation of modern American consumer culture involved not only introducing new products and establishing market demand for them, but also creating new domestic habits and activities, performed at home, away from stores and outside the marketing process. People who had never bought corn flakes were taught to need them; those formerly content to buy oats scooped from the grocer's bin were informed about why they should prefer Quaker Oats in a box. At the same time, they learned how packaged breakfast cereals fit modern urban lifestyles, suiting people seeking convenience, punching a time clock, and not in need of the calories of a country breakfast. Patrons of photographers and barbers, along with people who had never been photographed and men who had never shaved, had to be told how to incorporate cameras and safety razors into their lives by integrating picture-taking and shaving into their habits and routines.

The advertising industry that planned and coordinated these lessons underwent a substantial transformation at the end of the nineteenth century. Newspapers and magazines had published paid commercial messages since colonial times, but most had printed them in separate sections full of closely packed small ads, like classified advertising today; usually these simply informed potential customers that goods were available. By the turn of the century, new, mass-circulation magazines and newspapers were supported by advertising revenues and designed to highlight the ads—to function as advertising *media.* Advertisements grew in size, and their use of white space embraced new design principles. According to some contemporary advertising practitioners and to many historians of the subject, the new

———————————————— IIICIII ————————————————

In nineteenth-century magazines, advertisements for national brands such as Sapolio, an extremely popular and widely advertised scouring soap, appeared on dense pages of advertising like this one, from *Harper's,* 1870.

THOMSON'S
PATENT
"GLOVE-FITTING"

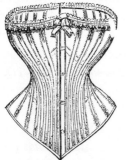

The Most Popular Corset ever introduced into the American Market.

The strongest proof of the excellence and popularity of this Corset is found in the *numerous* attempts to palm off *worthless imitations* as the *genuine imported* "*Glove-Fitting.*" We therefore call special attention to our stamp and trade-mark, which are always to be found on each Corset, and without which *none are genuine.*

N. B.—All infringements of Patent, or of our copyright in name " Glove-Fitting," will be prosecuted.

Waltham Watches.

Buyers of watches at retail should be on their guard against buying watches represented as " American," and which are usually advertised in connection with the words " Oroide," " Imitation Gold," and other words calculated to attract attention. Nine cases out of ten such watches are spurious, as our genuine movements are seldom, if ever, put into any thing but solid gold or silver cases. Large numbers of these worthless watches bear colorable imitations of our trademarks. To avoid imposition, buyers who do not know responsible jewelers should first procure a descriptive catalogue of the different styles of watches made by the American Watch Company, of Waltham, Mass. The catalogue contains, in addition, much useful information to watch-buyers. Address

ROBBINS & APPLETON, General Agents,
182 BROADWAY, New York.

ENOCH MORGAN'S SONS'

CLEANS
WINDOWS,
MARBLE,
KNIVES.
POLISHES
TIN WARE,
IRON, STEEL, &c.

Depot, 211 Washington Street, New York.

artwork contributed to a larger change: the goals of advertising shifted from an emphasis on providing information to an attempt to influence buyers by any means possible.

The change began during the 1870s, when *Scribner's* and *Harper's* instituted new practices, offering relatively low rates to advertisers who bought whole pages. Cyrus H. K. Curtis, publisher of the *Saturday Evening Post,* went a step farther when he founded the *Ladies' Home Journal* in 1883 and set subscriptions at fifty cents per year; *Godey's Lady's Book,* until then the leading American women's magazine, cost six times as much. Within five years, the *Journal* displayed more than twice as much advertising as any other women's magazine, and by 1900, Curtis boasted to advertisers that it reached a million subscribers. At about the same time, newspapers following the lead of publishers Joseph Pulitzer and William Randolph Hearst sought an even broader audience, daily reaching large numbers of people of all classes. Most cities supported several papers, competing for the public with their comics, features, and pictures, and competing as well for advertising. Their low fixed rates encouraged the use of large spaces, and fostered the layout of the modern newspaper.

Even the immigrants who did not read American newspapers and magazines saw billboards, probably the oldest of advertising media. During the decades after 1880, new systems offered advertisers and their agents better control over signposting; regional and national outdoor advertising firms began to guarantee that posters would actually be put up and kept up for the amount of time paid for. Poster lithography made it possible to reproduce color images on a scale and in numbers never before seen, while electric signs made the nighttime as commercially viable as the day. These new technologies enabled advertisers to create billboards so intrusive that they provoked public controversy about the use of visual space for commercial purposes.

While reformers campaigned against billboards on public property, advertisers extended their use of publicly visible but privately owned space. Sapolio inaugurated streetcar advertis-

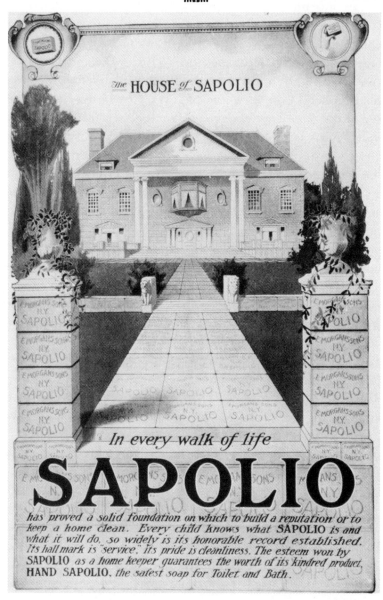

This Sapolio advertisement from the *Harmsworth Self-Educator Magazine,* 1907, shows the turn-of-the-century changes in design and space policy.

ing on New York's horse-drawn cars in 1884; for years the characters and jingles on its "Spotless Town" placards provided distraction for public-transit passengers. Artemas Ward, the trade-journal editor and copywriter who directed that Sapolio campaign, eventually set up one of several competing streetcar advertising firms that by the end of the century could place standardized cards simultaneously in thousands of trolleys, in cities all over the country.

As the nature of the media changed, advertising agencies introduced new services. For decades after the Civil War, they had functioned as space brokers: agents bought blocks of space in newspapers and magazines, and sold them to advertisers who created and designed their own ads. At the turn of the century, many agents began to hire artists and copywriters and to offer clients coordination with the agencies that handled outdoor and transit advertising. The most advanced agencies conducted campaigns—carefully planned maneuvers, often entailing rudimentary market research—and handled sampling and other nonprint promotions.

Increasingly, agents operated as self-conscious advertising professionals. By 1906, enough of them had gathered around Madison Square for *Printers' Ink* to pronounce it the "new hub of the advertising universe." The magazine itself promoted professional consciousness, as did local advertising men's clubs and leagues in major cities. In 1907, seventeen local organizations had joined the Associated Advertising Clubs of America. Within a few more years, advertising agents and advertising managers for manufacturers and publishers could join a number of national organizations that promoted advertising and provided legislative lobbying, employment bureaus, speakers, and clipping and information services for their members.

Advertising men used language that described market competition as war and the market as a battlefield. The American publicity director for Lever Brothers, Ltd., which operated the world's largest soap factory in England, spoke of "invading America" with Lifebuoy soap. His "first step was the construction

Sign painters and bill posters worked for companies affiliated with national agencies th
could put up advertisements all over the country and guarantee that they would stay up f
the contracted amount of time.

of a plan of campaign for the whole field"; the company "fired the first gun" in 1902. National Biscuit named the teams that dispensed samples and dressed store windows the "In-Er-Seal Squadrons" and "In-Er-Seal Cadets." In 1910, Shredded Wheat's advertising manager, Truman A. DeWeese, called newspapers "the infantry of our advertising campaign" and magazines the "artillery," with "the back covers in illustrated weeklies being the big guns." This rhetoric eventually became so standard that the word "campaign" took on a civilian connotation.

The campaign, a planned series of steps and maneuvers, offered advertisers the possibility of coordinating newspaper and magazine advertisements with billboards, streetcar ads, storewindow displays, and special promotions. Advertising agent

Charles Austin Bates introduced comprehensive planning in the early 1890s, asking prospective clients to fill out a "symptom blank," a series of questions designed to provide him with a complete understanding of the business. By 1905, Earnest Elmo Calkins and Ralph Holden had prepared a complete marketing plan, illustrated with graphs, charts, and sketches of magazine advertisements and window displays. Bates found clients hostile to his questionnaire, and Calkins and Holden never presented their plan to the Gillette company, for which it had been made, but within another decade, campaigns like the one for Crisco revealed the advantages of careful planning.

The most effective campaigns encouraged new needs and new habits, not by creating them out of whole cloth, but by linking the rapid appearance of new products with the rapid changes in all areas of social and cultural life. Buying behavior depended on new behavior at home and in the workplace, which manufacturers and their advertising agents consciously promoted in their emphasis on new product categories. "The problem was to sell the *Soup Idea*," a Campbell's representative wrote in the early 1920s about the company's first advertising twenty years before. That idea was bolstered by changes in American work schedules, by the introduction of other new convenience foods, and by gas and electric stoves and hotplates that could be used one burner at a time. "Copy policy has been designed to create reader interest and a distinct Campbell's individuality through the famous Campbell's Kids and the jingles," the spokesman continued; "simultaneously the ceaseless propaganda for soup-eating continues."

Colgate and the Florence Manufacturing Company, maker of the Prophylactic, the first widely advertised toothbrush, taught people to brush their teeth. A Colgate spokesman called his company's early advertising "pioneer work . . . in teaching the public the habit of caring for the teeth," while Prophylactic said "it has been our aim to educate the American people to keep their teeth and mouths clean." Both companies published booklets explaining dental hygiene, available through the mail and

Corporate promotional efforts dovetailed with attempts to teach dental hygiene in school, celebrated in this 1912 advertisement from the *Ladies' Home Journal.*

handed out at fairs and exhibitions. For Colgate Ribbon Dental Cream, introduced around 1905 and specifically formulated to eliminate "the old druggy taste" of previous dentifrices, a wide sampling campaign was designed to show "people who had never brushed their teeth and children who found it difficult to acquire the habit" that toothpaste could taste good.

One Colgate booklet, *ABC of the Teeth,* ended with an ad for other Colgate products and an offer for the company's pamphlet *How to Shave Yourself,* available for a two-cent stamp. The Hapgoods Sales Company, maker of the Razac safety razor, offered *The Face of the Well-Groomed Man,* with chapters on "How to Prepare the Face for Shaving; How to Shave; Simple Massage; Care of the Skin; Why the Barber makes Wrinkles." Gillette warned of "the dangers that men often encounter who allow their faces to come in contact with brush, soap and barber shop accessories used on other people." "Nobody knows your face as well as you do," the company asserted. "Nobody else can take as good care of it." Urging men to establish a daily product-using routine, the headline of one 1909 ad in *Town and Country* declared frankly, "You Ought to Shave Every Morning."

The Gillette razor, as this advertisement put it in text displayed below a portrait of King Gillette, "is not a mere device. It is a *public service* with a *personality* back of it." Gillette was indeed a personality, well known as a utopian thinker who wrote for influential radical magazines, and who in 1894 had published *The Human Drift,* which denounced competition and celebrated centralization as a natural human tendency. Before he invented the disposable razor blade that made him rich, Gillette had worked as a salesman, traveling first for Sapolio and later for a bottle-cap manufacturer. He remained eccentrically and simultaneously dedicated to making money and to societal perfection, developing his social theories in a series of books written during power struggles in the rapidly expanding business that bore his name. By the end of his life he had lost control of the company and much of his personal fortune, but his picture and signature continued to appear on razor-blade wrappers until the introduc-

King Gillette, the inventor of the disposable razor blade, appeared in many early Gillette advertisements, extolling his razor and warning against the dangers of barbershop shaves. This ad was published in 1907.

tion of stainless-steel blades in the 1960s. By that time, King
Gillette reigned in the land of myth and symbol, as renowned
as Betty Crocker and the Green Giant.

This colorful character spoke frankly and directly in the text
of early Gillette advertisements. After 1908, the diamond-and-
arrow trademark joined the battery of company symbols, while
the portrait was relegated to a cameo. Within a few years, full-
page advertisements without the founder's picture showed the
mark of a new and more modern art director, and a new sort of
didacticism. A series of ads during the summer and fall of 1910
pictured groups of men who could not patronize barbers—sail-
ors, railroad travelers, outdoorsmen. The men in these ads actually taught readers how to shave, demonstrating the "sliding or

---

Gillette explicitly taught shaving lessons in its advertising. This was one of a series of 1910 ads in *Town and Country* that showed men using the proper strokes.

You can have an object lesson in the use of the Gillette on any sleeping car in America.
Most men who shave on the train use the Gillette. They can shave quickly—with no stropping, no honing—shave smoothly and clean up all the corners, with no danger from the lurch or motion of the car.
A bridegroom on the Canadian Pacific acquired a three-days' growth of beard. Despair was written on his face. A kindly old gentleman loaned him a Gillette—and received the united thanks of two fond hearts.
Men who travel much become very practical. They go in for efficiency—get down to necessities.

Tourists and travellers are the staunchest advocates of the Gillette. It would be interesting to know how many thousand Gillettes are sold every year through their example and recommendation.
Be progressive. Keep a Gillette on your home washstand—take it with you when you travel. Spread around some of the Gillette sunshine. Wear the smile of the man who can shave without stropping or honing. Life is brighter when a clean face is an every morning habit.
Standard Set $5. Gillette Blades 50c. and $1.00

King C Gillette

GILLETTE SALES COMPANY, 80 W. Second Street, Boston
New York, Times Building   Chicago, Stock Exchange Building   Gillette Safety Razor, Ltd., London   Eastern Office, Shanghai, China   Canadian Office, 63 St. Alexander Street, Montreal
Factories: Boston, Montreal, Leicester, Berlin, Paris

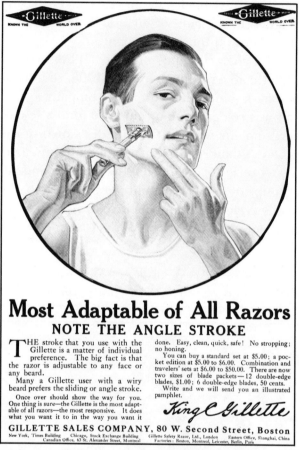

The first of the shaving-lesson advertisements, from *Town and Country*.

angle stroke," which one 1910 ad pictured explicitly.

Town and Country and the other magazines where Gillette advertised were addressed to affluent people. At five dollars, the least expensive Gillette cost about twice as much as a straight razor and somewhere between a third and a half of an industrial worker's weekly wage. The company's board of directors had originally settled on a three-dollar price, but changed it at the insistence of Gillette's major backer, who believed that a market could be created for an expensive razor. The company was so

successful that within four years dozens of manufacturers offered safety razors, most encountering more production problems than difficulties selling their stock.

One of these manufacturers, P. C. Sherman, who had turned
down an opportunity to invest in Gillette, hoped to make up for
this error by starting the company that produced the Sterling
safety razor and running it on the principle that "A safety razor
is a broad, democratic proposition." Advertising the five-dollar
Sterling not to Gillette's upscale market segment but in magazines addressed to a broader audience, he claimed that his product would pay for itself with the barber's fees it saved. It was sold
not in stores but through the mail, on the installment plan.
Applicants could get a razor free on approval if they sent letters
of reference, which the company actually followed up. ("If J.
Pierpont Morgan were to write in person, . . . no inquiry would
be needed," Sherman admitted.) This extensive relationship
with customers through the mail continued even after payment.
The company guaranteed that it would "keep the blades sharp,
free of cost, forever."

Gillette, in contrast, prided himself on and attributed the
success of his razor to "the idea of producing a blade . . . that
would be so cheap to manufacture that its cost to the consumer
would permit of its being discarded when dull, thus avoiding the
annoyance and difficulties of stropping and honing." His company created relationships with stores that not only sold his
razor but also his blades. The Gillette razor, in other words,
made money not only from the consumer's initial five-dollar
purchase but from his continuing investment in blades. King
Gillette's biographer claims that the seed of his idea had come
from William Painter, his boss at the bottle-cap company, who
had invented the crimped, cork-lined tin bottle cap and was
earning $350,000 a year in royalties. Painter's central advice to
Gillette was to conceive another disposable product.

People who could not save enough money to buy a Gillette
could still aspire to one. Razors and many other costly products
were available as premiums to those who accumulated enough
wrappers and coupons from the chewing gum, soap, and to-

bacco products that they could afford. Two hundred and fifty United Cigar Store certificates—the number issued with $62.50 worth of merchandise, or 1,250 nickel cigars—could procure a five-dollar Gillette in 1909. Premium catalogues also offered such turn-of-the-century high-tech leisure goods as stereo-scopes, phonographs, and cameras, which, like razors with dis-posable blades, required additional purchases beyond the initial investments: stereoscope slides, phonograph records, film, and developing services or equipment.

In part because of the profit to be made from turning amateur photography into a frequent habit, Eastman Kodak advertising taught perhaps the most explicit lessons on incorporating new products into modern life-styles. In the pages of the "better" magazines, the company courted men who wore ties and women who employed servants; during the early 1920s, a spokesman reported that Kodak had never used streetcar advertising and rarely employed billboards, two media generally used to attract the working classes. Much of the promotion was directed at young adults who took European vacations, boys who skied, and other adventurers. In 1893 Kodak published a booklet with ad-vertising matter at the back, *The Kodak at the North Pole,* a reminis-cence of a recent Greenland expedition by a real adventurer, Admiral Robert Peary, who did not actually claim to reach the Pole until 1909. "There are no Game Laws for those who hunt with a Kodak," the company reminded more modest explorers in a 1905 advertisement, proposing an activity in the wilderness for prosperous urbanites who bought their meat from the butcher. "The rod or the gun may be left out, but no nature lover omits a Kodak from his camp outfit."

At the same time it appealed to outdoor adventurers, Kodak established its place in the prosperous home. "The big idea behind the selling of Eastman Kodaks," an advertising writer pointed out in 1922, "is that every man can write the outline of his own history, and that the outline will be a hundredfold more interesting if it is illustrated." The development of that idea— or, more accurately, of the idea that every *woman* should create

If it isn't an Eastman, it isn't a Kodak.

Drawn for Eastman Kodak Co., by Edward Penfield.

Bring your vacation home in a

KODAK

Add to the after-delights of your holiday with pictures of the people, the places and the sports you are interested in. Every step easy by the Kodak System.

Kodaks,$5.00 to $108.00. Brownies,$1.00 to $9.00.

Catalogs of the
dealers or by mail.

EASTMAN KODAK CO.
Rochester, N. Y.

This advertisement, from *Town and Country* in April 1905, was drawn by noted illustrator Edward Penfield, when printing techniques still prevented Kodak from using photography in its advertising.

that history for her family—can be seen in a series of Kodak Christmas advertisements from 1904 through 1910. The company advertised throughout the year, but at Christmas, the Kodak could serve two special purposes, functioning as a desirable gift and recording the family celebration for posterity.

In 1904, "A Christmas Morning" (A) defined the photo opportunity to potential camera-owners who might not recognize it, provided a visual image of a woman taking photographs, and suggested cameras both as gifts and as tools for a family chronicle. The next year (B), the company offered more detailed directions, proposing "Kodaks on the tree" as gifts, and recommending things to photograph—the tree, the baby, the grandmother, the party. Soon the mounting pile of pictures

——————— A ———————   ——————— B ———————

A Christmas Morning

KODAK

Where there's a child, there should the Kodak be. As a means of keeping green the Christmas memories, or as a gift, it's a holiday delight.

Kodaks from $5.00 to $97.00. Brownie Cameras (They work like Kodaks) $1, $2, $5. Kodak Developing Machines, $2.00 to $10.00.

EASTMAN KODAK CO.

Catalogue free at the dealers or by mail.   Rochester, N. Y.

If it isn't an Eastman, it isn't a Kodak

KODAKS

on the tree; then Kodak pictures of the tree; pictures of the baby, of grandmother, of the Christmas house party—all help to keep green the Christmas memories.

Kodaks, $5.00 to $108.00. Brownies, $1.00 to $9.00.

EASTMAN KODAK CO.

Catalogs at the dealers or by mail   Rochester, N. Y. *The Kodak City*

*If it
Isn't
an
Eastman
it isn't
a
Kodak*

The Kodak Christmas Story

Wherever children are there's a Christmas story, yes, an all the year round story for the Kodak to record—a story that grows in interest as the years go by.

Let the grown folks with a Kodak and the Children with a Brownie join in building the family Kodak Book. And there's no better way to begin than with pictures of Christmas day.

Kodaks, $5.00 to $100.00.   Brownies, $1.00 to $9.00.

The Kodak Baby Book—now in press, ready in January—free at the Kodak dealers or by mail.

EASTMAN KODAK CO.

Rochester, N. Y., *The Kodak City*

———————————— C ————————————

became the basis of larger projects: the family photo album (C) and the library of memory books of which it was part, one for each child to be started at birth. "Make Kodak your family historian," the Rochester, New York company told magazine readers in December 1910.

Without saying in words that picture-taking was so easy a child could do it, the text addressed that issue (D). "Unless you are already familiar with Kodakery," it read, coining a noun form that

—————————————————————— D ——————————————————————

fortunately did not catch on, "you will find the making of home portraits much simpler than you imagine." Those still intimidated by the technicalities of camerawork might obtain *At Home with the Kodak,* a free book about home portraiture, available by mail or at Kodak dealers. Like many manufacturers of new products, Kodak addressed consumer resistance and apprehension.

The L. E. Waterman Company, which began its business in the mid-1880s and estimated that it sold 85 percent of the fountain pens in America by the early 1920s, faced two sources of resistance: the highly personal nature of its product and the possibility of leaky pens. This company placed a strong emphasis on courting and training salespeople at the stores that handled its pens, through advertisements in the trade media, letters to retailers, and booklets on salesmanship. Waterman competed with the hundreds of combinations of penholders and steel penpoints that individuals could choose to fit their hands and their writing styles. "Men often get married to their pen, and it is well that they do," the company told retail clerks in *Waterman Ideal Salesmanship* (1902), a hardbound book with many engraved illustrations printed on glossy paper. "A certain pen action and that one only will suit them. But pens are as different as individuals, and just as there is a wife for every man, if he will patiently look for her, so, only with no trouble at all in the finding, there is a Waterman Ideal Fountain Pen that will suit every taste and every habit in pen action." The clerk was to assume the trouble; he was told to keep a complete stock of the various barrels and points, watch customers closely as they tried them out, ask them many questions about their writing, and patiently suggest point after point and barrel after barrel until the match was made.

Customers who found pens that fit might still resist the product because they did not believe that any fountain pen would work consistently without leaking. In its instructions to clerks, Waterman justified their suspicions: the pens apparently did not work consistently without leaking except with careful and time-consuming attention. The company insisted, however, that if certain "simple conditions" were not "violated" the ink would flow as ceaselessly as the Hudson River, and urged salespeople to maintain their stock well enough to prove this, by keeping each pen clean and filled, ready to write. The "simple conditions" required keeping the entire display so clean "that no one would have a suspicion that there was any ink within a thousand miles until the nibs of the pen touch the paper." "Anything with ink in it must be treated respectfully," the company warned, "not gingerly by any means but just respectfully, with a due

Waterman advertised fountain pens for vacationers because they could be used anywhere. This ad appeared in *Town and Country,* June 1912.

regard to the nature of the substance, ink. This must be borne in mind from the time the goods are received till they are finally disposed of to the customer."

To help dealers whose maintenance of the displays was so essential to its product's success, Waterman provided adjuncts to the extra advertising it put in the magazines during the busy seasons: commencement, vacation, the opening of school, and Christmas. At Christmas, it supplied the cigar stores, hardware stores, and stationers who sold Watermans with gaily decorated folders imprinted with the retailer's name, illustrating the complete line of Waterman pens. This "most acceptable Christmas present" whose "quality, beauty, and unfailing reliability are lifelong reminders of your thoughtfulness" was priced from less than three dollars to over twenty-five, a range broad enough to accommodate many pocketbooks, but still very expensive for working-class people. Like Gillette and Kodak, therefore, Waterman did most of its consumer-magazine advertising in the "better" publications and addressed the copy to the prosperous. Vacation-season ads informed consumers that they could buy Watermans at "leading stores in every resort in the world," and listed addresses for company-run stores in foreign cities. "Plan now for your summer writing," Waterman entreated *Town and Country* readers in 1911, "and save the bothers of indoor-writing and the dip, dip, dip of the hotel pen."

The fountain pen's particular advantage, especially salient for travelers, was that it permitted people to write anywhere; this modern product extended opportunities for an activity that people had pursued for thousands of years. Safety razors and box cameras, too, promoted greater mobility: now men could shave while traveling; now photography could emerge from the studio. In various ways, such devices helped define modern lifestyles. The camera offered a completely new way of viewing the world; even the intimacies of domestic life could now be framed and stylized according to the new conventions of the amateur snapshot. Both the camera and the razor replaced the personal service of professionals with purchased products, to be operated by their owners; like shopping itself, shaving and picture-taking had once been accomplished in public places, in the context of face-to-face relationships. And all of these products were widely available: nearly everybody could afford corn flakes and cigarettes, and even expensive fountain pens and cameras could be had by the provident savers of soap wrappers. Large numbers of people adopted modern life-styles, duplicating the new habits of their neighbors.

Historians have pointed to the celebration and promotion of

Some companies celebrated their products' modernity. This Waterman advertisement, from *Town and Country*, 1914, celebrates technological achievement and its part in saving time, an important element of modern life.

modernity in the advertising of the 1920s. Their evidence suggests that the transformation of culture, from ideas and lifestyles based on local relationships and regional manufacturing to those contingent on mass production and a national market, took decades. Yet that transformation was well on its way before World War I, activated in part by the products themselves. In promoting those products, manufacturing companies in this earlier period were often direct in stressing modernity as an advertising theme. Other companies put a strong emphasis on converting the population to the modern ways of mass production and factory-made goods, using images that ranged from fanciful to factual and inviting the public to observe mechanized processes.

The Standard company was even more explicit in promoting modernity, in this advertisement from *McClure's,* 1905.

Some literally celebrated the "mass" in "mass production," bragging about the size of their output and the enormous quantities they distributed, and insinuating that everybody was buying their product. "Shipped in Train Loads," Quaker Oats boasted in a half-page ad in *Munsey's Magazine* in 1895. "Has the largest sale of any Cereal Food in the World." Some companies hung signs on the trains and on the cars: "The largest single shipment of one brand chewing gum ever made," Wrigley's told the folks along the Illinois Central line between Chicago and Sioux City before Christmas of 1905, "all for C. Shenkberg," a wholesale grocer. The *Sioux City Journal* informed its readers that the car contained 60,000 boxes, which occupied "2,500 cubic feet of space, one solid mass of chewing gum." Waterman boasted that the factory it opened in 1910 would produce "A

Many manufacturers used images of freight cars and trains to suggest the large quantities they sold. This image comes from a series of color lithographs reproduced in a booklet the Quaker Oats distributed at the World's Columbian Exposition, Chicago, 1893.

QUAKER OATS TRAIN CROSSING THE ROCKIES.

Million a Year," and mounted a major campaign using that phrase as a theme, coordinating color spreads in the leading national Sunday supplements, window cards for retail display, and a luncheon at the new facility, with two thousand invited guests who included dealers and Waterman agents.

Many other companies showed off their factories and the equipment they used to produce their goods, illustrating buildings, machines, and workers in their advertising. Typical pictures appeared in the four corners of an ad for Baker's cocoa published in the *Ladies' Home Journal* in 1899—"Mill No. 1" (an exterior view of a solid brick factory building), "Chocolate Machine" ("Capacity, 10,000 lbs. daily," with three aproned workers striking wooden poses), "Breakfast Cocoa Mill Room" (dozens of identical shiny machines receding to the vanishing point), and "Wrapping Baker's Chocolate" (similarly receding women workers, seated at tables doing handwork). Such illustrations, one *Printers' Ink* writer asserted in 1910, gave the public "an idea of stability. . . . There the factory stands, a most tangible and conclusive proof of the advertiser's ability to cope with demand. . . . Every reader of normal psychology must feel that here is a concern anchored to one spot by the weight of capital invested in national equipment. Suspicions of irresponsibility, of 'fly-by-night' policies, are allayed before they are born."

Food companies used their factories to allay suspicion not about the firm so much as about the products, inaugurating factory tours so that people could see for themselves the conditions under which food was processed and packaged. By 1907, 100,000 annual visitors toured the Shredded Wheat Company of Niagara Falls, New York, the "factory with a thousand windows," invited by the company in the fine print of magazine advertisements. As one of the "Wonders of Niagara, Scenic and Industrial," the building was said to compare to the falls in its massive dimensions; a 1903 flyer detailed the 3,000 tons of steel, 4 million bricks, 10 tons of putty, 300 miles of electric wire, and 35 tons of paint that had been used in construction—though this list accounted for only 844 of the windows. A 1915 souvenir

The largest man-
ufacturers of
pure, high-grade Co-
coas and Chocolates
on this continent.
Highest awards at
the great Interna-
tional Expositions.

Mill No. 1, Walter Baker & Co. Ltd.   ESTABLISHED 1780   *Chocolate Machine—Capacity, 10,000 lbs. daily*

WALTER BAKER & CO. Ltd.
Dorchester, Mass.

Baker's Chocolate

The pure product of
selected cocoa beans, to
which nothing is added,
and from which nothing
is taken away. Cele-
brated for more than a
century as a delicious,
nutritious and flesh-
forming beverage. Best
plain chocolate in the
market for cooking
purposes.

Done up in blue
wrapper, with yellow
label on the front and
trade-mark on the back.

REGISTERED TRADE-MARK

Vanilla Chocolate

Unequaled for smooth-
ness, delicacy and flavor.
Much used now at re-
ceptions and evening
parties in place of tea
or coffee.

Good to eat, good to
drink, and good for
cooking.

The most healthful
and invigorating food
for bicyclists, tourists
and students.

Done up in white
paper, tied with colored
ribbon, trade-mark on
the front.

BREAKFAST COCOA

Breakfast Cocoa Mill Room   *Wrapping Baker's Chocolate*

From which the excess of fat
has been removed. Abso-
lutely pure and soluble. Has
more than three times the strength
of cocoa mixed with starch,
arrowroot or sugar, and is
therefore far more economical,
costing less than one cent a cup.
It is delicious, nourishing,
strengthening, *easily digested*,
and admirably adapted for in-
valids as well as for persons
in health.

Put up in ½-pound tins.
Trade-mark on every package.

This Baker advertisement, from the *Ladies' Home Journal,* 1899, offers
typical illustrations of factory buildings, workers, and machines.

"ITS ALL IN THE SHREDS"

The Home of SHREDDED WHEAT.
NIAGARA FALLS, N.Y.

SHREDDED WHEAT—
The cleanest and purest of all cereal foods, made in the cleanest, most hygienic food factory in the world.

Shredded Wheat factory-tour souvenir postcard, 1907.

postcard informed visitors' correspondents that their friends and relatives had spent their honeymoons and vacations viewing machinery that baked over 2 million Shredded Wheat biscuits a day.

Other companies pursued an opposite image-making strategy, illustrating promotion materials with pixylike characters that implied the "magic" of mass production. According to *What a Cake of Soap Will Do,* published before 1895, Procter and Gamble adopted illustrator Palmer Cox's well-known Brownies and impressed their "mystic power" into service collecting cottonseed and coconuts, manufacturing Ivory soap, and distributing it to every house in the land. The elves who made Post Toasties even took care of the packaging, shouting and laughing as they painted cartons with a picture of a cozy fireplace scene, in *Tale of the Toastie Elfins,* a pamphlet published in 1914.

Other companies admitted that they produced their goods with machines, but used elfin characters in their promotion. Jell-O hired Rose Cecil O'Neill, whose Kewpies—the Smurfs of

Illustrator Palmer Cox's Brownies, familiar to readers of late-nineteenth-century magazines, were shown manufacturing Ivory soap in an illustrated poem that appeared in Procter and Gamble's *What a Cake of Soap Will Do*. Many companies used such images of pixies and elves, intimating that mass production was like magic and contrasting with other companies' use of factory images in advertising.

Cover for the recipe booklet *Jell-O and the Kewpies*.

their day—were the subject of her illustrated poems, published regularly in *Good Housekeeping,* and, reproduced as dolls, created a sensational fad. The mischievous Kewpies illustrated advertising and lightened the tone of Jell-O's recipe booklet, which had previously featured pictures of the six domestic scientists who created the recipes. The Campbell Kids, Kewpies in human form, could likewise be obtained as dolls. Sunny Jim, an old-man version of a Kewpie with an identical topknot, served as a trademark character for H-O Force, a wheat-flake cereal. Created by leading advertising agent Earnest Elmo Calkins, he appeared in antic predicaments in books like *Through Foreign Lands with Sunny Jim* (thirty-six pages, available for four coupons cut from the box, or ten cents in stamps). He dispensed sunny wisdom ("a

recipe for being happy" by living in the present) in a book of
Force recipe suggestions that went through at least two million-
book editions. Unfortunately for the company, the Force advertising served as an early example of clever promotion that won
public attention without increasing sales. "Everybody talked
about Sunny Jim," veteran copywriter Helen Woodward wrote
in her memoirs, "but nobody connected him with *Force.*"

Sunny Jim and the Campbell Kids lived in a land of trademark
characters that experienced a population explosion around
1900. Curiously, many of their compatriots represented not
modernity but traditional wisdom. Characters like the Quaker
Oats Quaker, dressed for business in a bygone era, intimated a
connection between new products and the presumed integrity of

---

Many companies used visual imagery that connected new products with
traditional wisdom, symbolized by older women. On this 1892 trade card,
Chase and Sanborn pictured a grandmother—remarkably like that of its
competitor, A & P—and set her the task of reading tea leaves.

WHAT VISION, DEAR MOTHER, IN YOUR CUP DO YOU SEE?
THE WHOLE WORLD DRINKING CHASE & SANBORN'S COFFEE AND TEA.

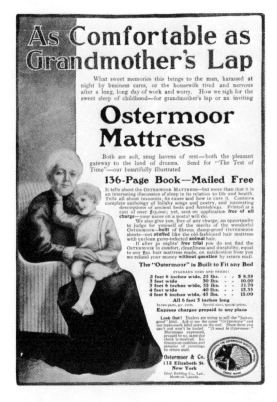

Other advertising grandmothers, like this one representing Ostermoor mattresses in *McClure's*, 1905, radiated love and comfort.

previous times. A number of companies gave advice through old-women characters representing traditional wisdom and old-fashioned comforts, beginning with the Great Atlantic and Pacific Tea Company's Grandmother, a trademark as early as the 1880s. Her portrait and her testimonial to A & P's tea and coffee ("my solace through life") appeared on the backs of collectable cards lithographed with pictures of flowers; in cameo, she may be seen on page 223. Some of her colleagues spoke directly to the issue of modernity. "Times have changed," Jell-O's white-haired, white-capped, and bespectacled "Aunt Em'ly" told *Ladies' Home Journal* readers in 1912. "Pie twice a day was all the style when I was a girl. . . . Now there isn't one of the children that doesn't like JELL-O better than pie, and I must say I'm glad of it. Pie is dreadful hard on stomachs." At Thanksgiving dinner, when

The Thanksgiving Dessert

HOW all eyes brighten when they see Grandma's mince pie! It is a tempting sight, giving to the home coming an appetizing reminder of past Thanksgiving feasts.

Made with Crisco a mince pie is a real delicacy. The lower crust is as tender as the flaky, brown top that covers it. Just as good and wholesome as it looks, it is easily digested.

CRISCO

Use Crisco for shortening if you wish the lightest, most delicious pastry you ever ate.

Crisco is an all vegetable product, having neither odor nor taste. It is the cream of edible oil, pure and delicate and gives only richness to foods.

Crisco Mince Pie

In Making Both Pastry and Filling Use Accurate Level Measurements

For Pastry

1½ cupfuls flour	½ cupful Crisco
1 teaspoonful salt	4 to 6 tablespoonfuls water

Sift the flour and salt and cut the Crisco into the flour with two knives until it is finely divided. Then add the water sparingly, mixing it with a knife through the dry materials. Form into a dough, roll on a floured board to about ⅛ inch in thickness. Use a light motion in handling the rolling pin, and roll from the center outward. The Crisco should be of such consistency that when scooped out with a spoon it rounds up egg-shaped. In making pastry it is advisable to use pastry flour. Brush over the lower crust with a little beaten egg white before adding the mince meat. (The egg forms a hard surface between the crust and filling but does not prevent crust from baking properly.) Bake in hot oven.

For Filling

4 tart apples	1 tablespoonful chopped citron	¼ teaspoonful nutmeg
¾ cupful raisins	¼ cupful Crisco	¼ teaspoonful cloves
¼ cupful currants	½ teaspoonful cinnamon	3 tablespoonfuls sugar
		¾ cupful cider

Chop apples, raisins, currants, citron and Crisco together until quite fine. Add spices, sugar and cider. Mix well together. Cover closely, and, to ripen, let stand several hours before using.

Send for "The Whys of Cooking"

Many housewives are thankful, among other things, for the household helps they have found in Janet McKenzie Hill's new book "The Whys of Cooking". Many of your own perplexing problems will doubtless be found among the questions she asks and answers in this handsome addition to the Crisco library. It contains 150 new recipes and the interesting Story of Crisco. Bound and illustrated in color. Makes a fine gift book. We will send it to you for five 2-cent stamps. Worth much more. Write Dept. D-11, The Procter & Gamble Co. Cincinnati, Ohio.

By 1916, Crisco was well enough established that its advertising could connect it to that most traditional of shortening tasks, the making of Thanksgiving pies.

pie was essential, digestion could be aided by using Crisco, endorsed by Grandma herself in a 1916 advertisement. The makers of cleaning products such as Colgate's and Old Dutch Cleanser similarly traded on traditional stereotypes of clean old-country Netherlanders, dressed in traditional costume.

The white caps worn by Dutch girls, grandmothers, and servants signified cleanliness, and that image blurred with reality at the Heinz plant in Pittsburgh, where many young women acted the part of "The Girl in the White Cap." Alone in a drawing on a souvenir postcard, surrounded by bowls of vegetables, she packed one bottle; together at the factory, her counterparts produced thousands. They dressed in uniforms and worked under surveillance by the public taking the famous Heinz factory tour, which attracted 20,000 visitors annually at the turn of the century.

Many more people availed themselves of Heinz hospitality at the Heinz Ocean Pier in Atlantic City. Until it was destroyed by a hurricane in 1944, this building, extending almost nine hundred feet into the ocean, was one of three such enclosed structures in Atlantic City and the only one that stayed open all year. About 15,000 people a day used its facilities at the height of the season, sitting in the sun parlor, taking advantage of the rest rooms, and writing home on free postcards showing scenes of the pier and of the Pittsburgh factory. The pier displayed the Heinz collection of artworks and curios, including busts of Socrates and Shakespeare, an Egyptian mummy, a pair of nine-foot elephant tusks, and many large paintings. A demonstration kitchen offered samples of Heinz products; a company representative delivered a lecture illustrated with stereopticon slides that offered views of the main factory and its workers. Naturally, none of these images revealed the strain from low piece-rates, seasonal overtime, and fast-paced machines that resulted in an average tenure of less than two years among both skilled and unskilled workers in Pittsburgh's canneries.

Obscuring the realities of industrial work, the factory images that manufacturers propagated helped to create a new attitude towards factories and mass production in general. That attitude

Two public relations images of the Heinz "Girl in the White Cap." At left, a souvenir postcard, one of many available at the factory in Pittsburgh and at the Heinz Ocean Pier in Atlantic City. Below, a photograph of real workers doing the same task, filling bottles with a grooved stick.

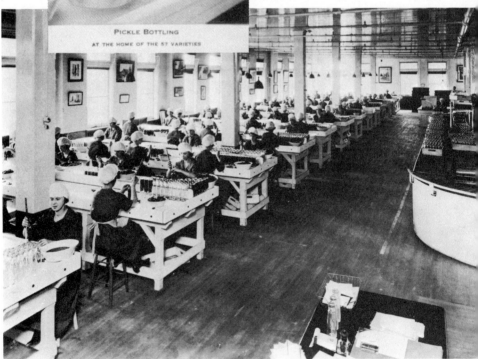

contributed to the making of a new material culture: new products, new relationships between the makers of goods and the
people who used them, and new daily routines. Positive images
of goods and factories not only improved sales but helped the
development of new attitudes towards manufacturers, reinforc-
ing the trademarks themselves. For individual marketers, however, the primary goal was not to promote mass production but
to sell goods. In service to that goal, they developed new principles, based on the concept that a market was a malleable entity.

CHAPTER 5

IIIIC3IIIIIIIIIIIIC3IIIIIIIIIIIIC3IIII

DESIGNING MARKETS

NEUTRALLY LOCATED ON THE BOUNDARIES BETWEEN TOWNS AND tribal areas, marketplaces in many premodern cultures operated as sacred spaces, presided over by gods particularly suited to market activity and protected by rituals associated with boundary crossing. Hermes, the ancient Greek patron of trade—a messenger, a thief, and a wily trickster—embodied, writes historian Jean-Christophe Agnew, "suspicion and apprehension toward strangers." Although trade moved from the periphery to the physical center of social relations in the Greek city-state— the *agora* was both its marketplace and its political, religious, and military meeting place—the boundary between the marketplace and the rest of the social world continued to define a special kind of space. Suspicion persisted, but commercial transactions depended on meeting strangers in a nonhostile environment, protected by rituals and by laws that regulated the fundamental confrontation, the contest between buyer and seller.

The ancient Greeks had no word for the market as an abstraction. The term took on abstract meanings during the rise of capitalism, which entailed the development of markets in two nontangible commodities, labor and money. "Market" came to refer to a process as well as to a place, culminating in the work of Adam Smith; in his *Wealth of Nations* (1776), people entered markets without literally going to marketplaces. By the early twentieth century, the word had taken on even more meanings and usages. It might still describe systems of relationships between buyers and sellers, but it was also used for the people in a geographical area, as in "the Cleveland market." "The market for Jell-O" might refer to groups of potential buyers or to actual ones. Businesspeople used phrases like "the cola market" and "the carbonated soft drink market" sometimes for large numbers of consumers and at other times for small groups of manufacturing firms. Twentieth-century usage even extended the linguistic abstraction so that it might not refer to trade at all: people were now said to be "in the market" or "on the market" for intangible things that nobody really bought or sold, such as trouble.

Again, the linguistic extension followed social practice. Market relations themselves had been expanding as more people joined the money economy, working for others to earn the wherewithal to pay for things formerly made at home or gathered from nature. By 1900, the market dominated American culture, and the term might well be applied to nearly anything. A secular realm without firm boundaries, its demands pervaded the interactions of daily life. The growth of the market was central to its survival, and this dynamic concept governed the thinking and the practice of the businessmen who concerned themselves with the markets for individual products in an economy and a culture abounding in goods previously unknown. Their fundamental problem in the early years of mass distribution was not establishing control over some defined (if abstract) territory: with so many new products, the marketing goal was less often gaining market shares than expanding the entire field. They had to stretch the boundaries of the malleable markets for soft drinks and safety razors by recruiting new buyers and by inducing current buyers to purchase more.

The initial effort to find new buyers entailed finding new

sellers. Even well-capitalized enterprises began small, moving
from local distribution to regional, national, or international
sales. For most companies, moving to new territories required
creating relationships with wholesalers. They further had to
establish distribution within the new regions, choosing authorized dealers or making sure that nearly every grocer or hardware store or druggist carried the product. In the attempt to
gain wider distribution, manufacturers created national sales
forces, mailed promotional matter to storekeepers, and initiated
consumer advertising, trusting that the requests it generated
would alert merchants to the products. Many companies, like
Procter and Gamble in its early Crisco advertisements, enlisted
consumers to supply them with the names and addresses of
potential dealers. "If your grocer hasn't them, let us know," Van
Camp's wrote in a 1905 pork-and-beans advertisement. "Sold
by all dealers," A. Stein and Company of Chicago claimed of its
Flexo garters, but equivocated in the next sentence: "Insist on
Flexo, and if the dealer hasn't them, send us his name and 25¢,
and we will see that you are supplied."

Organizing new distribution often involved assigning a product a new position with respect to competition or to groups of
consumers, a practice now called "repositioning." Around
1906, for example, the Pacific Coast Condensed Milk Company
hired the well-known Chicago advertising agent John Lee
Mahin, agreeing to spend $10,000 in advertising if he would
come to Seattle to consult on national marketing for Carnation
milk. The market for canned milk was limited by the product's
status as a standby for emergencies or for use on explorations
or in camp; sales to Klondike expeditions had dominated Carnation's early years. Mahin advised a campaign based on the
slogan "The Modern Milkman," establishing Carnation's competition not as the syrupy, sweetened condensed milk that other
companies put in cans but as the raw milk then under attack as
unclean. "When advertising methods were first discussed,"
Printers' Ink writer James H. Collins reported, "it was thought
that the slight flavor due to sterilizing would have to be ex-

plained. After a thorough study of the whole subject, however, the Mahin staff asked: 'Why be negative on the taste? All over the country there is agitation about the milk supply and eminent physicians are condemning the use of raw milk, no matter how fresh or clean it may be. Carnation Milk is ideal from the scientific standpoint. Let it go out on its merits.' " Another slogan, "Carnation Milk—from Contented Cows," downplayed the manufacturing process. By 1910, the company had four factories in Washington and two in Oregon; the next year, it began manufacturing at three new plants in Wisconsin and one in Illinois.

———

The first Eastern shipments of Carnation milk went around Cape Horn. Rather than permanently depend on the National Parks Transcontinental Highway, the company built Midwestern plants for its national distribution.

The Pompeian Company of Washington, D.C., consciously repositioned olive oil. Outside Italian neighborhoods, olive oil had formerly been a luxury product or a medicine, dispensed by druggists in bulk or packed in four-, eight-, and sixteen-ounce glass bottles. Pompeian introduced vacuum-packed cans ranging from half-pints to gallons, which cut the cost of packing and transportation, increased shelf life, and enabled the company to reduce the price, especially after it installed its own can factory. "The price proposition was almost the first angle of our business policy that demanded careful solution," the company's president, Nathan Musher, wrote, "because upon ability to lower prices somewhat and correct the prevailing estimate of olive oil as a luxury depended the success of our plans for popularizing olive oil." By 1914, the company had spent $1.25 million on consumer promotion: about half on streetcar publicity, and most of the rest on women's-magazine advertising and on booklets and cards that Pompeian produced in its own print shop.

Like Heinz, Pompeian mounted a large exhibit in Atlantic City, where it spent $15,000 to $20,000 on free samples. The company eventually abandoned free sampling, however, because it did not coordinate with the repositioning. The small samples provided enough for customers who would take a teaspoonful of olive oil as medicine, but not for the ones who would use it to make salad dressing. "So firm is my conviction on this score," Musher wrote, "that I say to the retailer, 'If you must give a free sample, give a quart can.' I have extended this privilege to a few retail merchants in the large cities that cater to a high-class trade . . . on a very restricted scale." The company continued to exhibit, selling small trial cans for a nominal price at such events as the 1914 Panama-Pacific Exposition in San Francisco, where it operated a miniature olive-oil plant.

Perhaps the most stunning example of early product repositioning is the story of Asa Candler, an Atlanta retail and wholesale druggist who in 1888, after attempting to market his own tooth powder and blood tonic, bought the recipe and the name for Coca-Cola, along with a stock of ingredients and advertising circulars. As *Printers' Ink* told the tale twenty years later, Candler purchased a headache remedy, sold to soda fountains as a syrup and mixed with carbonated water to make a "pleasant beverage." The new proprietor reasoned that "the chronic sufferer from headaches may have but one a week. Many persons have only one a year. There was one dreadful malady, though, that everybody . . . suffered from daily . . . which during six or eight months of the year would be treated and relieved, only to develop again within less than an hour. That malady was *thirst.*"

As a history of Coca-Cola, this version of the tale exaggerates Candler's marketing skill; in the words of one historian of the company, its advertising through the 1890s exhibits "a profound ambiguity on whether to extol Coca-Cola's taste or its curative powers." As an enlightening tale from the magazine that liked to call itself "the Little Schoolmaster" for the advertising trade, however, it served as a lesson in fundamental marketing concepts. By the time it was published in 1908, it was clear that wise marketers did not merely produce goods and buy advertising, although the techniques for shaping markets were not fully formulated and certainly not universally applied. Manufacturers and the advertising agencies that had begun to provide planning services in addition to copywriting had come to conceive of the market as malleable. They defined markets and positioned products and promotion plans to fit them.

Many companies provided consumers with suggestions for product uses they might not have thought of, not completely repositioning the product but putting out promotional literature that was aimed at attracting new customers and increasing the quantity demanded by current users. In the late 1880s, one Ivory advertisement showed it as a horse soap, while another suggested an adult "Bubble Party" as an amusing entertainment for the holidays, with prizes to be awarded to the lady or gentleman who blew the largest bubbles, using clay pipes and bowls of Ivory soapsuds. Although the company dropped this suggestion, it consistently emphasized its product's multipurpose char-

This poster, lithographed in color and stressing Ivory's multipurpose character, was copyrighted the year of the Yukon gold rush.

acter. "Is the Ivory a Toilet or a Laundry Soap?" inquired a
booklet whose cover showed the product floating among swans
and lily pads. "Laundry soaps have an unpleasant odor and are
too strong to use on the skin, and toilet soaps are too expensive
to use in the laundry," but Ivory was "so perfectly made" and
was "sold at such a reasonable price" that it could be used for
both. The booklet also recommended it for cleaning brass, free-
ing plants from insect pests, and removing ink stains from carpets.

Other companies gave out booklets listing dozens of possible
uses. The Cudahy Packing Company of Omaha, makers of Old
Dutch Cleanser, offered *Hints for Housewives,* with instructions
for treating bites from mad dogs and snakes, for taking ink out
of linen, and for using Old Dutch—on floors, windows, cutlery,
marble washstands, kitchen tables, carpets, and nearly all other
household surfaces. "By Finding a New Use for a thing, its value
to you is increased," the Southern California Fruit Exchange
proclaimed on the front cover of *How to Use California Lemons,* a
booklet aimed at altering the luxury status of that fruit, much as
New Zealand fruit cooperatives seventy years later would provide ideas for kiwi and star fruit.

Thanks in part to the home economics movement, which encouraged cooking by the book, many people sent for manufacturers' compilations of recipes, certainly the most popular form
of promotional material intended to increase the market by giving people ideas for using more of the product. Shredded
Wheat's compilation, *The Vital Question Cook Book,* 112 pages
long and imprinted with the grocer's name, had been published
in sixteen editions of 250,000 each by 1902. A book of chocolate
and cocoa recipes developed for the Baker Company by the
well-known cooking teacher Maria Parloa entered its twenty-
sixth and twenty-seventh editions in 1912, each of a quarter-
million or a half-million copies. In 1914, the company printed
French and German versions. Recipe contests encouraged consumers to participate in the development process. Around 1902,
the Genesee Pure Food Company ran a six-month contest for

"*NATURALLY ORGANIZED FOODS MAKE POSSIBLE NATURAL CONDITIONS* THERE IS NO OTHER WAY." H.D.P.

SUCH FOOD IS

SHREDDED WHOLE WHEAT BISCUIT.

and with them as the basis in general cookery the eye is pleased, the taste satisfied, the body is nourished in natural proportion, and natural conditions follow.

RASPBERRIES IN BISCUIT BASKET.
RECIPE NO. 136.

CREAMED SPINACH ON SHREDDED WHEAT BISCUIT TOAST.
RECIPE NO. 62.

EGG TOAST RECIPE NO. 28.

SHREDDED WHEAT BISCUIT JELLIED APPLE SANDWICH.
RECIPE NO. 249.

POACHED EGG ON SHREDDED WHEAT BISCUIT.
RECIPE NO. 26.

BISCUIT, WARM OR COLD, WITH MILK OR CREAM
RECIPE NO. 1.

Mr. James Ten Eyck, the father and trainer of the now famous "Ned" Ten Eyck, winner of the Diamond Sculls at Henley Royal Regatta, says:—"For good, tough, elastic muscle and at the same time to keep the body in good condition, there is nothing in my judgment equal to Shredded Wheat Biscuit. This food is free from previous fermentation, as found in light breads made from fine flour, which should always be avoided. I am convinced it is a perfect food to train on, and to live largely on before training, instead of any other kind of bread or cereals. I keep 'Shredded Wheat' in my house—would not be without it."

Speaking of Shredded Wheat Biscuit, Rev. Dr. Edward Everett Hale says there is nothing he more enjoys for his breakfast.

Rev. Dr. John Lindsay Withrow says: "Our table is constantly supplied with your delicious biscuit."

Recipe ideas from Shredded Wheat's *Vital Question Cook Book,* illustrated and reprinted on a card imprinted with the dealer's name.

Jell-O recipes, offering $1,200 in prizes of from one to ten dollars, judging entries on originality (20 points), artistic appearance (15), palatability and delicacy (10), and simplicity (5). Contestants in such competitions presumably bought more of the product to experiment with.

People who were already buying certain products might also be encouraged to buy more if marketers could create year-round demand for products perceived as seasonal. "When I first started out selling this preparation," the Coca-Cola general sales manager told *Printers' Ink* in 1908, "even Southern soda fountains were shut down four to six months in the year." Because his company had worked to build an all-year trade for itself and for its distributors, "the winter business is growing even in the coldest parts of the North."

Year-round demand provided manufacturers the distinct advantage of smoother coordination with supply, but it was not always easy to achieve. In 1919, the American Sugar Refining Company introduced Domino Golden Syrup, a product that could be manufactured throughout the year, unlike molasses, which was still made seasonally. The company's sales manager began to instruct the sales force to extend syrup orders beyond the winter pancake season. "Our belief is that the entire year is syrup season and the people must be educated to believe this is a fact," he wrote in a circular letter. After months of exhortations and claims, he finally suggested a summer use for the product, the Domino Syrup Nut Sundae, and dispatched his men to soda fountains. Although adding another channel of distribution complicated their work, the company's hope was that drug-store sundaes would serve as a product demonstration that might spur retail sales to people who wanted to make them at home.

American Sugar's failure to create lasting year-round demand for Domino Golden Syrup indicates that even a large company in a monopoly position, with a substantial promotional budget and a well-known advertising agency, could not take for granted its ability to make and enlarge markets. The fact that a successful product might eventually decline made the process and the concept of market design even more perplexing. That fact was obvious by 1910 to observers of Sapolio, probably the clearest early demonstration of what marketers now call the product life-cycle. In fact, all America had observed Sapolio, a scouring cleanser in cake form, actively promoted beginning in the early 1870s. The company that made it, Enoch Morgan's Sons, suffered financial difficulties in the 1873 depression. Three years later it incorporated, under a plan that allowed the Morgan family to keep half the stock in payment for trademarks and goodwill, and to distribute the other half to creditors. The company paid its first dividend in 1880, and both sales and advertising increased steadily. In 1884, George F. Morgan hired Artemas Ward, whom he had initially encountered soliciting advertising for the *Philadelphia Grocer,* which Ward owned and edited. Benefitting from an increased advertising budget and from Ward's energy and ingenuity, Sapolio entered a period of twenty successful years.

In 1900, Ward's new art director, J. K. Fraser, designed and wrote the verses for a series of streetcar cards featuring the inhabitants of "Spotless Town." "The series has been parodied and used in political cartoons and campaigns everywhere," Ward said two years later, "and 'Spotless Town' plays and entertainments are having a decided vogue at church fairs and other places." (The company provided a script, songs, and production directions in *Ye Booke of Spotless Town,* which went through two editions by 1909; for a dollar, it would send scenery, a map of the town, tickets, and "most of the materials, except costumes, for the make-up of the different characters.") In his 1929 history of advertising, advertising agent Frank Presbrey recalled the campaign's success: "Allusions to Spotless Town became common on the stage, in newspaper text and cartoon, in public speeches and in political controversies, until the phrase got into the language as a synonym for cleanliness, order, and perfection." With so much free publicity and with a large advertising budget, in 1905 Morgan sold over 16.5 million cakes of Sapolio

Good for the Spotter of Spotless Town! He spotted a spot on the Butcher's gown.
'T would not be meet, for justice' sake, to roast the Butcher at the steak,
And so behind the bars he'll go.
Bars of what?—— SAPOLIO

Two of the many inhabitants of "Spotless Town," and a verse typical of those that amused passengers on most of America's streetcars in the first years of the twentieth century.

in the United States, approximately one for every family in the country.

That year, however, a new product restructured the market, and Sapolio never did as well again. Since 1886, its principal competitor had been Bon Ami, also in cake form. At about the same time, soap powders began to appear on the market; although they were primarily used for dishes and clothes, such products as the heavily advertised Pearline and Gold Dust promoted consumer awareness of powdered cleaning products. In 1905, the Cudahy Packing Company introduced Old Dutch Cleanser—gritty like Sapolio, but in powder form, packed in a sifter-top can. Cudahy promoted its new product heavily, using many forms of local and national advertising and dealer displays, and becoming, in *Printers' Ink*'s words, "perhaps the most persistent and enormous sampler among the national advertisers." Sapolio responded with an advertising appeal to economy: "Get a cleanser that won't waste or shake—a cleanser that doesn't spill and can't put an atom where it doesn't change into shine." Nonetheless, sales plummeted. By 1910, they were 73 percent of their 1905 level, and by 1915, less than 50 percent.

The Bon Ami Company, in contrast, put out a powdered cleanser and offered cash prizes of from two to fifty dollars for new uses of both products. In 1915, it sponsored a contest with over $2,250 in prizes for lists of the best uses (not necessarily new ones) of both the cake and the powder and for essays on the subject "Which do you like better, Bon Ami Cake or Powder, and why?" The company received more than 25,000 lists and 6,000 essays, which it treated as market research data, tabulating replies into a chart that guided the advertising. A decade later, when George Morgan died and his son took over the firm that made Sapolio, the new president declared that his company's major problem was "the development of a new product whose manufacture and sale will render possible a fuller utilization of our manufacturing and marketing facilities and our good will." It took another decade for the firm to develop Sapolio Powder, which never had more than modest sales.

Most successful companies did attempt to exploit their equipment, find applications for their by-products, and make better use of their marketing organizations by generating additional products. Few relied for long on only one, working instead on creating markets simultaneously for a "line" or "family" of products. "A salesman can talk five or six allied lines to dealers and wholesalers at very little more expense than one; and a single trade-mark or good-will reputation is perfectly competent to support a line of products and advertise them at a far lower cost per unit than a single article could be exploited," *Printers' Ink* editorialized in 1911. Many companies used their factories, their trademarks, and their marketing organizations to offer at least what are now called "line extensions": new models, sizes, or flavors of an existing product, using the existing brand name. By 1909, for example, the same company that had invented the disposable razor blade was flaunting its latest "achievement," a new "edition" of the Gillette razor that might induce people who already had one to buy another.

Gillette Safety Razor
New Pocket Edition

HERE is news in-
deed — for the
two million men who
shave themselves every
morning with the
Gillette Safety Razor.

Our first announcement of the
latest GILLETTE achievement—*the
New Pocket Edition*—the GILLETTE
Safety Razor in such compact form
that it can be carried like a card case
in the waistcoat pocket, or slipped
into the side of a traveling bag.

Same size blade as before, same
principle; but neater, more work-
manlike, the most perfect shaving
implement in the world—as compact
and as beautifully finished as a piece
of jewelry—*and the blades are fine.*

If you are a GILLETTE user call on
some progressive dealer at once and
examine this new razor.

If you have never used the GIL-
LETTE now is the time to get ac-
quainted.

You can shave yourself in from
two to five minutes with the GIL-
LETTE—a clean, satisfying shave. *No
stropping, no honing.*

The pocket-case is of gold, silver
or gun metal. Plain polished or
richly engraved in floral and Empire
designs. Inside the pocket-case are
handle and *blade box*—triple silver-
plated or 14K. gold plated. Prices,
$5 to $7.50, on sale everywhere.

You should know GILLETTE Shaving Brush—a new brush of GIL-
LETTE quality—bristles gripped in
hard rubber; and GILLETTE Shaving Stick—a shaving soap worthy of
the GILLETTE Safety Razor.

New York, Times Bldg.
Chicago, Stock Exchange Bldg. **GILLETTE SALES CO.** *Canadian Office*
63 St. Alexander St.
Montreal
London Office
17 Holborn Viaduct, E C. **595 Kimball Building, Boston**

Factories: Boston, Montreal, London, Berlin, Paris.

Gillette Safety Razor
NO STROPPING NO HONING

This 1909 Gillette advertisement from *Town and Country* promotes what
is today called a "line extension," a new model of a product that uses the
existing brand name. The shaving brush and shaving stick, different products under the brand, are now called "franchise extensions."

Some manufacturers used line extensions to reach consumers along a broad price range. At the top of the 1910 Edison phonograph line stood the Amberola, with a sapphire "reproducing point," an oak or mahogany cabinet that enclosed the horn and held a hundred records, and a $200 price tag, about a third of a steelworker's annual wage. The lowest-priced Edison sold for $12.50. Each model appeared in the company's 1910 newspaper advertising in 420 cities. Ads featuring Amberolas compared them to other expensive musical instruments; the cabinetry was "even more charmingly designed" than a piano's, it did not require "a lifetime of study," and it surpassed a player piano (which, "when all is said and done . . . gives you nothing but piano music") by offering opera, orchestra, and band music. Copy illustrated with a cheaper model appealed to economy: "You might have bought an Edison Phonograph many times over," it read, "with the money you have paid for tickets for concerts, theatres, vaudeville shows and other amusement not nearly so satisfactory as the entertainment that comes out of the horn of an Edison Phonograph." Aimed at a much broader audience than elegant magazines, the newspapers that carried the ads also published record reviews, which the Edison advertising manager acknowledged as unpaid advertising, "favors" to the company. Continually apprised of the latest records, even working people who read the papers might aspire to phonograph ownership.

Some makers of less expensive goods were equally explicit about the relation between quality and price in their lines. The Hunt Brothers packed canned fruits in three grades: the Staple brand with blue wrappers, the Superior brand in white wrappers, and the red-wrapped Supreme brand; a description of the color scheme appeared on every label. More often, packaged-goods companies pursued different economic classes with what are now called "flanker brands": another version of an existing product under a different brand, advertised to a different segment. They did not necessarily describe the grades or even emphasize that both products came from the same maker.

In 1913, for example, Arbuckle Brothers, the world's largest coffee firm, introduced a new high-priced blend to New York and Chicago. The J. Walter Thompson Agency thought up the name, designed the package, and planned the advertising, calling the new brand Yuban, "the private coffee of the greatest coffee merchants." The next year, the agency recommended a new definition for Arbuckle's popular Ariosa coffee, which the company had distributed since before the Civil War. The agency suggested advertising Ariosa in national farm papers, sectional weeklies, religious papers, and daily newspapers in medium-sized cities: the publications aimed to attract the 51 million people who made up the poorer classes in those cities and all classes in towns and rural districts. Wealthier urban people would drink Yuban; a clear definition for Ariosa complemented the Yuban marketing strategy. When Arbuckle and J. Walter Thompson planned a third brand, the agency urged the company to name and promote it in ways that would not detract from the existing two. (Later marketers would come to call destructive competition between two brands made by the same company "cannibalization.")

Most manufacturers had a conception of the class base of their products, which informed their choices of promotional plans. "Originally we looked upon the Ingersoll as a timepiece for farmers and workingmen," C. H. Ingersoll said of his company's dollar watch in 1906. The firm soon discovered that people who could afford expensive watches used cheap ones as throwaways, taking them on fishing trips and military expeditions. Secretary of State Elihu Root had taken one to Labrador, and Thomas Edison, Ingersoll claimed, "buys a dollar watch, . . . squirts oil under the cap of the stem, and when it gets clogged with dirt buys another, breaking the old one with a hammer." Nonetheless, the company considered it most profitable to advertise to working people, its most constant source of sales.

Such concentration on segments of the market was in part a response to a particularly American marketing problem. In the United States, marketers confronted a genuinely multicultural population. About a third were foreign-born or of foreign parentage in 1900; even higher proportions of immigrants lived in the industrial cities of the Northeast. These people brought tastes and traditions with them from the old countries. In all of the large cities, ethnic and class differences challenged the manufacturers and their advertising agents. Variations in life-styles and tastes between city and country, between North and South, and between East and West further complicated matters. The new products held different places in the lives of Lower East Side immigrants, Northwest homesteaders, and the farmers who did their shopping in Ada, Minnesota. Marketers had a choice between, on the one hand, attempting to create standardized products that might be sold in all regions and to all classes and nationalities, and on the other, exploiting differences in tastes—

———————————————————IIICꓵIII———————————————————

Three Chicago shopping districts, from the *Chicago Tribune*'s pathbreaking market study, *Winning a Great Market on Facts,* published in 1916. Below, the Carpenter Street district. "To the residents of the immediate locality surrounding it, its stores have all the allurement the shops on Michigan Avenue possess for a different class of Chicagoans."

A "better grade" of neighborhood shopping district, "but yet by no means
a Michigan Avenue, as may be gathered from the appearance of the pedestrians in the immediate foreground."

———————————————————————————||ICⱯ|||———————————————————————————

Michigan Avenue between Madison and Washington streets, the heart of
the "Loop."

in modern jargon, positioning products for segmented markets. They did both.

Expanding from local to national distribution often required taking such regional differences into consideration. In 1906, William Wrigley had been in the chewing-gum business for fifteen years, producing several successful brands, each regionally popular: Juicy Fruit in Texas and the Southwest, Sweet 16 in the South. Rather than choosing to confront regional prejudice by making one of them into a national brand, he created a new flavor—Spearmint—that did not correspond closely to any of the existing types. His established connections with jobbers enabled him to add on this brand; retailers took it on because he

----

This sample card, introducing Juicy Fruit for national distribution in 1916, was mailed to over seven million households.

gave them free boxes; consumers tried free samples. Ten years later, when Wrigley was selling both Spearmint and Doublemint around the world, the company extended Juicy Fruit distribution, advertising in four out of five American newspapers. It further invested a quarter of a million dollars in a sampling campaign, mailing cards holding two samples of Juicy Fruit and one each of Doublemint and Spearmint to 7.5 million households. "While this brand has been sold for 24 years, it is not so well known in your section as the other two," the card read. "It has an odd flavor and is a great favorite with the ladies."

In 1910, a *Printers' Ink* writer argued that not only the products but the advertising copy should be designed to take sectional variations into account. Using the Pacific Coast as his example, he explained that a Coca-Cola advertisement designed to show the product as a thirst-quencher for scorching days would not work in the cool San Francisco summer. Furthermore, the less refined temperament of Westerners dictated less refined advertising copy: "the secret . . . on the Pacific Coast is to use *the loud pedal.* The average Far Westerner has little or no interest in *pianissimo* matters."

Problems multiplied for companies doing world marketing. A German farm-implement agent refused to use an International Harvester poster "showing a reaper drawn by tigers and driven by the Goddess of Liberty. He explained that tigers were not used for draught purposes in Germany, and that while women worked in the fields they were more modestly garbed." The Armour advertising manager wrote that a salesman in Madagascar reported trouble caused by a can picturing a little girl on the label, "the universal inference being that the contents of the can was *made from little girls!* Less extravagant cases may be cited, such as a similar inference from a horse on a label." A Chinese salesman wrote the company not to use red, a color of mourning; Armour abandoned blue and yellow in Norway because they were the national colors of Sweden.

Armour's international label problems stemmed from its attempt to standardize distribution among a vast range of goods.

The company had expanded its product line thanks to the traditional slaughterers' aspiration to use everything but the moo
and the squeal. It followed the imperatives both of the products
it made and of the raw materials it used in production, manufacturing sandpaper when it could not find a satisfactory market
for glue, and eventually buying forests, paper mills, and quar-
ries. By 1913, Armour made fertilizer, combs, grape juice, ammonia, strings for musical instruments, leather, perfume,
metal polishes, and proprietary medicines, and the company
was dispatching salesmen to the many outlets for all of these
goods. E. B. Merritt, who managed advertising for the entire
firm, worked against opposition from departmental managers to
institute a uniform label for Armour products, each previously
distributed under its own brand. The value of uniformity, Merritt wrote, lay in *"cumulative publicity.* The uniform label is the
first gun, or the first series of guns, in a world-wide and time-
long campaign of 'institutional advertising.' There is no latitude
left for the individual or the isolated brand." Each Armour product would presumably help sell every other one.

Other companies attempted to expand their markets and to
create diversified lines under a single brand by means of extension rather than consolidation. Many used their brand names
not only on line extensions—new flavors, styles, or models like
the Pocket Gillette—but also on what are now called "franchise
extensions," related products such as the Gillette Shaving Brush
and Gillette Shaving Stick. Starting only with irons, then adding
toasters, Hotpoint had by 1915 developed a family of twenty-
four products. Ranging in price from two to fifty dollars, the new
appliances all used the Hotpoint trademark in addition to such
individual names as "El Tosto," "El Grillo," and "El Perco."
("The prefix El was adopted for two reasons that are not generally known," a *Printers' Ink* writer explained, not entirely satisfac-
torily. "It is the Spanish equivalent for the English word 'the,'
and it is also suggestive of the word 'electric.' ") Ralston used
its products to sell each other, offering retailers quantity discounts on mixed orders. A small store could take five cases that

Some ads, like this one from *Collier's*, 1907, promoted whole lines of products from one manufacturer.

contained a combination of Ralston baking powder, Ralston gelatine, and Ralston cereal coffee, in addition to the company's staple Ralston breakfast food and nine other products, all in checkerboard packages.

Companies with many products could not necessarily afford to advertise them all. Colgate manufactured 225 products in 1910, advertising between 25 and 30 of them. Some firms concentrated almost solely on one product, as National Biscuit did with Uneeda. An article in *Advertising and Selling* recommended instead the strategy of rotating the products in the advertising, building a rather elaborate military metaphor. "Because Washington may have doted mostly upon his infantry," it ended, "or Napoleon upon his artillery, or the National Biscuit Company upon its Uneeda Biscuits, does not necessarily imply that the battles of war and of business cannot be won with the various units of an army or of a family of products *each* bearing equally the brunt of the battle." The Dennison Manufacturing Company, for example, advertised its crepe paper, glue, and tags each for portions of the year, the manager of the appropriate department working with the central advertising department during that time. Libby, McNeill, and Libby used this method to coordinate demand with supply. A particularly good harvest or a particularly good deal made in the stockyards could yield thousands of jars of olives or cans of tongue, which could be advertised with special copy inserted in the regular Libby space in magazines and newspapers.

As products multiplied and marketing strategies became more complex and expensive, advertisers began to assess their expenditures and attempt to approximate them beforehand by analyzing markets. As early as 1884, Schilling claimed to have estimated "the capacity of the United States for being supplied with Perfection Canned Teas," and to have based its importing and its marketing on that estimate. By 1905, when Earnest Elmo Calkins and Ralph Holden published *Modern Advertising*, they could cite numerous examples of manufacturers, advertising agents, and publishers who performed rudimentary tests on

A COUPON IN WHICH THE AGE OF THE INQUIRER IS AMONG
THE INFORMATION DESIRED.

A SQUARE COUPON.

COUPON WITH KEY IN
UPPER CORNER.

COUPON KEYED FOR PUBLICATION.

COUPON ACROSS BOTTOM OF PAGE.

FORMS OF COUPONS.

Examples of coupons, from Calkins and Holden, *Modern Advertising*, 1905.

advertising copy and studied population statistics to establish the groundwork for their campaigns. The booklets of hints and recipes, Calkins and Holden revealed, had an additional purpose as tests of whether advertising was actually being read; consumers sent for them using coupons or addresses with codes or "department" numbers keyed to the publications, enabling advertisers to compare results from different copy or from different magazines. "The present-day tendency on the part of experienced advertisers," they wrote, "is to get at the facts—to reduce the art of advertising to a science—to develop what may be called the mathematics of advertising." Advertising *was* an art, they assured their readers, but like other arts it must be based on theory and fact: "The statistics of advertising bear the same relation to preparing a successful advertising campaign that the mathematics of architecture bear to the designing of a great library."

Calkins and Holden quoted at length from an article, "The Psychology of Advertising," which had appeared in the *Atlantic* in 1904. The author, Walter Dill Scott, then a psychology professor at Northwestern and ultimately president of that university, had originally considered the topic in a speech to the 1901 annual dinner of Chicago's Agate Club, an organization of advertising men. John Lee Mahin, who was at the dinner, established his monthly *Mahin's Magazine* as a showcase for Scott's writing on topics in psychology and advertising; Scott turned his twenty-six *Mahin's* articles into *The Theory and Practice of Advertising* (1903) and *The Psychology of Advertising* (1908). He published the results of his own psychological experiments and those of Harlow Gale, a professor at the University of Minnesota, who had attempted to measure attention value in advertising as early as 1896, and had published his work in 1900. Gale studied what kinds of words and illustrations got the most attention from readers, establishing, for example, the greater power of a magazine's right-hand pages over the left.

In addition to this psychological work, Calkins and Holden cited market studies. *McClure's* had made a complete list of its subscribers in Cleveland, classified by occupation; *Ladies' World* had published photographs of every subscriber's home in selected towns. The *Northwestern Agriculturist* had sent out questionnaires to all subscribers, with prizes to those who responded, asking what brands they used. From the answers, the paper demonstrated that their subscribing farmers used high-grade goods: only sixteen said they owned Ingersoll watches, for example, compared with nearly two thousand Elgins and Walthams, both much more expensive brands. Ingersoll, Calkins and Holden noted, had not advertised in farm papers, concentrating instead on urban publications; the results of the survey showed a clear preference for goods the farmers had seen advertised in the media aimed at them. The popular Butterick magazines had in 1904 received more than five thousand responses to a similar questionnaire asking what brands its readers bought and why. Calkins and Holden called for additional statistical work that would enable advertisers to estimate markets. Even the Census Department, they pointed out, did not yet keep accurate and clearly classified records and tabulations of retail trade.

Calkins's and Holden's interest in statistics was shared by other advertising practitioners; the most advanced agencies used some statistical market study in planning campaigns. Before 1904, the Mahin agency sent questionnaires to publishers and retailers and tried different advertisements in different territories, testing them with keyed responses. Sometimes they did this as preliminary work, to be used as part of a presentation to an advertiser so that they might get the account. "Copy," said J. K. Fraser, the creator of "Spotless Town," who had gone to work for Mahin, "is just the surface of the campaign. All the machinery that produces results is below the surface, and the Mahin method deals almost entirely with this hidden machinery."

Mahin and other agencies combined research about product use with research about media, and kept careful records of the results they obtained from mail-order clients, applying the information to other accounts. With such data, magazine subscribers and particular parts of the population could be targeted, their buying habits tracked. Although methods were somewhat crude by today's standards, many business-research organizations did adopt the Hollerith machine, which tabulated coded data. Working on the principles established by these early practitioners employed by agencies, publishers, manufacturers, and universities, market research became not only a means of investigating markets but a tool for creating them, a literal needs creator. Discovering whether there was a market for a new product entailed finding out what people had, what they might want, what promotional plans they responded to, and what features of the product or its image might be reshaped to resemble what they wanted and induce them to buy. Researching a market thus became identical with discovering whether and how one could be called into being.

When Calkins revised *Modern Advertising* ten years after its 1905 publication, his own use of theory and statistics was considerably more sophisticated and he was able to point to many more instances of other people's work in the field. "The difference between advertising then and now," he wrote in 1915, "may be compared with the difference between a sailing vessel and a steamship. By good luck and favoring weather a sailing vessel can make a voyage almost as quickly and reach her port as safely as a steamship. But she will not do it so often and there are too many circumstances outside the control of her captain to make the voyage anything more than a courageous venture. . . . Even to-day advertising is not a scientific certainty. It is more scientific and more certain than it was."

Calkins dedicated this book to Cyrus H. K. Curtis, publisher of the *Saturday Evening Post,* the *Ladies' Home Journal,* the *Country Gentleman,* and other leading magazines, "the man who has done most to put the modern conduct of advertising on the right basis." The Curtis organization hired its first market-research director, Charles Coolidge Parlin, in 1911. Parlin first engaged in industry-wide studies of marketing structures, discussions of markets and channels of distribution in agricultural implements, textiles, foods, and automobiles. "Anyone with a food product problem who does not consult this report," counseled J. Walter Thompson's Cincinnati office in the agency's weekly newsletter when Parlin's food investigation appeared in 1916, "is, in Cincinnati's opinion, passing by a very valuable tool." The New York office responded with a claim that the report was inaccurate, not as good as its own investigations.

Other newspaper and magazine publishers hoped to induce advertisers to buy space by offering information about their readers. Here leadership came from the *Chicago Tribune,* whose Merchandising Service Department published in 1916 an illustrated booklet called *Winning a Great Market on Facts,* which re-

From *Winning a Great Market on Facts:* "A typical resident of district No. 18, where the population is largely foreign born and dependent almost entirely upon their local stores as the source of supply. These consumers look to their storekeeper for advice in the choice of their products. His recommendation of goods goes a long way to advance the sale of any product." District number 18 was the Carpenter Street district; another view may be seen on page 140.

ported the results of a massive house-to-house survey that had begun in February 1913. Although its sampling techniques were somewhat primitive by today's standards, the survey presented marketing facts by residential districts, discussing and offering figures on rents, buying habits, and the number of dealers in each line for each district. The booklet also presented the many services of the department. It offered retail merchants advice on good business practices and criticism of their advertising and store displays, through a service bureau and through a business paper called *The Co-Operator.* In return, the storekeepers displayed a sign in their windows, "We Sell Products Advertised in *The Tribune.*" To manufacturers, the *Tribune* offered extensive

1

NEWSPAPER DIRECTORY BLANK

CLEAR   CONFUSED

1   U. S. Postal District _18_   .01   Date **FEB 16 1914**   .02   No. _927_

2   Name _Conway, Peter_   Residence _2637 Rice St_
     (Householder)

3   Nationality _Irish_   Clubs _____

4   Business _motorman_   Business Address _-- Chicago Car Co--_

5   Which does the household buyer like best? goods by the___ 1. ☐ package, or___ ☑ bulk (pound or quart). Why? _Find it cheaper in end - have more in house & can economize_

	MEATS	GROCERIES	FRUIT VEG.	DRUGS					CLOTHING CLOTHES	SHOES	DRY G'DS		
6. Look at the card and tell me—"What do you buy downtown?"	∠	∠								∠		∠	∠
7. Why? _don't buy much except at sales._													
8. What do you buy at your neighborhood store? — _Buy mostly_	∠	∠	∠ ∠		∠	∠	∠						
9. Why? _in neighborhood_													

10   Which has the household buyer the most confidence in.... 1 ☑ Articles recommended by your dealer, or.... 2 ☐ those you see advertised?

11   Why? _I think in what dealer has. If they is owner has cheap it not as good & find as sale cost groceries to_

12   Is there anything you buy where you have a kick—on weight, quality, delivery, credit, service, price—or anything else?

13   What is your plan for finding out where to buy goods to the best advantage?.. _Papers & butter are advertised as 3¢ cheaper & when you get it the quality is bad._

14   ☑ Do you, or.... ☐ do you not read the ads before you go to buy? ... _Naturally — But I don't pay much attention. Believe must on faith_

15   ☐ Do, or.... ☑ do not ads cause you to buy something you hadn't thought of before?

16   Have you asked for an advertised article recently and had the dealer offer you something "just as good" or "cheaper"? ...... 1 ☑ Yes. ...... 2 ☐ No. What was it? _Butter & Coffee_
     Where advertised? _local circulars — window_   Anything else?

17   In the case of the......(naming each) what did you do? .... 1 ☑ Take what he offered ...... 2 ☐ Purchase with the privilege of returning ...... 3 ☐ Refuse the article and forget all about it ...... 4 ☐ Go somewhere else and purchase ...... 5 ☐ Wait for the dealer to order. _but found it poor quality & didn't go back_

18   Have you answered any advertisements recently? ...... 1 ☑ Yes ...... 2 ☐ No. How? ...... 1 ☐ by calling at store, ... 2 ☐ telephoning, ... 3 ☐ ordering from canvasser, ... 4 ☐ writing, ... 5 ☑ presenting coupon or ticket to dealer, ... 6 ☐ filling out and mailing coupon to manufacturer? What, if you remember? _Book cases advertised in magazine_ _Book_

19   Look at the card and tell me what influences you the most in buying goods. (The 2nd — 3rd — 4th—5th—6th—7th.)
1 ☑ Recommendations of dealer.
2 ☐ Canvasser.
3 ☑ Demonstrations.
4 ☐ Samples.
5 ☐ Window displays.
6 ☑ Shopping.
7 ☑ Newspaper advertisements.
8 ☐ "Weekly" advertisements.
9 ☑ Magazine advertisements.
10 ☐ Street car cards.
11 ☐ Bill boards.
12 ☐ Electric signs.
13 ☑ Circulars _through mail from grocers_

20   Which influences you the most in buying goods? ...... 1 ☐ Advertisements in Weekly Magazines, Monthly Magazines, Bill Boards and Street Car Cards Combined, or ...... 2 ☑ in Newspapers?

Key to Check Marks: { V = Voluntary.   S = Suggestion.   P = Prejudiced.
(After each answer, check in proper RIGHT HAND COLUMN.) { A = Answered.   F = Facetious.   ? = Doubt.

This questionnaire was used in the *Chicago Tribune* market research study reported in *Winning a Great Market on Facts.* Chicago Car Company motorman Peter Conway, "typical of the class of consumers who are obliged to watch their pennies carefully," frequently bought in bulk, rarely shopped downtown except at sales, and had more confidence in neighborhood dealers than in advertisements.

trade investigations. Researchers had investigated Chicago distribution for a salad-dressing manufacturer, for example, and were able to inform the company that although nearly 100 percent of the stores carried the product, only 40 percent of customers bought any prepared dressing at all. The Merchandising Service Department further provided maps of the city for manufacturer planning and guide maps to neighborhoods for the use of salesmen.

Manufacturers could also buy research services from the most progressive advertising agencies, which advanced the work that Mahin had pioneered. J. Walter Thompson first published a compilation of census figures, *Population and Its Distribution,* in 1912. Population statistics, the agency maintained, formed the correct basis for the quotas manufacturers must set for salesmen and territories. "What should this quota be—what are your sales possibilities? Facts, not guesses, must frame the answer." The information offered was limited, however, to lists of cities and their population, arranged by states. In 1915, the agency formed a research department and began its own consumer and trade surveys. Within a year, the department offered clients a 650-volume library. It carried trade publications, chamber of commerce reports, agency portfolios, and samples of work done for clients, and kept additional files on trades and industries, markets, clients and competitors, and media. The second edition of *Population and Its Distribution,* in 1918, included 196 pages of charts and statistics on population and population density, by regions and states and by nativity and race. Additional pages gave figures on wholesale and retail trade.

Around 1915, the Eastern Advertising Company, which controlled nearly all of New England's streetcar advertising, published the even more comprehensive *Advertisers Hand Book of New England.* This compilation offered data on literacy, school expenditures, manufacturing activity, population density, nativity, occupations, and incomes. For every town served by streetcars, it listed numbers of passengers, estimated annual volume of retail sales, and numbers of dealers in fourteen leading lines of

A Hyde Park grocery store, displaying the *Tribune*'s sign on its door, with a window decorated for Halloween.

business. "It puts New England under the microscope," the introduction declared. "It enables an advertiser to select the exact spots where he wishes to concentrate . . . and then to plan his sales and dealer work locally—to use up every scrap of value for his money spent in street-car advertising. . . . He can calculate the distances and time necessary for salesmen's work. . . . He can concentrate on the exact type of population he desires . . . and he can calculate the number of dealers he might sell, or the volume of trade in his line that he can hope to do in a given trolley system district."

Some manufacturers made their own forays into market research. Sampling and demonstration teams sometimes interviewed consumers while introducing a product, like the crews Nabisco sent house-to-house before 1906, who asked three simple questions: "Have you ever heard of Uneeda Biscuit? Have you ever used Uneeda Biscuit? If so, do you still use Uneeda

Biscuit?" The company tallied the results, and the president used them to justify and plan his advertising strategy. In 1911, R. O. Eastman, the Kellogg advertising manager, formed a consortium of more than forty major manufacturers to cooperate in a postcard questionnaire on magazine readership. The next year he developed a more elaborate questionnaire, hiring Kellogg salesmen to moonlight as interviewers.

Most companies used salesmen to make less formal reports on trade conditions. Charles Coolidge Parlin, writing in *Printers' Ink* in 1914, implied that manufacturers resisted research departments because they thought they could get sufficient information from their salesmen. Salesmen, however, "have a salesman's view-point and a salesman's prejudices," he wrote. "They see a part of the truth too clearly to get a fair vision of the whole truth." A research department could see what both the salesman and his boss missed. Earnest Elmo Calkins concurred: "Reports of salesmen make a good starting-point. They reflect the dealer attitude, which in turn reflects the consumer attitude. It must not be forgotten, however, that both salesman and dealer are cogs in an old-established machine. They run in certain grooves and are not so valuable in reflecting new conditions and new attitudes. Better still is the work of the real investigator: the man who collects and classifies facts as automatically as an adding machine."

"Real investigators" came from the ranks of a group of men who moved among positions in academia and business. When the representative of Chicago's Agate Club invited Walter Dill Scott to speak at the club's 1901 dinner, he had already been turned down by two prominent psychologists, Hugo Muensterberg of Harvard and Edward L. Thorndike of Columbia, who had declined the invitation because they were reluctant to participate in the direct application of their psychological work to commercial purposes. Over the next two decades, however, more academics (including Muensterberg) established business ties. Probably the best-known example is the pioneer behaviorist John B. Watson. When he lost his Johns Hopkins job for

sexual misbehavior in 1920, he had already done some private
consulting and had worked with Walter Dill Scott in a psychological consulting company. Full-time business work, he wrote
a colleague, "will not be as bad as raising chickens or cabbages."
A few months later he went to work for J. Walter Thompson.

In a burgeoning field, jobs could be had in teaching and
"pure" research, and in doing applied work for manufacturers,
publishers, and advertising agencies, as employees or as private
consultants. Kellogg's R. O. Eastman moved to agency work and
then, in 1916, opened the Eastman Research Bureau. J. George
Frederick, managing editor of *Printers' Ink* between 1909 and
1911, left to devote full time to the Business Bourse, a research
organization he had founded a few years earlier; he continued
consulting after he became editor of *Advertising and Selling* in
1913. Frederick organized the Psychology Roundtable, a fore-
runner of the Economic Psychology Association, of which he
was the first president; there he collaborated closely with Harry
Hollingworth, a Columbia faculty member who published
widely in the field. L. D. H. Weld, who made conceptual contributions to marketing before 1920, working at the University of
Minnesota and briefly at Yale, eventually worked for Swift and
Company and the McCann-Erickson advertising agency; similarly, Ralph Starr Butler, briefly a professor at the University of
Wisconsin and for a longer time at New York University, went
to the U.S. Rubber Company and the General Foods Corporation. Paul Nystrom, who also taught at Minnesota, worked for
the Associated Merchandising Corporation, returning to academia as a Columbia professor. Arch W. Shaw, the *System* editor
and Kellogg board member, taught at the Harvard Business
School and organized the Harvard Bureau of Business Research
in 1911.

Shaw called for more business and university cooperation in
"Some Problems in Market Distribution," the article that had
introduced the functional middleman concept. Scientists could
have businessmen's specific problems brought to their attention
through university-based research bureaus, he suggested. He

maintained that much of the billion dollars spent on advertising in the United States was wasted, a problem that could be solved only by careful testing of advertising material and by careful analysis of the market, broken down by region and by economic strata. Statisticians, he pointed out, had a unique understanding of mass phenomena. "The engineer does not choose material for a bridge by building a bridge of the material and waiting to see whether it stands. He first tests the material in the laboratory. That is what the business man must do."

Calls for scientific attitudes towards marketing were closely related to intellectual fashions in other areas of business and of social life. This was the heyday of efficiency experts practicing and preaching "scientific management," an approach to work that entailed scheduling tasks and defining standards. Notions of efficiency infused thinking about society in general and prescriptive writing about fields as far from the arena of profit as housekeeping and education. The first edition of J. Walter Thompson's *Population and Its Distribution* began with a reference to Harrington Emerson, one of the best-known efficiency engineers, disparaging the "slow, irregular, unprogressive" life of early steamboat towns. In contrast, the first railroad towns "were wide awake, clocks were in every home, and life went forward with brisk regularity—all because the scheduled arrival and departure of trains set a standard which the entire town conformed to. So with your sales organization."

An *Advertising and Selling* article calling for an institute for advertising research contrasted the scientific approach with witchcraft. Many thousands of people, it pointed out, had been tortured and burned at the stake "by a 'Popular Opinion' which was as *sincere* and mistaken as 'Popular Opinion' on *other* issues *can* be in the year 1912. . . . 'Popular Opinion' is based largely upon vague Tradition, simple 'Say-so,' Ready-made-Beliefs, Hand-me-down Axioms, 'Guff,' 'Con' and Dogma of the dog-gone variety, instead of being based upon *Investigated Information,* Unbiassed *Evidence,* and Sure Knowledge of *clearly-proven Facts.*"

From the start, opinion on analytical methods was mixed. *Printers' Ink*'s 1903 review of Walter Dill Scott's first book maintained that "the book contains nothing particularly new. Advertisers have reached all of the Professor's basic laws by the very serviceable kind of psychology called 'horse sense,' and his principles, while reduced to scientific fact, are all drawn from actual advertisements. . . . He is following the advertiser, not leading him." The magazine began to change its position around 1910, under the editorship of J. George Frederick. A decade later, however, Frederick complained in his book *Business Research and Statistics* that "the average business executive . . . has not yet fully grasped the profit and economy of making full and constant use of research and statistics." He accused research workers of a similarly bad attitude, "narrow and circumscribed and uncreative. It is sometimes a mere hack statistical outlook, unacquainted with practical business aim and necessity; sometimes too academic and inelastic in application."

The argument over scientific marketing reflected a larger question about human nature. The economists who had followed Adam Smith had come to believe in "the market" as an impersonal realm of autonomous decision-making, where individuals operated rationally, according to self-interest: seller exchanging with the highest bidder, buyer purchasing at the best price. A conception of human nature compatible with this view of "economic man" prevailed in the thinking of some advertising practitioners at the end of the nineteenth century, but others were coming to conceive of buyers as irrational, a view that predominated by 1910, adopting the language and methods of applied psychology. The makers of branded products were particularly interested in combatting consumers' rational interest in purchasing at the best price. Competing with bulk goods and private labels required brand identification that was stronger than price sensitivity. In other words, people had to be willing to pay whatever the cost in order to get Ivory or Van Camp's.

The psychological school, interested in the phenomenon of

suggestion, concentrated on the effectiveness of trademarks and advertisements. University and company researchers tested subjects' memories of trademarks and slogans, following Hugo Muensterberg's 1909 recommendation that psychological testing could be of use in problems of trademark law. Copy testing and analysis was led by Harry Hollingworth, a psychologist teaching at Columbia and New York University. In 1913, he published *Advertising and Selling: Principles of Appeal and Response,* with sections on capturing interest, holding attention, and provoking responses, and chapters entitled "The Nervous Basis of Mental Processes" and "Sex and Class Differences of Interest to Business Men."

Despite the best efforts of psychological theorists, the question of effective advertising was so elusive that some researchers asked the public directly. In 1907, *Everybody's Magazine* offered ten prizes of twenty-five dollars each for the best essays in answer to the question "Which is the most effective advertisement in this November issue of *Everybody's Magazine*—and why?" Two years later, Colgate sponsored a contest comparing an ad appealing to rationality with one based on suggestion. Nearly 60,000 people entered. "Of course you will be anxious to know which really was the better ad," the company admitted in its announcement of the winners. "We are sorry to be unable to tell you, for since the opinions were almost equally divided, the question still remains practically unanswered."

Colgate sold toothpaste using both kinds of advertising. The essential concerns of successful marketing were not psychological; they went beyond the issues raised by the debate between suggestion and rationality and beyond measurements of memory, attention span, or suggestion. Nor were they limited to the nature of advertisements. The new marketing principles concerned broad cultural issues. They involved conceptualizing the market as dynamic and malleable, constantly changing as new products were incorporated into people's daily lives. "The demand for candles," Ralph Starr Butler pointed out in a 1914 textbook, "is not keeping up with the increase in population,

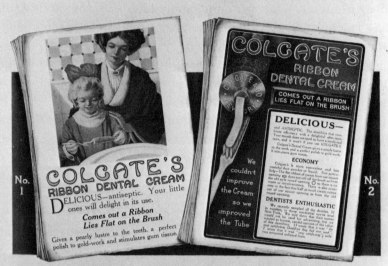

WHICH IS THE BETTER "AD"?

$750.00 for the Best Answers

(Fifty-eight Prizes)

1 First Prize of $100.00	10 Fourth Prizes of $15.00 each
2 Second Prizes of $50.00 each	15 Fifth Prizes of $10.00 each
5 Third Prizes of $25.00 each	25 Sixth Prizes of $5.00 each

What is a good advertisement? *We* are not sure, and we want *you* to tell us.

Ask us what a good toilet or shaving soap, perfume, dental cream or toilet and nursery powder is and we *can* tell you.

Three generations of Colgates, from father to son, for over a century have been conducting this business under the Colgate name. We *know* how toilet articles should be made, and we are making them that way.

For many years also we have been making advertisements — good, poor and indifferent. We *ought* to know something about them. But — we realize that we still have much to learn. A Colgate advertisement *ought* to reflect the Colgate spirit. It ought to please and interest you in its appearance. It ought to convince you in its text. And it *must* be absolutely truthful or it *cannot* be a Colgate Advertisement. What kind of an advertisement best fulfills these conditions?

We believe that you can tell us and we have taken this method of getting your opinion.

Above are two Colgate advertisements of entirely different character.

No. 1 is pictorial. Its value depends upon its suggestive power.

No. 2 is descriptive. It goes into details about our Dental Cream and the Ribbon Tube.

Both kinds of advertising have given us results, both have been favorably commented upon.

But which sells the more Dental Cream?

It is to *you* that we are advertising and it is from *you* that we want the answer because we believe that you (the majority of you) know far better than the best advertising "expert" just what kind of an advertisement influences you to purchase.

This Is Our Offer

Write us a letter of not over one hundred words giving your opinion as to the better of these two advertisements. Base your opinion on the appeal to purchase which they make to you. Ask yourself which one would be the most likely to influence you to buy our Dental Cream and give us your reasons.

The letters which give the most common sense reasons in plain, simple wording will get the prizes. You don't have to know anything about advertising to compete, in fact you'll be handicapped if you do because we believe that we can recognize the "advertising man's" view point and it's just that view point that we *don't* want.

Prizes will be Awarded by the Following Judges:

Mr. Caspar Whitney, Author and Editor, Collier's Weekly   Mr. Keith Evans, Advertising Manager of Woman's Home Companion
Mrs. N. H. Kinkaid, Assistant Editor of The Delineator   Mr. Frank Seaman, Advertising Agent

Contest closes on November 1, 1909. All letters must be received on or before that date. Write on but one side of paper and sign letter *plainly* with your full name and address, which will not be counted in the "one hundred words." Direct your letter thus —

Dept. H, (Contest) COLGATE & CO., 55 John Street, New York

Makers of the famous Cashmere Bouquet Toilet Soap

* On the back cover pages of the October Woman's Home Companion, Delineator, Designer and New Idea Woman's Magazine we ask for similar opinions about two of our Talc Powder advertisements. No person is eligible to compete in both contests.

Nearly sixty thousand people entered this 1909 contest, evenly divided between partisans of the suggestive and the descriptive approaches.

because newer methods of illumination are driving candles from the field." Nearly all such new technologies, Butler explained four years later, started as luxuries. At the beginning, there was not much demand for automobiles, phonographs, tractors, or typewriters. "The far-seeing manufacturer," he declared, "will refuse to limit his vision to the expressed demand for his product, and will find in the field that he wishes to cover, if he will only seek them out, a constantly increasing number of people to whom his product can be made to appeal as a necessity."

With this advice, Butler articulated the central concept of modern marketing: an expanding market that was not defined by supply and demand but shaped by energetic manufacturers who understood that markets could be developed. Techniques like market segmentation and targeted promotion emerged in tandem with this idea of the malleable market, which was founded in and reinforced by the new roles of consumer and dealer. Yet the new ways of selling emerged not from theoretical concerns but as practical responses to the problems of marketing in a diverse culture and an economy dominated by new kinds of goods.

Booklet cover showing the American Cereal Company pavilion at the 1893
Columbian Exposition in Chicago.

CHAPTER 6

IIIICƆIIIIIIIIICƆIIIIIIIIICƆIIIII

SALES
AND
PROMOTIONS

DURING THE SUMMER OF 1891, THE AMERICAN CEREAL COMPANY dispatched a special fifteen-car freight train from its mill in Cedar Rapids, Iowa, carrying 126,000 two-pound packages of Quaker Oats to Portland, Oregon, where the company had not yet sold its product but had left a half-ounce miniature package in every mailbox. An advance man preceded the train by a few days, visiting local newspaper offices in towns along the route to brief reporters on the train's approach, buy space in the paper, hand out samples, and hire newsboys for the day the "special" passed through. The train stopped briefly in each town, where hundreds or even thousands of people gathered to receive tiny cartons from the newsboys' canvas bags and to watch a show featuring a man standing on the engine, dressed like the Quaker on the package.

Two years later, the company installed its display at the World's Columbian Exposition in Chicago, where it distributed a souvenir booklet that compiled lithographed scenes of modern grain farming, processing, and distribution. At the St. Louis World's Fair in 1904, the company introduced Quaker Puffed Rice by shooting it from eight bronze cannons. Hired hands roamed the fairgrounds, handing out four-color pictures of

Niagara Falls and Independence Hall, suitable for framing. On the reverse, a map of the fair highlighted the Quaker exhibit, where, as at state fairs and regional expositions, the company gave away samples of cooked oatmeal.

American Cereal was a major national advertiser, spending about $100,000 during the year of the Columbian Exposition on streetcar placards, trade journals, magazines, and newspapers. Twenty years later, the Quaker Oats Company was still second only to Procter and Gamble among corporations purchasing national magazine advertising. These companies and the many others that followed their marketing leadership constructed campaigns based both on advertising and on other forms of promotion. People saw advertising regularly on their way to work and in the newspapers and magazines that linked them with the public world. Special trains and world's fairs made products into public attractions, with souvenir samples to take home and try. Another kind of giveaway, the premium, ensured brand loyalty over time. The year-round activities of the sales force established personal relationships with retailers, bringing marketing campaigns into the stores. All these promotional tactics played distinct and complementary roles in the creation of the market and the adaptation of the distribution system to branded mass-produced goods.

Nearly every company used some kind of giveaway scheme, a practice that had begun decades before with lithographed trade cards and booklets from patent-medicine companies. Collecting the small, full-color trade cards was a popular hobby during the 1880s and early 1890s. They came in packaged tea, coffee, and soap, but were more often obtained from retailers, who got them from drummers. Single cards usually pictured the products, but not always, and could be quite elaborate affairs, die-cut with movable parts. Arbuckle Brothers inserted cards in coffee packages that could be collected into fifty-card sets picturing animals, American history, or a trip around the world; Singer made puns on its company name with a series of songbird trade cards and another of opera singers. The many cards produced for the Columbian Exposition in 1893 obscure the fact that by

KIRKMAN'S BORAX SOAP

FOR THE LAUNDRY, BUT GOOD ENOUGH FOR TOILET USE. TRY IT IN YOUR NEXT WASH.

Trade cards with movable parts, like these two from Kirkman's Borax Soap, were known as "mechanicals."

then the trade card was on its way out, its importance as an advertising medium eclipsed by the new mass-circulation magazines.

Advertisements in these magazines almost always offered some kind of printed matter through the mail, in part as a copy-testing device: with or without corner coupons, advertisers kept track of which ads in which magazines brought the most requests. Many booklets consisted solely of advertising, but others had their own utility. Patent-medicine companies continued to provide the booklets of medical advice they had offered since the 1830s, and even companies with no cooking-related products to sell gave recipe books away. Written guidance for other aspects of modern life could be obtained from hundreds of commercial sources. In one 1905 magazine, the makers of Ostermoor mattresses offered a book about sleep ("Tells all about insomnia, etc."), Cuticura would send *How to Care for the Skin and Scalp,* Nestlé's provided *Book for Mothers,* and Eaton-Hurlbut Papers

Front cover of Kellogg's 1909 *Funny Jungleland.* Pages were divided in three, so that the animals' heads, torsos, and legs could be exchanged, creating "moving pictures."

issued *The Gentle Art of Letter Writing.* Dozens of other companies offered booklets of recipes, tourist information, and catalogues.

Children were special targets for promotional materials. At least one trade card instructed the "lively little card collector" to show the card to mother. Others were intended as toys, incorporating paper dolls or puzzles; the movable "mechanicals" often had children's themes. "There is a big juvenile equation in the chewing-gum business," *Printers' Ink* wrote in 1910, lauding Wrigley's for advertising copy that "has something of the Mother Goose quality." Five years later, the company published its own *Mother Goose,* featuring characters like Little Bo-Spear, who had lost her deer. Quaker Oats concocted wholly original "nursery rhymes," about boats full of oats sailing on cream and babies growing big thanks to good breakfasts. Colgate reproduced more traditional Mother Goose verses, confining the advertising to the back pages. Kellogg issued *Funny Jungleland,* a book of corn-flake doggerel and "moving pictures"—pages divided in thirds so that heads, torsos, and feet could be switched around; the company distributed eight carloads of the booklet within a few months of its first offer in 1909.

Toys were among the inexpensive items imprinted with trademarks that came to be known as "specialty advertising." Manufacturers expected specialties to have a longer impact than ads in newspapers and magazines, which were likely to be thrown away. Fans would be used throughout a summer, calendars and almanacs lasted a year, penknives or bottle openers even longer. Shredded Wheat offered a celluloid "Ladies Work Basket Mea-

"Specialty advertising" from Quaker Oats, a match striker. This inexpensive but useful item might be displayed publicly over a long time.

sure and Book Mark," stamped, like many manufacturers' booklets, "Compliments of" the retailer. Other objects were more directly associated with the products, and required cash payment or proofs of purchase. In 1901, Welch's offered a "self-pulling" corkscrew for one quart or two pint grape-juice labels or ten cents in stamps. Fifteen years later, the Karo syrup company advertised an aluminum-griddle offer in seventeen women's magazines and twenty-seven farm papers expected to reach about 72 million readers, as well as in many local newspapers and on billboards all over the country. Consumers paid eighty-five cents and enclosed labels from fifty cents' worth of Karo, and long before the campaign reached its peak, its success motivated company plans to offer a candy pot and a preserving kettle to promote other uses for the product.

The American Cereal Company packed pieces of china in its boxes. Between November 1900 and March 1902, the company purchased nearly 2.5 million sets of china from the manufacturer, which in 1904 built twelve additional kilns to supply Quaker. In 1905, the company began to pack lettered coupons into its Pettijohn's wheat cereal, offering a free stereoscope to consumers who collected all the letters in the word "Pettijohn"; the next year, the boxes contained stereoscope slides of scenes around the world. Unlike griddles and calendars, and unlike the children's rings and kitchen gadgets that Quaker also packed in its cereal, these premiums induced multiple sales. People attempting to collect sets of dishes or slides would not switch to some other breakfast food, and they might persuade friends to buy the product so they could trade duplicates.

According to one contemporary observer, Quaker's practice of packing premiums in boxes was exceptional. More commonly, manufacturers attempting to induce multiple purchases enclosed coupons or required consumers to send wrappers; often they asked only for cut-out trademarks, a practice intended to reinforce trademark recognition. In the late 1890s, Procter and Gamble offered sentimental pictures, without advertising and suitable for framing, in exchange for ten Ivory

Procter and Gamble included this card with samples requested and sent through the mail. "Should you want more of the 'IVORY SOAP,'" read the reverse side, "your family grocer can easily get it for you, as every whole-sale grocer sells it. We take this opportunity to say, some grocers are so short-sighted as to decline to keep the 'Ivory Soap,' claiming it does not pay as much profit as inferior qualities do; so if your regular grocer refuses to get it for you, there are undoubtedly others who recognize the fact that the increased volume of business done by reason of keeping the best articles more than compensates for the small profit, and will take pleasure in getting it for you."

A page from Dunham's Cocoanut's 1893 premium catalogue. A "whole
certificate" was printed on the label of the one-pound box.

wrappers. For thirteen empty Knox Gelatine boxes sent to the
factory during 1904, that company would exchange an entry
ticket for a drawing with much more substantial prizes: a Steinway piano, an expensive sofa, and a sewing machine.

By 1893, a few firms had established elaborate premium programs, with catalogues picturing hundreds of items. Dunham's
Shred Cocoanut gave specific instructions for redemption, in-

sisting on certificates cut from the front of the package and letters following a prescribed form. The catalogue also offered a few recipes and an explanation of the premium program: "Why do the manufacturers of Dunham's Shred Cocoanut make such liberal offers to consumers, and why should they give away such valuable premiums? To all such questions we reply, that in this, as in many other ways, we are *advertising.*" "Save Your Labels," the back cover read. "Ask your friends to save them." With friends' help, people might aspire to items requiring the purchase of twenty to thirty pounds of coconut.

Books and magazines were especially popular premiums. Colgate published the titles of the several-hundred-volume Octagon Library on the backs of Octagon Bar laundry soap wrappers in the 1890s; twenty-five trademarks would fetch *Paradise Lost, Through the Looking Glass, Jane Eyre,* and many works now obscure. Boxes of Force and other H-O products contained "library slips," coupons issued by the Magazine and Book Company of New York, which handled premiums for many manufacturers, permitting consumers to consolidate proofs of purchase from different standard goods. For consumers who preferred watches or furniture to books, H-O ran its own premium program. Colgate also extended its premium program to people not satisfied with a choice between Milton and Brontë. In 1911, it published an elaborate catalogue entitled *The Right Way to Wash Clothes,* with extensive washing advice, "important facts about soap making," and thirty pages of premiums to be obtained for coupons from Octagon soap powder, Colgate's lemon and vanilla flavoring extracts, Bee laundry soap, and Colgate's White Floating Soap.

Unlike the many companies that gave away cheap merchandise specifically manufactured for premiums, the United Cigar Stores, the retailing arm of the American Tobacco Company, stressed its trademarked goods. "Wherever possible," the company maintained in one premium catalogue, "we have secured articles bearing the name or trade-mark of the maker identified with the manufacture of the best article of the kind." The United Profit Sharing Corporation, organized in 1914, extended the

Consumers who saved Wrigley's wrappers could redeem them for premiums through the United Profit Sharing Corporation.

United Cigar program to other manufacturers. In more than 150 cities, redemption stores would exchange goods for coupons printed on Wrigley's gum wrappers and packed inside household products including Economy canvas gloves, Durkee's salad dressing, Rubberset brushes, Wesson Oil, and Washington shirts.

Premiums were the traditional promotional tool in the tobacco industry. In 1889, the year before it united with four other manufacturers to form the American Tobacco Company, W. Duke Sons and Company alone spent most of its $800,000 advertising budget on premiums. The expenditure reflected the degree of competition, as did the wide variety of attractive goods that continued to characterize tobacco premium offers. In 1904, the Floradora Tag Company of St. Louis, which serviced premiums for manufacturers including P. Lorillard, offered baseballs, playing cards, cigarette holders, and fishing line for 25 to 50 cigar bands, coupons, or metal tags from chewing tobacco. In the same catalogue, four models of Studebaker farm wagons could be had for 6,200 to 11,200 proofs of purchase.

Until 1907, the forty-four people who worked in the R. J. Reynolds premium office handled a similar range of goods. Liggett and Myers operated redemption stores from New York to Portland, Oregon, and in 1913 created a corps of traveling premium men, who set up temporary redemption stations in small-town tobacco stores.

That year, however, Reynolds launched Camels. According to industry historians, this brand established the modern cigarette industry, with innovations in the product (a blend incorporating Burley tobacco, a variety that could absorb flavoring "sauces") and in its marketing. Unlike other inexpensive brands, which came in packages of ten, Camels were packed in the twenty-

Two pages from the 1908–1909 United Cigar Stores "Profit Sharing List." This company emphasized branded, standard goods as its premiums.

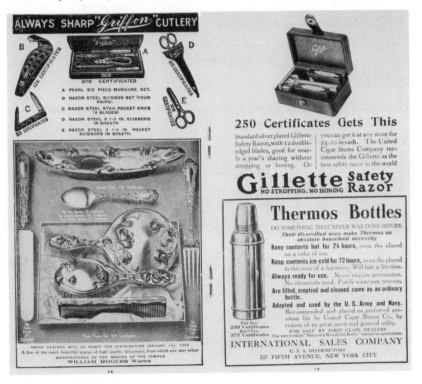

CENTRAL PROFIT-SHARING STATION IN NEW YORK, 44 WEST 18TH STREET.

The United Cigar Stores' main redemption station, from the 1914 catalogue.

cigarette packs that eventually became standard. Reynolds relied for its promotion not on premiums but on advertising,
primarily in newspapers and on billboards. Indeed, the company celebrated the abolition of premiums with the disparaging
inscription "Don't look for premiums or coupons . . . ," which
remained on the package decades after other firms had stopped
offering them.

In other industries, companies with more than one brand gave
premiums with those positioned for poorer market segments;
"premium brand" did not mean the best. Arbuckle gave premiums with Ariosa, paying publishers to enclose premium circu-

lars in their magazines, where ads emphasizing premiums alternated with ones touting the quality of the coffee. One spoon offer brought nearly 50,000 requests. In 1916, Procter and Gamble offered premiums with at least four brands of soap and one of washing powder, but not with Ivory or with Lenox, said to be the largest-selling laundry soap in the world. The brands that gave premiums, *Printers' Ink* explained, were sold in "the poorer class of stores, which are often run by foreigners who understand little English." Premiums provided immigrant workers with matching dishes, pretty things for the house, and children's toys, and gave manufacturers of expensive goods a wider market. A United Cigar Store representative testifying before the House Ways and Means Committee commented that the

---

Front and back cover of 1909 Star soap premium catalogue. Star was sold outside metropolitan areas; P & G marketed other premium brands for New York and Chicago.

Erector Sets and Thermos bottles his company marketed "go to a class of people who would not otherwise buy these goods."

"Scarcely a middle-class or wage-worker's family may be found, at least east of the Mississippi, where some kind of coupons are not saved and some kind of a free prize not expected," declared political economist I. M. Rubinow in 1905, describing premiums as a "moral epidemic." "Premium Mad," Philadelphia's *Grocers' Review* headlined an article the same year, in an issue reporting opposition from other grocery trade journals and from retailers' organizations. Opponents succeeded in getting premiums outlawed in many states, but as these laws were consistently struck down by the courts, they agitated also for federal legislation. A rider attached to the 1897 Dingley tariff bill prohibited packing coupons into product containers; directed at cigarette premiums, this prohibition was removed in 1901. The 1914 House Ways and Means hearings concerned four bills that had been introduced with the support of thirty-eight of the smaller tobacco and cigar manufacturers. By 1915, the battle had been joined by the National Retail Dry-Goods Association, representing more than 350 department stores; Marshall Field's and Macy's would not carry any merchandise bearing premium coupons. The American Newspaper Publishers' Association passed resolutions against them, and the *Saturday Evening Post* refused to sell advertising space to premium companies.

"It is not evident, on the face of it," wrote Rubinow, "why the retail grocery-dealers should find the system of premiums objectionable." His explanation revealed to readers ignorant of the costs of retailing a central fact of branded distribution: premium goods, like all popular branded goods, offered less profit to the retailer. The usual opposition to premiums, however, focused less on self-interest and more on the hidden costs of premiums and the dangers of educating people to expect something for nothing. Some expressed concerns about the survival of small-town business that would later infuse protests against mail-order houses and chain stores. "Our Association, for one," the retail grocers of Olean, New York, resolved in December 1904, "does not propose to distribute advertising matter for any manufacturer in our opinion calculated to injure our fellow-merchants in other lines of business." A large Chicago manufacturer who used premium coupons called the antipremium propaganda "simply ludicrous," based on "the same arguments which have, under one guise or another, been directed against advertising of standard, trade-marked merchandise. The merchant doesn't want the consumer to be influenced by the manufacturer. He wants to control the situation—but he can't."

In March 1916, the Supreme Court reversed the consistent trend of the lower courts, upholding the right of the states to impose laws prohibiting or taxing premium systems. Three decisions announced simultaneously left conditions uneven from

---

The Hamilton Corporation ran premium plans for many manufacturers, who packed their popular coupons for both consumers and retailers in many household products. This advertisement, describing the coupon plan as a form of advertising, appeared in the *American Grocer* in 1910.

state to state. As of 1933, premium goods could not be inserted into packages sold in Montana, or into food packages in Nebraska; coupons were illegal in Idaho and Washington, but the Idaho law was not enforced; Wisconsin demanded that items given as premiums be manufactured by the company offering them; and other states imposed other stipulations.

One of the major legal issues was whether prohibition and taxing were discriminatory; in other words, whether coupons and premiums were sufficiently different from other forms of advertising and selling to justify special legislation. Unlike most of the lower courts, the Supreme Court said that they were. "Advertising," explained the Court, "is mere identification and description, apprising of quality and place. It has no other object than to draw attention to the article to be sold, and the acquisition of the article to be sold constitutes the only inducement to its purchase." University of Chicago lecturer C. S. Duncan, who later wrote major texts in marketing and market research, charged the Court with ignorance of modern merchandising. "The cloth is cut too short for a fit in this garment," he wrote. "There is no place for the educational advertising campaign, the development of new wants; there is no place for the advertisement whose purpose is to sell a *certain make of goods* where there are a half dozen choices of equal quality at the same place. . . . Has the learned judge never delved into the new business of advertising? Does he not know of the eager study of methods of appeal, of the principles of psychology, of art, of color effects, of design, of the power of words?" Duncan took his stand with the Chicago manufacturer. "After all," he asked, "is not the source of all opposition the plain and simple fact that the premium-giving system is too successful?"

Premiums enabled manufacturers to "induce continuous patronage," a phrase frequently used both in the premium catalogues and in magazine articles discussing premiums. To establish that patronage in the first place, they relied on sampling. It was perhaps the most traditional promotional method, with roots in common retailing practices; grocers had always

This Colgate advertisement, published in *Collier's* in 1907, offered a sample shaving stick in two ways: a conventional proposition (send four cents) at the bottom of the ad, and a free offer hidden in the next-to-last paragraph of the text, intended as a copy-testing device.

offered slivers of cheese to potential customers. Sampling was calculated to encourage trial and was considered especially effective for introducing new products. For decades, manufacturers had sent samples through the mail, hired people to distribute them door-to-door, and given them away as the closing flourish of factory tours. Some huge sampling campaigns reached many more people than print advertising: in 1909, *Printers' Ink* estimated that the Cudahy Packing Company, "the most persistent and enormous sampler," had reached three-quarters of the American population at least twice with full-sized free samples of Old Dutch Cleanser.

Every issue of every general-circulation magazine from the late 1880s through World War I offered readers the opportunity to send for samples of coffee, soap, complexion powder, canned soup, mucilage, toothpaste, varnish, or shirt collars. Companies with goods too expensive to sample offered fountain pens, mattresses, lamps, safety razors, stoves, water heaters, and shoe trees for free trial periods. Mellin's Food, a popular baby food that also courted doctors by exhibiting at the annual meetings of the American Medical Association, offered samples in the mail "free to any mother." Some samples really were free; other companies demanded payment in coins or stamps. *Printers' Ink* warned manufacturers not to charge too much: "many concerns constantly fly in the face of human nature," it cautioned, by asking consumers to pay the retail price plus postage. "This is straining the power of advertising entirely too hard."

Free samples and other giveaways drew crowds at the smallest country fairs and at big-city trade shows; along with the Ferris wheel and the Eiffel Tower, American manufacturers' samples lured tourists at world expositions in Paris, St. Louis, Chicago, and elsewhere. World's fairs offered manufacturers a variety of opportunities to showcase their goods, to enter them in competitions, and to disseminate samples and promotional material. Heinz had three different exhibits at the 1901 Pan-American Exposition in Buffalo: one serving food, one displaying photographs of the workers, and one exhibiting the goods the com-

arge manufacturers exhibited at small fairs as well as at huge expositions. Here a Sher-
in-Williams paint exhibit appears among the stalks of grain and other farm produce in a
notograph from a 1908 county fair.

pany produced for the American and British armies and navies.
Many companies spent $20,000 to $30,000 at the World's
Columbian Exposition in Chicago, and some spent much more.
To house its display, the American Radiator Company created
a two-room structure supported on Corinthian columns and
decorated with pure gold leaf, satin wallpaper, hardwood floors,
rare palms, and Turkish rugs. Even small companies spent as
much as they could afford on elaborate exhibits, ingeniously
designed sample containers, and expensively produced souvenir cards and booklets.

An small company's exhibit at the Jamestown Exposition in Norfolk, 1907. "The Bigg tea-pot on earth, holding a million cups," read the caption on this double-imaged sli made for viewing with a stereoscope, a popular entertainment at the turn of the centu

Some manufacturers' promotions contributed to the "visions of empire" and the racist stereotypes that historian Robert Rydell has identified as a central theme of these world's fairs, evident also in the midway shows and the government-sponsored exhibits. Singer's Columbian Exposition souvenir booklet displayed page after page of pictures of Singer products juxtaposed with images of foreigners, dressed in traditional costumes and posed with their sewing machines; the company reprinted these on trade cards the next year. Around the fairgrounds, people dressed in similar costumes, on exhibit for months on end, attempted to recreate normal daily lives as residents of model villages simulating Lapland or Borneo. American blacks living in actual slave cabins transported from their original sites played banjos and sang songs at fairs in 1897 in Nashville and 1898 in Omaha. Nancy Green, a former slave, appeared among the manufacturers' displays portraying Aunt Jemima at these and most other large turn-of-the-century fairs.

She stood outside a giant flour barrel, singing, flipping sample pancakes, and telling tales of bygone days in the slave South. The Missouri miller who made the pancake mix claimed to have received more than 50,000 merchants' orders at the Columbian Exposition, where Green first did her act. She left her position as a domestic servant for a Chicago judge and spent the rest of her life in the role.

Some food manufacturers recycled their world's fair exhibits at food fairs, usually sponsored by retail and wholesale grocers' associations. Held in cities all over the country beginning in the early 1890s, these events featured displays, demonstrations, and giveaways sponsored by manufacturers, pure-food organizations, government agencies, cooking schools, railroads, and

---

A typical illustration from Singer's Columbian Exposition souvenir book, which also pictured the company's various models of sewing machines. The company later used the many images of foreigners and their sewing machines as trade cards.

ONE OF THE GREAT EMPORIUMS OF THE EAST, AND CAPITAL CITY OF THE PHILIPPINE ISLANDS, IS LOCATED ON THE ISLAND OF LUZON. IT WAS FOUNDED BY LIGASPI IN 1571. THE INHABITANTS ARE INDIANS AND SPANIARDS. ITS MANUFACTURES AND EXPORTS ARE CIGARS AND CHEROOTS, ALSO CORDAGE MADE FROM THE FILAMENTS OF ABACA. THE CITY HAS A VERY ORIENTAL APPEARANCE, THE HOUSES BEING BUILT ON PILLARS ABOVE THE GROUND TO ADMIT THE FREE PASSAGE OF WATER UNDERNEATH IN THE RAINY SEASON. THE SPANISH INHABITANTS, AS WELL AS THE NATIVE INDIANS, USE AND PRIZE OUR SINGER MACHINE, WHICH HAS FOUND ITS WAY TO THIS ISLAND OF THE SEA.

farm cooperatives. They provided careers for the graduates of cooking schools, who traveled from state to state running manufacturers' booths and preparing samples, and for their teachers, whose demonstrations and lessons were among the food fairs' highlights. More than 12,000 people attended one Madison Square Garden show on a single day, and nearly 300,000 during the two weeks it was open. The Boston Retail Grocers' Association claimed that half a million people had attended the four fairs it sponsored before 1901.

"One could make quite a satisfactory luncheon, if so disposed, by going diligently from booth to booth," the *New England Cooking Magazine* wrote of a Boston fair in 1894, listing the possible courses in order, from soup or bouillon to tea, coffee, and bonbons. At an 1893 show in Brooklyn, Hecker's passed out empty flour bags, which fairgoers used to collect samples from other companies. "The grab for samples," the eminent Philadelphia cooking-school teacher Sarah Tyson Rorer explained to the advertising community in *Printers' Ink*, "is not so much that women want so much for nothing." She attributed it instead to the attractive miniature packaging, recalling that at the 1876 Centennial Exposition she had stood in line for three hours to get an advertiser's toy brick. "A good show is in a large sense an educator," she declared. "It brings the housewife into closer contact with the best of everything." Admission fees to these fairs limited contact with the best to housewives with some discretionary income; the Madison Square Garden show cost fifty cents, ten times the price of most popular entertainments.

Manufacturers introducing goods to a broader market distributed samples house-to-house, an expensive promotional method that local authorities sometimes thwarted by arresting samplers under antipeddling statutes. With retailer assistance, such problems could be avoided by issuing samples with coupons. Coca-Cola moved out from its base in Atlanta by writing to soda-fountain operators 20,000 at a time, offering free glasses and advertising displays, and asking for the names of 100 customers. Each of these customers received a letter and a coupon

The small rectangle at the bottom of this Coca-Cola card could be cut out and used as a coupon, good for a free glass of Coke at a participating drug store or soda fountain. The company redeemed coupons for millions of glasses in its initial crusade for distribution.

for a complimentary Coke, which the druggist or candy-store owner could cash in for five cents. From 1894 to 1900, the company redeemed coupons for over 9 million sample Cokes. Although it also used billboards, streetcar and trade-journal advertising, and many specialty items (the calendars, clocks, pocket knives, and drinking glasses beloved by later collectors), it relied on the coupons for achieving broad distribution and maintaining good relationships with dispensers.

Although not all coupon campaigns depended on such extensive retailer cooperation, they all required some: for coupons to be redeemed, the goods had to be in the stores. Van Camp's ran 3 million coupons in New York and Connecticut newspapers in 1909, offering for each a full-sized can of evaporated milk to the redeemer and ten cents to the grocer. Although many observers believed the campaign was "enormously extravagant and unwise," citing one woman who was said to have gotten 141 cans, others maintained that the unrestricted redemption attracted grocers as well as consumers, putting the milk on the shelves of many dealers who had not handled it previously. Three years later Quaker printed more than 21 million coupons for free Puffed Rice and Puffed Wheat in ninety monthly magazines and newspaper Sunday supplements. Trade-journal advertisements listed the magazines and exhorted grocers to stock up. "We urge orders of not less than two cases each—four cases in all—of Puffed Rice and Puffed Wheat. That will mean 144 packages and those cannot go far in a free coupon demand."

In 1915–16, Procter and Gamble spent the largest appropriation ever made for a single brand of soap on a campaign for its Star brand that combined the techniques of coupons, samples, and premiums. Two weeks after a house-to-house sampling directed at every housewife in each targeted town, a second canvass gave her a coupon that entitled her to two cakes for the price of one. Three cakes made a start on the Star habit, three wrappers a start on the premiums, and "a sizable proportion of the community is supplied with laundry soap for some time to come." Both of the house-to-house crews also visited retail stores, the first to check on whether they stocked the product, the second to place and install store and window displays. About three months after the first canvass, more coupons were distributed from house to house.

Coupons, premiums, and samples went to retailers and their clerks as well as to consumers. A writer whose father ran an Ohio grocery store remembered substantial Christmas gifts from Chase and Sanborn: "an inlaid tea caddy, a silver coffee service, a silver tray." Colgate published a separate premium catalogue for barbers. Large quantities of Wrigley's gum were packed with cheese cutters, scales, chewing-gum showcases, or furniture. Knox Gelatine held a retailers' drawing for a racehorse or $5,000. "Now think what $5,000 would mean to a host of retailers!" the contest publicity read. "It would put them on their feet financially at once; would clean up old losses; and locate them

A retailer promotion from Wrigley's. This showcase was one of many such offers; merchants ordering large amounts of gum could also get cheese cutters, rocking chairs, and other store and home furnishings.

Coupons for free merchandise, like this one for Doublemint gum, were used to introduce new products to retailers as well as to consumers. Several years earlier, William Wrigley had mailed similar coupons to retailers as part of the vast promotional effort for introducing Spearmint to a national market. "Get this trial box for nothing, and if it goes, stock more," read the letter accompanying the coupon. "If it doesn't, forget it."

———————————————————————————————————

on 'Easy' Street." The *Grocers' Review* disagreed. "For a valuable (?) premium," it warned in 1905, "the retailer will overstock himself with goods of doubtful character and act as an agent to cut his own business throat." Quantity prices presented a similar temptation and a similar danger. Many manufacturers offered them, and others announced free deals and rebates in trade journals or by direct mail, available for a limited time to retailers who bought in large quantities.

Other retailer promotions came in the form of "dealer helps," a term defined by Harvard's Paul Cherington in 1913 as "any effort made by the national advertiser . . . to help the dealer convert into sales the consumer-interest created by the national advertising campaign." The small retailer's daily mail brought his share of the tons of dealer literature manufacturers sent out:

booklets, copies of advertising, letters, postcards, announce-
ments of sales. Regularly published house organs had large
circulations; in 1911, the *Dutch Boy Painter* went to 95,000 dealers and house painters. Many of these magazines confined their
contents to jokes and promotional pitches, but others offered
real help. *Modern Sanitation,* which the Standard Sanitary Manufacturing Company sent to 32,000 plumbers, offered technical
pieces by sanitary engineers and a series entitled "Bookkeeping
for the Plumber," 15,000 copies of which were later reprinted
and distributed.

As part of a campaign promoting "modern bathrooms" and
attempting to induce homeowners to tear out and replace zinc
bathtubs and iron sinks, Standard sponsored a dealers' contest
with $1,000 in prizes for showroom displays. Manufacturers
commonly sponsored such display contests and even more commonly offered display materials as dealer helps. After technological improvements cheapened plate glass in the mid-1890s, even
small stores had display space visible from the street. Following
the lead of large urban department stores, which had emphasized window display during the 1880s, manufacturers hired
designers to help retailers use that space. By 1907, window-
trimmers had a national association, local and regional clubs,
three trade schools in New York and Chicago, and a magazine—
the *Show Window,* founded in 1898 by L. Frank Baum, a former
traveling glassware salesman who eventually resigned after the
success of his *Wizard of Oz* to write sequels. Although most
full-time trimmers worked for department stores, ambitious retailers and major manufacturers shared their interest in display.

Financial arrangements varied among manufacturers and
retailers displaying their products. The Victor Talking Machine Company sold its window displays, issued monthly and
shipped to dealers around the world. Shredded Wheat's three-
dimensional cardboard replica of its factory, with Niagara Falls
and a field of grain in the background, was free, but it remained
nominally company property so that it could be reclaimed from
dealers not using it. The manufacturer of Karo syrup paid retail-

ers cash for display space in their windows. Ingersoll sold glass showcases for as little as a dollar, but gave away 40,000 free holders that each accommodated six watches. (An eight-inch Ingersoll "Jumbo watch," with dog chain attached, was originally produced for retail display, but became so popular that the company manufactured it for sale, and sold more than 50,000.) The Bissell Carpet Sweeper Company included easels, show cards, posters, and circulars imprinted with the retailer's name with orders for certain numbers of carpet sweepers.

Bissell also supplied customers with electrotypes, or "electros," printing plates that many manufacturers provided for dealers to use as illustrations in local newspaper advertising.

–––––––––––––––––––––––––––––––– ⅢⅭⅢ ––––––––––––––––––––––––––––––––

Golden Sun coffee display in Owen and Seiler's Detroit store, 1913.

Calumet card used as part of a rather less professional display at the J. E. Hasson and Company store in Aliceville, Alabama, 1915.

The manufacturer of Hoosier kitchen cabinets went further, and offered to handle and place all of its dealers' advertising; the company sent proof sheets with timed ads, and information on other furniture makers who would contribute electros. An Iowa clothing-store owner complained that much of the advertising material manufacturers sent him failed to appeal to farmers and "robbed him of his individuality." Its tone suggested that the dealer had been honored by being chosen to sell the product, whereas he wanted to tell customers that he had done the choosing of a firm that made products he knew they would like. "I will not use electros . . . which advertise a manufacturer's product too obviously," he added, explaining that he illustrated his ads with stock cuts ordered from a catalogue. "I can't afford to have people think I am cheap."

THE CHECKERBOARD MONTHLY.   7.

Ralston Purina Club Member's Contest.

$10.00 in Prizes—Read carefully.

We show you, below, a new advertising cut to be distributed FREE to our customers.

A picture sometimes tells more than words, but the best advertising is a combination of both; in which the picture illustrates and makes graphic the idea contained in the reading matter, and helps to attract attention, and the reading matter is pointed and convincing and appropriate to the illustration.

Write for this cut and then send us a copy of your local paper, containing this advertisement with your wording.

This cut is mortised to receive a few sentences advertising **Purina Health Flour.**

The rapid increase in the use of this Flour is almost phenomenal, and shows that its quality is superior. **Purina Health Flour** makes a delicious, light-brown loaf of close-grained bread, which has an appetizing, nut-like flavor, and is much more nutritious than white bread. For rolls, muffins, etc., it is absolutely unsurpassed. This is a product which every grocer can recommend as unique in its superiority.

Our Advertising Department is going to call on the members of the **Ralston Purina Club** to give us some good, snappy reading matter to go with this cut, and in order to get **every member** to send us an Ad., we are going to give **$5.00** for the advertisement considered best by Mr. Walker Evans, Jr. and Mr. J. G. Cole, advertising men of this city. For the second best, **$2.00** and the next three, **$1.00** each.

You have advertising ideas. Now try your hand at expressing them, and you may get **$5.00** for your trouble.

Any Grocer in the United States, handling **Ralston Purina** products, can have the cut free. The contest, however, is open to Ralston Purina Club Members only.

Every month we are sending out thousands of the little booklets, "Get Out or Get in Line," "Mary and John," "Why Some Men Fail," "Breezy, Grocer's Clerk," and will continue to send them until the supply is exhausted.

The price of these booklets is 10c each, but every Grocer in the United States who will send us his name and address, will receive any one of them free.

On the last page of this issue you will see our current Magazine advertisement. The adoption of the **"Ralston Purina Miller"** will enable us to put out the most startling and interesting advertisements in the Magazines. Every month the "Miller" will have some common-sense remarks on the pure food proposition and will tell the people all about the different Checkerboard products. Every month the advertisement will be different, and our Miller will soon become a National Character. **Watch Him.**

The membership in the Ralston Purina Club is steadily increasing. Many of the members expect to see each other face to face when they visit us in 1904 to see the World's Fair.

This page from the May 1903 issue of Ralston Purina's house organ, the *Checkerboard Monthly,* announces a contest for grocers, with cash prizes for the best copy to go with a typical manufacturer's electrotype.

Although most retailers did display some products on their counters and in their windows, they threw out more dealer helps than they used. The editor of a hardware trade journal maintained that the average small-town hardware dealer "is literally swamped with advertising matter." A retailer might read a house organ or ignore it; it might arrive on a slow day or a busy one. "Just as your bundle of advertising dope is being delivered by the express man," one advertising manager reminded *Printers' Ink* readers, the merchant "may be telephoning to the doctor about the baby's measles—and that baby is far more important to him than your *de luxe* edition of 'Why everybody should buy starch in labeled packages.' " Another article urged manufacturers to avoid spelling errors when they imprinted retailers' names on consumer advertising matter and to find out about store-name changes and merchants' slogans. Stock display material, this writer advised, was most often used in the "backward, unprogressive store" with "the disreputable appearance of a poorly conducted junk shop." A piece entitled "Advertising and the Unappreciative Retailer" claimed that storekeepers used posters to wrap up merchandise.

Sick babies and busy days exacerbated a major reason for ignoring dealer helps: merchants' animosity against advertised goods. As late as 1916, the J. Walter Thompson agency newsletter described hostility as the general attitude of retailers towards new-product introduction and advertised goods in general, explaining that retailers believed they paid for the advertising. Many regarded all promotional schemes as efforts to turn stores into product advertisements and retailers into operatives for manufacturers, what the *Grocers' Review* described in 1904 as "bare faced attempts to get between the grocer and his trade." "Trade (or rather customers)," the writer maintained, "is not looked on as a grocers' asset any more by the advertising manufacturer. The customer belongs to him by virtue of his advertising. The grocer is a sort of present necessary evil between the manufacturer and the people who consume his product." Manufacturers' salesmen took a "proprietary air" towards retailers

who resisted advertised goods, suggesting that their companies'
direct relationships with consumers would create requests
that the retailers would not be able to resist. "You will have to
sell it sooner or later," the salesmen commonly told the storekeepers.

At the same time, from the manufacturers' standpoint, the
sales force was intended to operate as a weapon against retail
hostility, establishing ongoing personal relationships between
storekeepers and company representatives. Firms that did their
own wholesaling needed agents in the field for the same reasons
that wholesalers had used drummers: sales forces for these manufacturers took care of distribution problems best handled personally, like loss and damage claims and credit questions. Even
firms that continued to patronize wholesalers for their transportation and warehousing functions used their own salesmen to
mobilize retailers in support of marketing efforts. Just as retailers feared, manufacturers' traveling salesmen tried to induce
storekeepers not merely to sell but to promote their goods: to
suggest them when customers asked for other brands, to allow
demonstrations that took up space, and to devote windows and
counters to artful arrangements of pyramided cans and packages. Like the wholesalers' drummers, they also reported to
their companies on market conditions, explaining to display
designers about packages that deteriorated in sunny windows,
or telling advertising managers that retailers who refused to
incorporate large electros in their newspaper advertising might
agree to use smaller ones.

In larger stores, salesmen were expected to establish relationships not only with proprietors but with clerks, who actually
responded to customer requests and handled the goods and
therefore did the substituting that worried manufacturers.
Storeowners resented salesmen taking up their employees' time,
and high turnover further complicated the work of courting
clerks. But manufacturers persisted; many clerks moved from
store to store rather than out of retail trade, and ambitious ones
might open their own stores later in life. Morton Salt suggested

that its salesmen give clerks free packages; Heinz had special pencil clips for them. Johnson and Johnson required salesmen to keep track of drug-store clerks and let the company know about new ones, so that each would receive the firm's sales manual.

Above all, manufacturers used personal contact to bring marketing campaigns to the point of sale. Advertising was presented to sales forces at conventions and by mail, and a big part of the salesman's job was to show the advertising to the merchant. Heinz sent salesman proofs of new ads, with instructions to post them in stores. The advertising manager for a Rochester, New York stove works maintained that in some campaigns consumer advertising was a bluff, intended more to make dealers stock up than to influence their customers. In a sample dialogue for salesmen, Morton Salt even admitted that advertising raised prices, suggesting that salesmen justify a price increase because it paid for the ads. "The raise is really for your benefit," a fictional salesman explained to a merchant, because without it "we would not be able to spend our money getting your customers to want MORTON'S SALT instead of Bag Salt."

Salesmen attended workshops to learn how to make displays and competed with each other for window and counter space, much as manufacturers and their salespeople now compete for supermarket shelf space. Coca-Cola's fifty-four salesmen dressed 30,000 drug-store windows in 1907. With a larger sales force—about five hundred men in 1911—Heinz could change displays often enough to coordinate them with magazine advertising. For each advertising campaign, every salesman decorated about twenty grocery-store windows and placed interior displays in about thirty stores, so that Thanksgiving advertising featuring mincemeat, for example, was supported by 25,000 store displays. By 1915, the company offered even more service—and took more control. Its salesmen, like those working for manufacturers in modern supermarkets, would take charge of regular stock on the shelves, picking out damaged or deteriorated merchandise, arranging cans and bottles, and urging merchants to reorder low stocks.

Every Saturday, each Heinz salesman set a table with china and linen in one of his better stores and spent the day offering samples of the company's "57 Varieties" and telling customers about the model kitchens at the Heinz plant in Pittsburgh. Such demonstrations—some amounting to in-store sampling, others exhibiting features of the product or its packaging—were sometimes conducted by special crews, but many companies' regular sales forces were urged and often required to do them. They put consumers in direct contact with manufacturers' representatives, who carried empty packages, leakproof dispensers, and test tubes with them as demonstrating equipment. The Heinz men compared the looks of different vinegars, and washed canned baked beans to show that sauce adhered to the Heinz product. The Morton sales manual urged its staff to split open empty salt bags to expose the stitching, and to put grains of salt under a magnifying glass. "The majority of package food products in this country, that have been successful in a large way," the American Sugar Refining Company told Domino salesmen in 1920, "have been persistently demonstrated in stores and in homes." The company required weekly demonstration as part of the campaign for Domino Golden Syrup and stressed the importance of dealer cooperation. "Interest the grocer and make him enthusiastic to the extent that he will advertise the event in the local newspapers, and in addition, send out circulars to the homes."

Salesmen learned how to interest retailers at training sessions organized by their employers to prepare them for profitable visits. Most companies followed management methods introduced by the National Cash Register Company, which organized the first sales conference in 1886 and inaugurated formal training eight years later. At the training school and at annual conventions, salesmen studied standardized presentations, role-playing the merchants' parts as well as their own in arguments

Heinz salesmen at the 1902 convention's closing banquet.

that took as long as two hours. By 1910, companies commonly
provided instructions and motivation to their sales forces at
conventions and training sessions that complemented special
salesmen's house organs, circular letters, and daily personal
correspondence. Manuals for sales managers routinely included
guidance for holding effective meetings.

Conventions were to be carefully planned, from the roll call
at the start to the rousing finish. More than three hundred salesmen attended the fourteenth Heinz convention in January 1902,
leaving behind "only enough men to carry on the business at its
lowest ebb," according to the company magazine *Pickles,* which
devoted its next issue to reporting on the convention. Heinz
hired special trains from both east and west, and quartered the
men for eight days at Pittsburgh's leading downtown hotels.

After a tour of the plant the first afternoon, the sales force listened to about twenty talks a day, for seven working days: "Our Seed and Vegetable Farms and Salting Houses," "Pickling Vinegar—The Most Effective Way of Selling to the Merchant," "Broader Salesmanship," and others. They ate lunch daily in the employees' dining room, where the women factory workers who usually ate there served as waitresses. Although the company provided professional vaudeville one evening, others were devoted to working sessions. On the final afternoon, "there was more enthusiasm than could be seen at most political conventions and almost continually there was cheering and singing." The closing banquet featured ice cream in the shape of pickles, leather-bound souvenir books, and speakers including Theodore C. Search, president of the National Association of Manufacturers, O. J. Gude of the nation's largest outdoor advertising firm, and H. J. Heinz.

Such methods cost a great deal of money, one manual on sales management acknowledged, but it cost more "to operate a lot of poorly trained men with little or no enthusiasm." Between conventions, the manuals recommended building enthusiasm with competition, another method initiated by National Cash Register. In 1900, that firm set standards for comparison among different territories and assigned each agency and each salesman a quota. Those who exceeded their quotas were eligible for prizes and lionized at sales conventions; such rewards were in part intended, as a generally admiring book about the company's sales policies put it, "to form habits and tastes that only more money could satisfy."

Expense accounts reinforced those habits. Most books on sales management advised reimbursement of actual expenses, and after the turn of the century most wholesalers and manufacturers adopted the practice. Salesmen with fixed accounts might avoid work that required extraordinary expenditures, such as visits to out-of-the-way towns, and they might economize by staying in cheap hotels, tarnishing their employer's company image for extra cash. Employers therefore chose reimbursement

despite its major drawbacks: it created clerical labor for salesmen making and managers checking reports, it constituted a
potential source of friction, and it cost a lot of money.

As manufacturers organized large sales forces, they hired
managers and developed methods for keeping track of them.
Armour and Company employed four thousand salesmen
worldwide in 1913, "the most wonderful merchandising machine in the world," according to the company's advertising
manager. Although this was almost certainly the largest, sales
forces in the hundreds were not uncommon. Manuals, some
explicitly adopting the jargon of scientific management, suggested map-and-tack systems for following salesmen's movements and a variety of daily, weekly, and monthly reports.

In most companies, sales management developed separately
from advertising, and the relations between the managers of
sales and advertising departments were often troublesome matters of company politics. Two managers who handled both advertising and sales described the typical disharmony in *Printers'
Ink* in 1910. "Usually the ruction is started by a sales manager
who has little or no knowledge of advertising," one wrote.
"Ninety-nine per cent of our advertising men have never carried
a sample case," complained the other. Their solution represented a growing consensus, explained by a writer in *Advertising
and Selling* three years later: "The necessity of securing harmoni-
ous unity of effort between advertising and personal soliciting
makes it extremely desirable to have both branches of effort
directed by one man. No two people are ever in complete har-
mony."

Even this writer, however, took a partisan stand. He recommended that every advertising manager spend some time on
the road ("Such a trip will knock a lot of foolishness out of
him . . .") and that "no advertisement ever should be published
without the approval of the sales department." Truman A. De-
Weese, the director of publicity for Shredded Wheat, advised an
opposite approach. "The relation between the advertising manager and the sales organization should be one of complete,

confidential co-operation," he wrote, going on to grant greater power to the advertising department. "The advertising manager should evolve, originate and formulate the selling arguments that are to be used by the sales organization. . . . If the advertising department is what it should be the salesmen will be merely distributors. It is their job to keep in touch with the trade. They don't need to sell goods. The goods are already sold."

DeWeese was reiterating a position that had threatened salesmen for some time. Early champions of national advertising had argued that it would eliminate commercial travelers, then usually in the employ of wholesalers, or that it would reduce their work to order-taking. "It is a good deal easier to sell goods by advertising than it is by traveling men," Earnest Elmo Calkins wrote in 1905. "Inquiry at the counter and vacant shelves are a stronger demand for goods than any amount of force exerted by a drummer."

Within five years, however, most writers gave at least rhetorical expression to the idea that, in the words of a traveling salesmen's magazine, "The Old Idea That Advertising and Salesmen Were Opposed to Each Other Has Passed Away." Arch W. Shaw described sales and advertising as "different modes of accomplishing the same end," enabling producers to take over the middleman's selling function. Hugh Chalmers, an auto executive and a former National Cash Register vice-president, brought the idea to oratorical extremes in an address to the 1909 convention of the Associated Advertising Clubs of America. "The relation of salesmanship to advertising," he declared, "is the closest relationship—closer than friends; closer than a team under a single yoke; closer than brothers; closer than man and wife, as there can never be separation and divorce; all salesmanship is advertising, and all advertising is in part salesmanship; they are the twin screw engines that drive the ship of business; they are like a chemical compound, each contains the other and is itself the thing contained."

Individual company decisions about the strategic balance of sales and advertising varied from industry to industry. Then as now, the makers of appliances and other expensive, infrequently purchased items concentrated on sales, while packaged-goods producers, marketing products with a low purchasing risk, led the forces for advertising. Yet even the manufacturers of cereal and soap depended on the relationships that salesmen created with retailers for introducing new products and extending distribution to new geographical areas or new retail outlets. As companies aimed to introduce new products constantly, salesmen became constantly necessary. As manufacturers extended their numbers of lines and created market segmentation within a line, they relied on salesmen to explain the proliferating brands to the trade.

Observers and practitioners argued about the relative importance of sales and advertising—and they continue to do so, calling them "push" and "pull" strategies. But in fact the developing system required coordination of the two no longer really separate functions. Managers from sales and advertising departments cooperated in launching marketing campaigns and presenting them to sales forces. By 1910, advertising managers and advertising agents were always among the principal speakers at conventions, and the most enterprising agencies worked closely with sales managers. In 1916, six New York staffers from J. Walter Thompson (including Stanley Resor and Helen Lansdowne, who both spoke) traveled to Chicago for the Libby sales convention, attended also by the agency's Chicago office. Before 1920, N. W. Ayer and Son, the Philadelphia agency that handled accounts for National Biscuit, Domino, and other major corporations, issued *Advertising and the Salesman,* a booklet for their clients' sales forces that explained why "advertising increases the importance of your job."

Massive, successful campaigns required well-coordinated advertising and sales, and generally employed promotional techniques that depended on salesmen's work. Salesmen who convinced dealers to display a manufacturer's logo in local newspapers provided their employers with a way to expand local advertising and concentrate on trouble spots in a national campaign. Salesmen reporting from the field could persuade national advertisers to increase their own expenditures on media that could be controlled nationally but would show up locally: streetcars, billboards, and newspapers. And salesmen's displays and demonstrations brought national campaigns to the stores themselves, where their work checking on stock and courting clerks ensured that a customer who asked for an advertised product would walk out of the store with it.

Well-coordinated advertising and sales were indeed, in the *Grocers' Review*'s words, "bare faced attempts" to intervene in the relationships between retailers and their customers and in their decisions about merchandise. Many articles in the trade press reiterated this view and the merchants' resentment of manufacturers' attempts to turn them into "automatons," dispensing products that paid them little or no profit. Yet even potent new marketing techniques did not protect manufacturers from continuing power shifts in the distribution system. They could dominate the old system based on regional wholesaling and small retailing but not the new mass distributors—the department stores, mail-order houses, and chains that were better equipped to handle the enormous output of mass-production processes.

CHAPTER 7

THE
NEW
RETAILING

"SELLING AND DISTRIBUTION," THOMAS EDISON TOLD AN INTER-
viewer in 1910, "are simply machines for getting products to
consumers. And like all machines, they can be improved with
great resulting economy. But it is the plain truth that these
machines for distribution have made the least progress of all
machines. They are the same in many instances that they were
forty and fifty years ago. . . . The average selling machine has
become unwieldy and ancient." An ideal one, the inventor proclaimed, should get goods "quickly, economically and satisfac-
torily to those who want them." To that end, Edison was
perfecting the Samaritan Market, a device based on the slot
machine that would dispense tea, sugar, and even coal in standard quantities.

Edison's criticism highlighted the thousands of "unwieldy"
small stores and the persistence of old-fashioned distribution
practices based more on community relationships than on efficient systems for moving merchandise from factories to kitchens
and parlors. Yet distribution had in fact changed profoundly by
1910. Even the smallest stores and the wholesale merchants who
serviced them sold Ivory and Sapolio, responding to manufacturers' new marketing methods, which had created direct rela-

tionships between manufacturers and consumers and brought customers into stores with specific demands. Furthermore, small retailers, wholesalers, and manufacturers had all witnessed the development of three genuinely new merchandising forms: the department store, the mail-order house, and the chain store. Like wholesalers, these were large, powerful companies that often combined manufacturing and distribution, and represented a countervailing force to manufacturer power. Like other retailers, the mass marketers served basic functions in people's daily life and integrated individual consumers into the mass market. But they created new merchandising techniques capable of organizing that market, techniques that could genuinely be described as mass distribution and that posed a threat to traditional methods.

Department stores, mail-order firms, and chains did rest on Edison's principles of speed and economy, and their systems proved capable of organizing the flow of large quantities of merchandise. The three bore a "strong family resemblance," two *Printers' Ink* writers asserted in a fourteen-part series on chains published in 1914, "embodying exactly the same principles of *concentration* in buying and management, and exercising the same power of *manipulation* in selling." They all purchased directly from manufacturers, bypassing wholesalers and either labeling merchandise with private brands or buying in sufficient quantity to demand concessions from their suppliers.

These mass merchandisers shared three characteristics that became fundamental principles of modern selling. First, their customers bought at prices set by the merchant before the sale; nobody bargained with Marshall Field's or Sears. The one-price system enabled department stores and chains to hire large sales forces composed of low-paid, inexperienced workers. "The old dicker and bargain policy still found in many one-line stores of the old-fashioned type," the University of Minnesota's Paul Nystrom explained in 1915, "required salespeople with considerable skill in handling customers." Secondly, the prices were set at levels calculated to make profits by "turning stock," moving the goods through the system. Merchandise that sat on shelves took up space that could be used over and over again by fast-selling stock, and represented capital that could reap continual profits if it were invested in things that sold. Textbooks often gave the pushcart peddler as a simple example: if he bought four dollars' worth of goods and sold them for five dollars by the end of the day, he made a dollar, or 25 percent on his original investment. If the peddler sold the goods by noon, reinvested his four dollars, and thereby sold out twice by the end of the day,

----

The clearance sale, advertised in this photograph of Seattle's Bon Marché about 1895, provided department stores with a way to get rid of slow-moving merchandise and achieve stock turn, yielding space and capital for merchants to invest in new stock. Price cards in the windows declared the store's allegiance to the one-price system; departmen-alization facilitated accounting.

his four-dollar investment earned two dollars, or 50 percent. More complicated examples pointed out that fixed costs like rent made profits even higher on stock turned often.

The third characteristic of mass retailing was departmentalization. By putting different kinds of stock in different departments, the mass merchandisers devised accounting systems that enabled them to audit the contribution that particular departments and even particular pieces of merchandise made to the profits of the enterprise. Unprofitable goods and departments could be dropped, and employees could be evaluated according to numerical measures of their performance as well as on their personalities.

The New York dry-goods merchant A. T. Stewart built the largest early establishment to succeed using these principles, although he may not have been the first to try them and his store offered too limited a range of merchandise to be called the first department store. Beginning in the 1820s with a small shop, he moved to his four-story "Marble Palace" in 1846 and to an even larger building in 1862; when completed six years later, it covered a city block and rose eight stories. Stewart ran leading wholesale and importing businesses by 1840, and within another decade manufactured clothing for his own store and others. He contracted to make Northern uniforms during the Civil War, and by 1869 employed nine hundred seamstresses and owned textile mills in the United States, England, and Ireland.

During the 1860s, 15,000 to 60,000 customers a day passed through Stewart's store, served in 1869 by 1,000 retail clerks. "Not one of them has his discretion," Stewart told industrialist Peter Cooper. "They are simply machines working in a system that determines all their actions." The clerks did not make change, but handed customers' money to runners who took it to central cashiers. Nor did they negotiate about price: Stewart operated on the one-price system by 1846 and possibly earlier. He set prices at levels that would move the goods, and probably introduced the clearance sale to move old stock as early as 1837. "Although I realize only a small profit on each sale," he told another New York businessman, "the enlarged area of business makes possible a large accumulation of capital and assures the future." By 1869 and probably before, Stewart kept separate accounts for his various departments, making it possible to determine which goods made money.

Stewart's store was an anomaly at first, but during the 1860s and 1870s, other urban merchants both in the United States and in Europe adopted the new policies. Rowland H. Macy announced the one-price policy in 1858 and two years later began to expand beyond dry goods. Macy's first opened a new "French and German fancy goods" department to sell chinaware, toys, pocketbooks, and other merchandise. By 1877, twenty-four departments sold an even greater variety, including house furnishings, books, and flowers. At Macy's and elsewhere, departments contributed to the rationalization and specialization of space, finances, and labor. Separate departments had their own buyers, stockkeepers, and sales staffs. They kept separate accounts and were expected to show a profit, to pay for their own merchandise and labor, and to contribute their shares of the heating bill, the office costs, and other general store expenditures.

Macy's remained small by later standards through the 1870s, and even large stores like Stewart's and Marshall Field's were dwarfed by their wholesale operations. Many opened mail-order divisions, boasting that customers could come to their stores and inspect the goods; Macy's started mail order in 1874, and its catalogue, 127 pages in 1881, had grown to 311 pages a decade later. During the 1880s and 1890s, most department stores expanded their retail operations, centralizing accounting, employment, advertising, credit, and delivery. Many continued their wholesaling and mail-order operations, but erected new, larger retail stores that became central features of downtown life.

Like world's fairs, writes historian Neil Harris, big-city department stores "were mass encounters with the art and objects of the modern world, dramatic, persuasive, self-consciously designed to produce a maximum effect." They began to emphasize

FOR INFORMATION ABOUT ORDERING GOODS BY MAIL, SEE 3D PAGE OF COVER.
FOR INDEX, SEE LAST PAGE.
IF ANY OF YOUR FRIENDS DESIRE A COPY OF THIS CATALOGUE IT WILL BE SENT FREE
WHEN REQUESTED.

Downtown shoppers congregate in front of Jordan Marsh, one of Boston's leading department stores, on the first page of the company's 1885 spring and summer mail-order catalogue.

display for its own sake, using windows, mirrors, lighting, and colored fabrics to create a festive atmosphere. Marshall Field's installed electric lights in 1882, the same year the Edison Company opened the nation's first commercial power station. Within five years, department stores in smaller cities, like Albany's Whitney and Company, were lit with electricity.

Also during the 1880s and 1890s, department stores created an array of new services. Macy's already provided a soda fountain and a lunchroom, but now restaurants became common; Marshall Field's 1890 tearoom, "designed to suit a lady's taste," provided an atmosphere of "quiet elegance." Before the turn of

Crowds gather to look at Macy's Christmas windows, New York. From *Frank Leslie's Illustrated Newspaper*, December 20, 1884.

the century, stores provided telegraph offices, public phones, lost-and-found departments, post offices, ladies' parlors, free checking, child care, and first-aid stations. Nearly all offered charge accounts. Some provided live background music, sponsored lectures and plays, and incorporated branch libraries. "Under the guise of 'service,' " Paul Nystrom wrote in 1915, "the modern department store has come to be a sort of club house and amusement place for women." He added "silence rooms for nerve-tired shoppers" and beauty parlors to the list of common services and pointed to unusual stores that offered opera performances, employment services for domestic help, and banking and brokerage services. For those who chose to stay home, department stores provided telephone service; in 1907, Wanamaker's in Philadelphia took orders twenty-four hours a day.

By the end of the century, the big stores rivaled large factories in size. Marshall Field's and Macy's both completed new stores in 1902, each with over a million square feet of floor space. Macy's employed three thousand workers in 1898; Jordan Marsh was the fourth largest employer in New England in 1900. Marshall Field's had ten thousand employees, and a quarter of a million customers a day in its busiest season. Most of the new employees were women for whom the stores were neither clubhouses nor amusement places; their employment contributed to the stores' female milieu.

"The modern department store is a wonderful business mechanism," Nystrom wrote in 1915. "At its best it represents very high efficiency as a trade-getting and profit-making institution." Few of the nearly four thousand stores that called themselves department stores rivaled Field's or Wanamaker's, but they all attempted to profit from high turnover, departmentalization, and the one-price system. Even in small cities, they employed advertising specialists and used large amounts of newspaper advertising space, offering "specific, concrete presentation of information" that emphasized price. When they bought branded goods from manufacturers, the larger stores demanded advertising allowances, initiating the "co-operative advertising" allotments that by the 1920s manufacturers offered even to small stores using their trademarks in local advertising. For the most part, however, and in nearly every line, department stores (like wholesalers) sold privately labeled goods in open competition with manufacturer's brands. One large store, which marketed private-label hosiery that imitated the well-known Onyx line, advertised its own brands at bargain prices on the annual sale days that Onyx advertised in national publications.

Even the largest department stores with the most sophisticated selling systems remained regional entities, primarily catering to urban customers. Before the 1920s, when automobiles brought country people to town for shopping, most rural dwell-

One of the thousands of smaller stores that operated on the principles of departmentalization and high turnover: the Kinley Department Store, Upper Sandusky, Ohio.

Privately labeled pineapple from Brooklyn's Abraham and Straus.

ers encountered mass merchandising in the form of mail-order catalogues. "Here was an organization whose great arms embraced the world," wrote Edna Ferber in a 1917 novel about Fanny Brandeis, a woman executive at a Chicago mail-order firm that might have been Sears, Roebuck or Montgomery Ward. "Haynes-Cooper, giant among mail-order houses, was said to eat a small-town merchant every morning for breakfast. 'There's a Haynes-Cooper catalogue in every farmer's kitchen,' " Fanny's mother, herself a small-town merchant, had explained. " 'The Bible's in the parlor, but they keep the H.C. book in the room where they live.' "

Montgomery Ward began first. "Our business," the catalogue explained, "was organized in 1872 to meet the wants of the Patrons of Husbandry, from whom we then received our main support." This was the leading national farmers' organization, better known as the Grange, organized in part on principles of cooperative purchasing and eliminating middlemen. Membership brought some privileges at Ward's, "The Original Grange Supply House," which sold Grange paraphernalia among its wide variety of goods. All customers received merchandise COD and paid only if they were satisfied after examining what they had bought; Grangers had a ten-day grace period. By 1884, a

240-page catalogue listed nearly 10,000 items; rapid expansion including a new warehouse brought the number to 24,000 by the early nineties.

Montgomery Ward, then, was already successful in 1886, when Richard Sears began selling watches; Sears hired watchmaker Alvah C. Roebuck the next year. After several other ventures, the two established an office in Chicago, adopted the name Sears, Roebuck, and Company, and added jewelry, silverware, firearms, sewing machines, clothing, and other merchandise to their catalogue in 1893. Two years later, plagued by illness and stress, Roebuck sold out to Sears for $25,000. Two Chicago businessmen joined the firm, bringing new capital that financed continued growth. "Nearly everything in merchandise can be found in this book," the company claimed in its 786-page 1897 catalogue. Twenty-four special catalogues carried complete descriptions of even more goods, including blacksmith tools, furniture, groceries, books, and sewing machines, a much wider range of merchandise than the department stores sold. By 1900, Sears had surpassed Ward. Five years later, it embarked on a successful marketing campaign in Iowa, offering customers premiums for persuading others to order from the catalogue. Richard Sears became personally determined to "Iowa-ize" America, and the company extended the plan across the country, state by state.

In 1906, Sears owned or held a major interest in sixteen manufacturing plants. That year it moved to a new plant on a forty-acre tract in Chicago, with buildings connected by pipes, wires, railroad tracks, and underground tunnels. The Merchandise Building housed a clothing factory and could receive a sixty-car train; freight handlers worked night and day, in any weather. Two thousand people opened and processed more than nine hundred sacks of mail a day; the express companies, railroads, telegraph companies, and post office all managed branches on the grounds. Sears operated its own printing plant and the second largest power plant in Chicago after the Edison Company.

At the new plant the company instituted a scheduling system that enabled it to ship merchandise within forty-eight hours of receiving an order, even on mixed orders for merchandise from different departments. Machines opened 27,000 letters per hour; gravity chutes and conveyer belts carried the goods. At least as early as 1911, Sears applied systematic methods also to merchandising, maintaining a card index that showed what every customer had ever bought, indicated address changes, and often contained other information about the family. The firm used the index to classify customers—in essence, to segment its already existing market—in order to decide who would get which catalogues. By 1915, the largest mail-order firms kept files on 4 to 6 million customers.

Before the turn of the century, companies wishing to do mail-

This stereograph is one of a series showing operations at the T. Eaton Company, a depart ment store in Winnipeg, Canada, around 1910. About forty-five people processed ma and kept the card files. "Thousands of letters are handled daily," the stereo card explain on its reverse, "and no mistake is ever made that cannot be detected and rectified."

No. 24. SECTION OF MAIL OPENING.

order business could buy addressed envelopes or mailing lists
with millions of names, classified by occupation and other considerations. Although Sears and Ward were indisputably the
largest retail mail-order merchants, such mailing lists and other
promotional techniques permitted other companies to compete,
some with considerable success. The Spiegel, May, Stern company, still selling goods by mail a century later, was founded in
1882 and for many years specialized in mail-order installment
selling. The Larkin Company, a Buffalo soap manufacturer since
1875, began selling by mail a decade later, advertising "Thirty
Days Trial and Pay If Pleased," and offering lamps, desks, and
other premiums to customers who sent large orders. Eventually
the company expanded, not by increasing its soap business, but
by offering other grocery products, selling only for cash in lots
of ten dollars or more, and encouraging customers to form
buying cooperatives. For the most part, Larkin manufactured
and bought goods to label with its own brand. "This is probably
the biggest move ever made toward selling groceries direct from
factory to consumer for cash," commented the *Grocers' Magazine,*
although Larkin did sell some nationally advertised products. By
1914, the company had established branches in Philadelphia,
Chicago, and Peoria as well as the original Buffalo branch, and
had lowered the minimum to five dollars.

Mail-order houses met considerable opposition from local
business interests. During the 1880s and 1890s, some urban
retailers had protested the rise of department stores, demanding special taxes or laws that would restrict the lines of merchandise a store could handle. These bills failed, but they set
precedents for later, more powerful protests against mass merchandisers that called on small-town loyalties. By the turn of the
century, local newspapers regularly attacked the mail-order
houses as foreign interests that would destroy local business.
Sears and Montgomery Ward responded directly, in their catalogue copy. The 1899 Sears spring catalogue stated on its cover:
"This book tells you just what your storekeeper at home pays for
everything he buys—and will prevent him from overcharging

you on anything you buy from him." Ward's 1902 catalogue reprinted an agricultural paper's comments that "the farmers of today are tyrannized over by the country merchants to a far worse extent than they realize."

During 1906 and 1907, small-town businessmen organized "trade-at-home" clubs; Midwestern commercial associations banded together in the Home Trade League of America. "There is such a thing as 'tainted' dry goods, 'tainted' groceries and 'tainted' furniture," wrote William Allen White, editor of the Emporia, Kansas *Gazette* and a nationally renowned spokesman for small-town life. "All of such that are not bought at home, of men who befriended you, of men to whom you owe a living, are 'tainted' because they come unfairly." The Sears catalogue in those years promised protection from charges of betraying local merchants. Goods arrived from Chicago in plain wrappers with no return address, because "many people object to having the name of the shipper spread across every box or package, so that when it is unloaded at the station or express office everyone can see what they are getting and where they buy it. . . . We have learned that thousands of our customers need the protection that the omitting of our name affords. This applies especially to townspeople."

Three of "McGuire's Anti-Mail-Order Cartoons," a series of magic-lantern slides copyrighted in 1914 for use in trade-at-home presentations.

The issue heated up in 1910, when election victories by Democrats and insurgent Progressive Republicans put into Congress a majority favorable to legislation that would establish a parcel post and thereby authorize the post office to handle packages weighing more than four pounds. At committee hearings, both sides used arguments that had been developing for years. Parcel-post supporters described the difficulties of modernizing rural life for farmers who had to travel to the nearest railroad freight station to pick up packages. Opponents (led by the four large private express companies) described the legislation as money in the pockets of Sears and Ward, and warned that government package delivery "is likely to change fundamentally our conception of government." Trade journals for retailers, traveling salesmen, and manufacturers called the measure "a severe blow to retail merchants." Active agitation both for and against parcel post lasted until the legislation passed in August 1912.

Local merchants' organizations fought the catalogue stores with publicity. When Larkin opened a sample store in Louisville, Kentucky, so that mail-order customers could examine the goods, members of the Retail Grocers' Association organized opposition. They distributed 75,000 cards warning customers

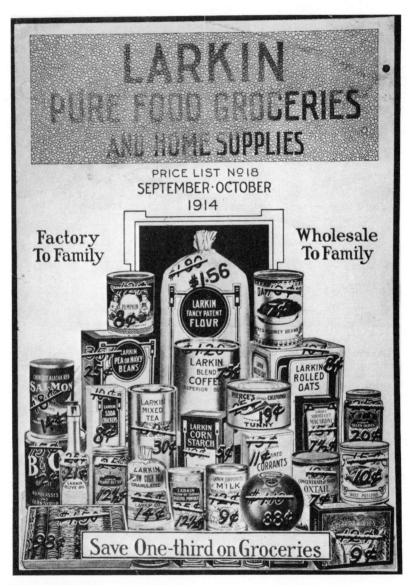

The Larkin Company of Buffalo, New York, expanded its mail-order soap business into a large retail mail-order grocery firm. It restricted business to customers who purchased substantial amounts, encouraging them to form cooperative buying clubs with friends and neighbors.

that "you and your friends pay for the FREE prizes, and you get equal and better values for less money in Louisville." In February 1912, members of the Cedar Falls, Iowa Commercial Club paraded through town, marching to band music and displaying banners proclaiming "Cedar Falls makes good" and "We thought we were buying cheaper, but we know better now." The parade ended with a mail-order catalogue bonfire in the town square. A few months later, the merchants of Peabody, Kansas, advertised that they would match any mail-order prices, and urged customers to bring their catalogues and order blanks to the stores.

Ada, Minnesota merchants "all had vastly exaggerated notions" of the volume of mail-order trade, according to a University of Minnesota study made six months after parcel post began operating. About 65 percent of farm families and 41 percent of village people had ordered something by mail, but they did not order much: less than 3 percent of the region's total trade went to mail-order businesses. Still, some merchants "felt very bitterly that farmers should send away at all, and were apparently sincere in their declarations that they had no moral right to do so." As for parcel post, the study declared, more merchants than farmers had used it so far. A few years later, the same researcher found that only a handful of New Haven, Connecticut families bought groceries from Sears and Montgomery Ward.

"From the perspective of a present-day vantage point," the leading historians of Sears wrote in 1950, "one can feel that the inadequate system of retail distribution would sooner or later have cracked under its own dead weight even without the mail-order companies." Retail trade was bound to change in a culture and an economy based on "better roads, motion pictures, improved communications, the automobile—in short, the whole march of technological progress." The protests, they assert, came from merchants who "saw their position deteriorating," and they suggest that these men "opposed change." Similarly, Daniel Boorstin describes the movement against parcel post as

Meet Your New Grocery Man

MR. SYDNEY MURCH
Manager of the World's Largest Grocery

HERE is the man who is going to make it his personal business to cut your grocery bills in two. You will find that he will take a bigger interest in you—in seeing that you get fair, square treatment—heaping values and heaping measures, than any other grocer you ever had. When you make out a grocery order, know that this man is as much interested as you are in having the goods just right. Know that he will, through his assistants, see that the right goods are shipped, that they are packed carefully and that they are shipped promptly.

Know also that he personally guarantees the absolute truth, the positive correctness of every statement made in this Grocery List, and better yet, know that the big house of Montgomery Ward & Co., with its 39 year old reputation for square dealing, stands back of Mr. Murch.

And **finally (and most important), know** that if, for any reason, you are not entirely satisfied with anything you buy, here is the man who is going to see that the matter is adjusted to your liking. We will take back the goods and either exchange them for others or we will promptly and cheerfully refund every penny of your money as you prefer.

You deal with some grocers simply because you like them personally. You would undoubtedly deal with Mr. Murch for the same reason. No man would go further out of his way to please you. But Mr. Murch makes a far stronger bid for your trade than personal friendship. He offers to save you from 20 to 50 per cent on every bill of groceries you buy. That makes it well worth your while to know Mr. Murch and to deal with him.

Mr. Murch stands at the head of a grocery store that is as large as a thousand corner grocery stores all rolled into one. Where the corner grocer buys and sells by the pound and the can Mr. Murch deals in tons and carloads. Now Mr. Murch does not make his strongest plea to your personal sympathies. He will never seek to coin your friendship into trade. He makes his plea direct to your pocket book—your bank account. All he asks is one trial—one small order. Not that he needs that order, but he knows that once you sample his goods, once you make a careful comparison, once you figure out how much you save each day—each week—each month by trading with him, he will have you for a permanent customer.

That's what Mr. Murch wants. He wants you as a permanent customer. He wants to add you to the three million odd regular customers he now has. But he wants to do it, insists on doing it, on a "make good" basis. He asks for a trial, for a chance to prove that on your first order he will save you a worth while amount.

Try him!

If you are not satisfied, you lose nothing—not a penny, for you have simply to bundle up the order and ship it back to us, charges collect.

Turn now to the big array of bargains this book offers. Take a blank sheet of paper and make out an order. Give your new grocer this one chance to prove that he can save you from 20 to 50 per cent of your grocery money.

TO YOU | WHO ARE STRUGGLING TO MAKE BOTH ENDS MEET

Give This New Plan a Trial You have tried a good many plans and schemes for meeting the constantly increasing cost of food supplies, and none of these plans has met with any real success. But here is a plan you have not tried; one that is as certain to work as tomorrow's sun is to rise.

You have been cutting the cost of living in the wrong place. You have been cutting in quality—buying cheaper goods than you once used on your table. Either that, or you have been economizing in the amount you have bought. You have cut out the desserts. You have allowed smaller portions to each person.

These are the **wrong ways** to economize. These are the **wrong places to cut the cost of living.**

Buy just as much as you formerly did—furnish your table just as liberally. See that every **article is** of top notch quality. **But** (and here's the vital point) buy where prices are from 1/3 to 1/2 lower than those you now pay.

You are going to look out for your own interests, the interests of your family, before you look out for those of anyone else. That is only natural. It's simply the world old law of self preservation.

Now, you do not love any grocer so well that you will rob your own purse, your family's table, to trade with him. If you find out that you can save at least 20% to 50% of your month's grocery money by trading somewhere else you are going to change grocers. And no broad minded, unselfish person can blame you.

Montgomery Ward & Co.'s customers are troubled little by the increased cost of living. This is practically an empty, meaningless phrase so far as they are concerned. You will readily understand why after you have carefully looked through this Grocery List, carefully compared the prices with those you have been paying elsewhere.

GIVE OUR NEW PLAN A TRIAL. You are protected from any loss or disappointment by our liberal, iron clad guarantee—"Your money back if you are not satisfied."

Make out your order now. You have been keeping house long enough to know about how much of each article you will use during the month.

When you have the order made out total it up. Then compare the amount you pay us with the sum you paid for your table supplies last month.

This Man Saved $9.33 on a $17.60 Purchase

MONTGOMERY WARD & CO., Chicago.

Gentlemen: I wish to say a few words in favor of your goods, which we received in good time. We think we certainly got good value for the money. We took the groceries in the $17.60 order and at the prices we would pay for equal value and quality here, we figured that we saved $9.33 on the price of the order. The Coffee is far better than we pay 35c a lb. for, and we do not think that the tea can be equaled for 49c. We have tried several items, and feel satisfied that we could not buy equal value for less than one-third more. Yours truly,

Sherman Seal,
Box 172   LaSalle, N. Y.

Montgomery Ward & Co., ^{CHICAGO AND KANSAS CITY} Chicago Ave. Bridge, Chicago

Montgomery Ward grocery catalogue, 1911. The catalogue was seventy-two pages long and listed some dry goods as well as groceries.

"rearguard actions": "Its spokesmen spoke for the dying past of the general store, the village post office, the one-room schoolhouse and the friendly corner drugstore."

In fact, small-town merchants and the business organizations they joined usually led their communities' forces for local economic development. In the many boards of trade, chambers of commerce, and commercial clubs that formed in towns and cities of all sizes, merchants established social and business contacts with other local businessmen and financial interests. These associations promoted progress through economic growth: road-building, sewer systems, train depots, post offices, tourism, settlement, and irrigation projects. They sponsored Christmas shopping campaigns that built business despite inclement weather; they promoted regional prosperity by bringing extension agents to advise farmers on the latest agricultural methods; they solicited industrial growth and factory-building. They crusaded not only against mail-order houses but against peddlers and other less-established business people, fostering the growth of Main Street, where they had their businesses. Each of these campaigns represents their attempts both to defend their immediate financial interests and to expand their horizons. Though they may have refused to acknowledge or failed to see it, the good roads they promoted and the mass-merchandising techniques they attacked were of a piece, two aspects of a transformation that reverberated throughout the culture.

Nearly two decades later, small businessmen joined a campaign in opposition to chain stores that echoed the anti-mail-order protests, with local merchants again urging patrons to trade at home, battle big business, and save the American way of life. This time, both sides used up-to-date techniques, reaching the public over the radio and by means of well-organized public relations campaigns. Opposition to the chains rallied around William K. "Old Man" Henderson, Jr., the owner of a Shreveport, Louisiana radio station with a clear channel and sufficient wattage to broadcast his opinions across the South and Midwest. Henderson organized a national group of retailers, the

Merchants' Minute Men. By 1930, Minute Men and their fellow merchants had organized local "trade-at-home" campaigns in more than four hundred towns, and the question whether chains served or harmed the public interest had become the national college and high school debate topic. The National Chain Store Association responded with a public relations campaign, distributing pamphlets and issuing a monthly bulletin to more than 400,000 editors, marketing teachers, state officials and legislators, and libraries. Individual chains and chain organizations sponsored many such campaigns over the next decade, culminating in the three-year, half-million-dollar, "elaborately casual publicity program," in the words of one historian, that the Carl Byoir firm created for the A & P.

This controversy was a response to a marketing phenomenon as significant as the mail-order houses, although only the most careful observers of retail trade understood the importance of chains before the 1920s because most were still small and confined to regional trade. By the end of that decade, more than seven thousand national, regional, and local chain-store organizations did more than one-fifth of America's total retail business. The largest and best established, the Great Atlantic and Pacific Tea Company, had begun in the 1860s as a tea-and-coffee firm, offering premiums and adding new retail stores almost from the start, and conducting a large mail-order business that was both advertised and attacked in national periodicals. In the 1880s and 1890s, the A & P gradually expanded into other grocery lines, beginning with baking powder and flavoring extracts. By the turn of the century, the company operated nearly two hundred stores in twenty-eight states and the District of Columbia. Other successful chains were still much smaller. Cincinnati's Great Western Tea Company, later the Kroger Grocery and Baking Company, ran thirty-six stores in 1902. Frank W. Woolworth opened his first successful five-cent store in Lancaster, Pennsylvania, in 1879; he had seven stores in operation by 1886, twenty-five by 1895, and fifty-nine in 1900. That year McCrory had twenty stores and Kress had eleven, but S. S.

An 1883 card advertising A & P baking powder. The back lists addresses of about 150 company stores.

Kresge, which would become the second largest variety chain, was still a single store.

By 1912, chains were under attack as part of the movement to protect the public against big business. Critics who charged that Wall Street interests dominated chain activity had plenty of evidence about the larger firms, especially Woolworth's, whose directors included Henry Goldman, of Goldman, Sachs and Company; A. Barton Hepburn, chairman of the board of Chase National Bank; and Philip Lehman, of Lehman Brothers. These three men also served together on the boards of Sears and two other companies. "When a man with a business investment of three thousand dollars is told to compete with a man having a business investment of three million dollars—he is told to do the impossible," Frank H. Freericks, a former pharmacist and an attorney for the National Association of Retail Druggists, told a Senate committee. "Unrestricted competition in its broadest sense . . . is nothing short of a cruel joke." At least two grocers' magazines printed Freericks's testimony. "Perhaps we do not feel the pressure so keenly now as the druggist does," wrote the *Grocers' Review*, "but unless we stand together and take concerted action now, there will be no opportunity to do so later."

The next year, the A & P instituted new kinds of stores that would kindle rapid expansion. Until then, most chain groceries employed as many as six clerks and offered typical services: credit, delivery, and telephone ordering. In addition, many chains operated systems of peddler wagons, and later automobiles; from five to twenty salesmen worked out of each store, soliciting sales on commission. The A & P had thousands of peddler routes, Grand Union more than 3,500. One writer maintained that "the strength of the big chains was in the country and small-town districts covered by the traveling system."

In contrast, one manager and one assistant operated the new "Economy Stores," which closed when they went to lunch. The stores eliminated premiums, trading stamps, and the traditional grocery services, operating exclusively on a cash-and-carry basis. These economies were passed on to shoppers, who paid lower prices at the new, uniformly designed red-fronted stores than at the older A & P stores. Under the new policies, the company opened hundreds and even thousands of stores every year until it reached a peak in 1930 of 15,700 outlets, over twice the number that McDonald's had in the United States in 1988. Other chains followed suit, building their businesses with new stores that abolished credit and delivery.

In 1914, the editors of *Printers' Ink* considered the growing chains important enough to publish an unusual fourteen-part series that provides a snapshot of the phenomenon. The authors counted more than two thousand chains with three or more stores each. The Riker-Hegeman Corporation of New York, a drug chain with 105 stores, was growing at the rate of more than three per month. Woolworth's dominated the variety trade with 774 outlets, but Kress, Kresge, and McCrory each had more than 100. Although chains ran fewer than 5 percent of American grocery stores, they were particularly strong in urban areas, doing more than a quarter of the business in many cities; in Philadelphia, chains accounted for between 60 and 70 percent of the grocery trade. In all, five hundred grocery companies ran eight thousand stores. Substantial numbers of chain stores operated in the tobacco, newsstand, variety, and drug trades, and the authors found smaller numbers in numerous other fields, including piano stores, clothing stores, ticket agencies, funeral parlors, lumber yards, and bookstores.

Like department stores and mail-order houses, chains depended on modern accounting systems, departmentalization, high stock turn, and the use of low-cost labor. The United Cigar Stores required daily reports from each store; men from headquarters appeared without notice to check on their accuracy. The *Printers' Ink* authors likened the chains' employee training systems to "the building of a machine—an efficient, high-powered machine—in which the personality of each individual is merged in the house personality." Systematized work methods enabled chains to hire immigrants and women at low wages. Even managers' freedom and individuality were submerged in the systems, which determined merchandising and employment policies. "The Riker-Hegeman manual tells the manager that his place is in the front of the store, making sure that every patron who enters is assured a welcome and immediate attention. He has, in short, about the status of a floorwalker."

Chain employees ran high-volume operations. The average druggist turned stock three or four times per year, while the Riker-Hegeman chain claimed twelve. The most prosperous and up-to-date independent grocers and tobacco stores turned their stock fifteen or twenty times a year; some grocery chains claimed as much as forty-five, and the United Cigar Stores claimed fifty.

In the variety-store field, chains and independents showed more similar results. This was due to the concerted efforts of the variety wholesalers, whose survival depended on training their retailer customers to compete with the phenomenally successful Woolworth's and its substantial competitors Kresge, Kress, and McCrory. Butler Brothers, for example, a large jobber with branches in many cities, published an extensive series of manuals on how to do business, emphasizing the importance of stock turn to modern merchandising.

Chain-store locations were chosen systematically, and real-estate specialists negotiated sales and leases. The Child's restaurant chain, with eighty outlets around the country, waited as long as five years for particular locations, chosen on the basis of *"data on virtually every available place in the country."* United Cigar employees stood on street corners counting pedestrians. The busiest corner in America turned out to be State and Madison in Chicago (142,000 people between 7 A.M. and midnight), followed by New York's Broadway and Forty-second Street and rather less crowded corners in Philadelphia and Boston. The United Cigar system further incorporated information about who populated the crowds; some busy corners swarmed with the wrong market segment, workers with "a low purchasing capacity." The company's real-estate subsidiary bought whole buildings to secure good locations, and reaped substantial nonselling income; its stores were "often hardly more than holes in the wall" of large, company-owned office buildings.

Most of the bigger chain companies owned or were owned by other firms. Like manufacturers and wholesalers, these large retailers contributed to the "chaos in distribution" by refusing to keep to their assigned places in the old-fashioned manufacturer-wholesaler-retailer system. The chains lowered costs and increased efficiency by doing their own wholesaling and by buying manufacturing facilities; sometimes manufacturers and wholesalers bought or created chains as outlets for their goods. The United Drug Company owned at least three candy makers, several other manufacturing firms, and another chain, the National Cigar Stands. Sears briefly tried a chain of retail food stores in Illinois in 1904. The Kroger Grocery and Baking Company packed meat, roasted coffee, and manufactured candy and canned foods. Like large wholesalers, chains labeled goods with private brands.

Even without such direct connections to sources, systematized and massive buying power enabled chains to obtain financial advantages based on sheer size. They asked for and got extra discounts from the manufacturers and wholesalers that supplied them. They demanded—and sometimes simply took—extensions of time for payment, financing their operations in part on the credit of the jobbers and the manufacturers. Chains further enjoyed tax advantages unavailable to independents, a major issue for legislative reform as opposition to chain stores developed. Some states, for example, required corporations to pay local taxes only in the cities where they were incorporated, not in the places where they operated stores. Under such laws, A & P and Woolworth's conducted tax-free businesses in municipalities that assessed small merchants for revenues.

All of the chains' financial advantages—tax breaks, discounts on quantity buying, real-estate holdings, sophisticated financing schemes, Wall Street financial backers, and low operating costs—enabled them to cut prices on trademarked, nationally advertised goods. The extent of price-cutting varied from trade to trade. The chain variety stores—"five-and-tens"—really did limit their merchandise to things that could be bought for a nickel or a dime, and could not charge four or nine cents without altering that policy. But the *Printers' Ink* investigators called drug chains "pronounced price-cutters," and most grocery chains cut prices as well. In a 1915 court case, Cream of Wheat charged that the A & P Economy Stores sold its cereal for twelve cents, two cents less than the price at the regular A & P stores.

Cut prices on standard advertised products posed a fundamental challenge to small merchants, whose customers might well wonder why they should pay higher prices on identical cans of Campbell's soup or cakes of Ivory. Although the new A & P stores had abolished credit and delivery, most grocery and drug chains still offered those services as well as low prices. Small retailers could compete with price-cutting only on the basis of location, personality, and their position in the community.

Price-cutting threatened manufacturers' power as well, by emphasizing price and challenging brand loyalty. A newspaper advertisement touting two cents off a ten-cent box of Kellogg's corn flakes made the chain store look more attractive than the independent grocer even if it did not actually coax customers away from their neighborhood stores. Worse for Kellogg's, it reduced the product to the level of other corn flakes and other breakfast cereals and might suggest to consumers that Kellogg's was only worth eight cents. Marketers created their products as much in the process of setting prices as in designing packages. Yuban differed from Ariosa, Ivory from Star, in all the elements of what is now called the "marketing mix": the products themselves, the promotional strategies, the targeted retail outlets, and the price. Marketing for branded products aimed to establish strong brand loyalty that could overcome price sensitivity: belief in the qualities of Kellogg's or Ivory that would induce consumers to pay whatever those products cost.

Manufacturers feared that price-cutting made their products more susceptible to substitution when the neighborhood grocer or druggist suggested some less expensive brand that paid him better margins. If Kellogg's was advertised for eight cents, then the eight-cent private brand might really be as good as the local merchant claimed. The chains, too, substituted; some chain stores advertised low prices on branded goods but encouraged clerks to recommend the private label.

Some manufacturers took firm stands for traditional distribution, refusing to sell to chains that cut prices and committing resources to court battles when chain stores filed suit, as the A & P did in the Cream of Wheat case. Kellogg refused to sell directly to any retailer, whether a small independent or a large chain. Other manufacturers filled trade magazines with rhetoric. "Price cutting is a species of commercial debauchery that rests upon the relentless doctrine of the survival of the fittest," the Bissell Carpet Sweeper Company's advertising manager wrote in 1910, "upon the narrow, cold-blooded principle that mer-

chandising is a sort of commercial warfare; that 'all's fair in war'
and 'the devil take the hindmost.' "

Other manufacturers were less alarmed. Heinz left negotiations with chains to its branch managers. H. H. Good, an executive for Carter's Little Liver Pills, celebrated the volume of
business the chains brought. "There may be a possibility of their
growing so large as to dominate the manufacturer but that is
very remote at present," he asserted. "What we are after now is
business, and we must use the best channels to get it." A representative of the Bon Ami Company had a similar reaction:
"Theoretically I believe the chains will become a menace to the
manufacturer in the future, but that is too far distant to think
about now," he declared. The firm offered a jobbing discount
to any chain with twenty or more stores.

Wholesalers recognized the chains as another manifestation
of the general trend towards "eliminating the jobber," because
large chains did just that, handling their own warehousing, shipping, and financing. The secretary of the California Wholesale
Grocers' Association called them "nothing less than 'revolution.' " Some jobbers began their own chains, buying out retail
debtors to save themselves from loss. Others acquired stores in
new territories in order to find local outlets for their private
labels. In most fields, wholesalers formed trade associations to
bargain with manufacturers about policy. Some, like the Butler
Brothers variety firm, coached their retail customers in modern
merchandising to help them compete with the chains.

Retailers received such lessons from a number of quarters:
manufacturers' house organs and other "dealer helps," materials from wholesalers' and retailers' associations, and
commercially published trade magazines and books. These organizations had an interest in keeping small retailers from failing, and in keeping the system of which they were part from
"cracking under its own dead weight," in the words of the Sears
historians. Despite the success of the mass merchandisers, distribution was still for the most part carried out in single stores
operated by individual retailers. In 1919, chains accounted for
only 4 percent of total national retail sales. Four years later, the

proportion had grown to 8 percent; department stores accounted for about 16 percent, and mail-order houses and company stores about 4 percent each. As late as 1923, over two-thirds of American retail business was still done through general stores and small, single-unit stores selling one line of goods, such as hardware, drugs, groceries, clothing, or furniture. For more than a decade their proprietors had been told—in trade journals, at meetings, and by salesmen, bankers, and others representing the larger firms they did business with—that they could not in the long run beat the mass merchants and could only survive by imitating their methods.

These retail advisers recommended the one-price system and urged that prices be publicly displayed. Price-marking signified that the store renounced the outdated principle of "making the price suit the buyer" and the outdated practices of bargaining and secret price marks, the *American Grocer* editorialized in 1909. "A price attached to every article begets confidence; aids the customer in making a selection; is easily seen; saves time for purchaser and seller." Price cards and price tickets "give any store an air of prosperity and up-to-dateness," the *Grocers' Magazine* commented three years later, remarking that they would "answer many questions that otherwise the busy clerk would have to stop work and answer."

Both the 1910 and the 1920 editions of Butler Brothers' *Success in Retailing* strongly recommended marked prices, but only one of its photographs of actual variety stores displayed more than one price placard. The book lambasted the secret price mark. Customers might not know the code, but they understood the system. "The wool is not pulled over anyone's eyes. Even the old Polish woman, with a shawl over her head, suspects that it is there for a purpose, and she does not buy for fear she may pay the long-price." "A thing despised, discredited, almost universally discarded," the secret mark "still hinders the progress of an unthinking few, who keep it from its proper place, on the bottom of the scrap heap." Apparently unwilling to alienate the "unthinking few" among the firm's customers, the book went on, "Of course, there are good men who still use it—because they don't begin to realize how much it costs or what it means."

Writers took even greater pains to describe the meaning and significance of stock turn, a more complicated mass-merchandising concept. "Why do not more merchants get rich?" asked Butler Brothers in its 1916 *Butler Way System Book.* "The answer can be told in just three words: LACK OF TURNOVER." Retailers who remained in the dark about stock turn would overbuy when salesmen offered them quantity prices. They would tie up their money and storage space, owe extra interest to wholesalers and manufacturers, and risk losing money on merchandise that went out of style or got damaged in the back room. "The man who started in business with $5,000 and buried half of it in the ground, was better off than the man who buries half his capital in dead stock which doesn't move," the makers of Buster Brown shoes instructed salesmen to tell retailers in 1917: at least, buried money did not incur rent or other costs of doing business. Manufacturers of branded products that offered little profit to the retailer were especially concerned with turnover lessons. Because Life Savers, for example, cost storekeepers more than the many other brands of nickel candy, they had to sell more. A company representative told investigators that the trade had been "diligently educated to the wisdom of concentrating on the leader of the line" (that is, to the wisdom of pushing Life Savers) and "the greater profits due to turnover" from the more actively advertised product.

Keeping track of stock turn required keeping track of stock, and to do so, modern merchandising demanded record-keeping. By 1915, the average grocery store carried between 750 and 1,000 different brands of merchandise, while large fancy groceries might sell 5,000 different items. With so many stockkeeping units and so many small sales, appropriate systems were difficult to devise. Still, commercial manuals for storekeepers detailed complicated procedures that would keep the careful merchant apprised of his needs when the salesmen showed up and relieve the even greater difficulties of physically taking stock.

More realistic retail reformers understood that many small merchants kept no records at all, and urged storekeepers to

begin at the most elementary level, making some kind of nota-
tion about every transaction. In a 1917 manual for the "countless" stores too small to hire bookkeepers, accountant Eugene
Herz insisted on "making a sales slip for every sale—cash or
charge," but acknowledged that most of his readers kept records
only of charges "and some may desire to continue to do so."
Sales slips protected against disputes, a speaker named W. T.
Abell told the Philadelphia Retail Grocers' Association at an
evening meeting in 1912. Customers would no longer come
back "to make claims for articles they think they bought and
which you cannot prove they didn't." Nor could clerks be
trusted; they faced temptation "every hour,—yes every few minutes—of the day in the general grocery store." The good employer had a moral obligation to provide a system that would
keep his clerks' fingers out of the till and spare them both from
conflict. Writing everything down "is no doubt a habit hard to
form. . . . Some of you may not be able to write," Abell told the
most organized group of retail grocers in the country. "Well,
you are not too old to learn and it would pay you."

Illiterate shopkeepers could hardly be expected to master
double-entry bookkeeping, but for those who could aspire to it,
writers presented elementary record-keeping as the first step
towards full-fledged accounting, which retailers could learn
from a wide range of self-study publications. The Ingersoll
watch company offered *System and Cost Accounting for the Retail
Jeweler* in 1914; many other manufacturers addressed such booklets to specific kinds of retailers. Two years later the Federal
Trade Commission issued a nineteen-page brochure, outlining
(although hardly teaching) a system of accounts appropriate for
the small retailer. This pamphlet was one of many that it published on standard cost-accounting procedures in various fields
of business. At the other end of the scale, the A. W. Shaw
Company offered a nine-month, eighteen-lesson correspondence course in retail merchandising. "This Course is not for
John Wanamaker and his rivals," its authors assured purchasers.
"This Course is for the average retail business." Each lesson

consisted of a "lecture" that might run over fifty pages and a workbook establishing some piece of the books for the hypothetical Miller Merchandise Company. The publishers provided examination questions, sample forms for record-keeping and various types of correspondence, and even imitation money, and they encouraged students with questions to write to Robert B. Schreffler, the chief editor of the course. Lest the system seem too grand for the small retailer who thought he was getting along without it, its authors flattered his ambition and assured him that it offered "a concrete method of training for mental vigor."

Record-keeping at the level of detail taught in the Shaw course was well beyond any actual requirements for conducting a successful small business before 1920. Although small shopkeepers did fail by the thousands, other thousands existed and even prospered without sales slips, let alone double-entry books. Along with illiterate merchants and sloppy storekeeping, the retail advisers encountered a tradition of seat-of-the-pants skill that had as much to do with human relationships as with numbers. For merchants who had the aptitude for bargaining with traveling salesmen and shrewd customers, for dealing with people who asked for credit but could not or would not pay, and for picking merchandise that would sell, written records represented a burden.

Eventually most storekeepers learned to keep records, not for "mental vigor," but because larger firms expected and demanded that they do so. "Banks are paying more and more attention to the accounting methods used by the merchant to whom they extend credit," the FTC warned. "Even if he is successful but can not show it because of his bookkeeping methods the bank will not consider him a desirable credit risk." Retailers who kept inventory records would be able to get insurance, which would contribute to their standing with creditors, and they could inform insurance companies about losses in case of fire, still a common hazard, especially in country general stores heated with wood stoves. By 1916, Butler Brothers ex-

GROCERS' MAGAZINE

THE Grocer who tries to keep his business in his head can't keep ahead in his business.

His brain can't stand the strain— it's built to remember facts—not figures.

The human mind is never completely accurate.

The National Cash Register thinks with a brain of steel.

It keeps track of every detail of every sale—stops leaks and checks losses.

A store using a National Cash Register is run on system—it's bound to yield profit to its owner.

Over One Million have been sold

"Get a Receipt"   Write for Booklet   *"Get a Receipt"*

The National Cash Register Company
Dayton, Ohio

3

National Cash Register advertisement from *Grocers' Magazine,* 1912.

pected its customers to have the information necessary to report
to Dun's or Bradstreet's, the two agencies that gave small business credit ratings. "A sentimental sense of pride or a feeling of
independence" might deter old-fashioned merchants from making such reports, but "outside or hearsay information" was
rarely sufficient for a credit rating. "A BLANK RATING IS A DANGER
SIGNAL TO THE CREDIT MAN," the *Butler Way System Book* warned.

Often the first and most persuasive missionary to confront the
retailer in the interests of record-keeping was the cash-register
salesman, usually an agent for the National Cash Register Company. Butler Brothers recommended the machines only for
large stores, and suggested buying them second-hand. "Just as
soon as you start into business," its *Success in Retailing* cautioned,
"you will probably be solicited—and cleverly solicited—to buy
one. . . . You may be almost hypnotized into buying." These
"sharks," as one disaffected NCR salesman called his former
colleagues, owed their abilities to the company's pioneering
training systems, sales management methods, and sales principles. The company discarded the concept of market saturation:
no group of merchants could ever have enough new cash registers. When new prospects became difficult to find, salesmen
were to convince current cash-register owners that they should
trade up to better machines.

Expensive models could cost as much as a small retailer's
stock, and effective salesmen emphasized that end of the line.
E. C. McCann, an Indiana NCR salesman, won third prize in the
Beech-Nut Packing Company's national essay contest for salesmen's success stories. "Meeting the Price Argument" described
his interactions with Mr. D., "a grocer who had eight children
to care for and no one but the family working in the small store."
Six weeks after purchasing a $200 register, D. had tried to return
it because he was having trouble meeting the payments and was
not convinced of its benefits. McCann induced him instead to
exchange it for a $400 machine. Thanking Beech-Nut for "the
seventy-five good U.S. dollars" he won for his essay, the salesman claimed it made him "more ambitious to do more of that

sort of selling that 'benefits both parties to the sale.' "

"Don't try to sell a systematizer without a system," NCR president John H. Patterson wrote in a list of "Don'ts" that he published for his sales force. Expensive technology would not sell itself to old-fashioned retailers in small stores. NCR salesmen introduced themselves as representatives of the company's "system department," and taught business methods with a variety of company materials. Before 1891, the firm introduced the *Hustler,* a house organ addressed to retailers with a circulation that reached 1.5 million. At various times, the company published the magazine in seven languages and in separate editions for groceries, drug stores, meat markets, and other retail lines.

Pushing business systems and window-display ideas replaced the earliest selling strategy for cash registers. They had first been marketed as "thief-catchers" that would enable employers to apprehend clerks who had their hands in the till. In response, retail clerks and saloon bartenders organized protective associa-

---

The bottom and the top of the line from National Cash Register, 1911. In between, the company offered eighteen other models.

Detail-Adder

Total-Adder—Receipt and Sales-Strip Printer

With separate adding counters and cash drawer for each clerk.

No. 215.　Price $20

No. 572-4.　Price $500

"Father, good-bye," the dying man said,
"But first to you I must tell

How your open cash
drawer drew me on
To the road that
leads to Hell."

NCR had softened the "thief-catcher" motif by 1909, but used the argument of the storekeeper's moral responsibility to his clerks in *The Storekeeper's Dream,* an expensively produced book of color paintings on glossy paper.

tions, destroyed NCR advertising, and taught each other how to make the machines perform incorrectly. For a time, NCR hired Pinkerton detectives—a corps then conspicuous for violent activity against organized labor—to catch the "thieves" who outwitted the "thief-catchers." The *Hustler*'s "Clerk's Corner" column, begun during the height of the clerks' rebellion, represented an attempt to court the clerks instead, appealing to their ambition by offering them retailing lessons that might help them get ahead with their employers or open their own stores.

Other manufacturers of business technologies provided instructions and rationales for their use. The American Sales Book Company mailed out 175,000 copies of *Where Have My Profits Gone?,* arguing for the place of the receipt and the sales record in modern business. The Burroughs Adding Machine Company's System Service Bureau provided model bookkeeping plans for all kinds and sizes of businesses; finding retailing "an almost virgin field" in 1913, the bureau prepared materials for small merchants, as it had for large industrial firms. Burroughs offered retailers a thirty-six-page booklet, *How to Figure the Cost of Doing Business,* along with pamphlets and tables on figuring selling prices and net profits. The pocket-sized "Burroughs Blue Book" contained blanks for every conceivable transaction. *Stopping Store Leaks* described a complete bookkeeping system that depended on dividing stores into departments, keeping separate records of sales by different clerks, keeping stock records, and making both daily and monthly calculations. The resulting figures could hardly be arrived at without an adding machine, but the small retailer may well have wondered whether he really needed to assign a precise proportion of his clerk's wages to every pair of suspenders or can of soup. Burroughs assured him that he did. With an adding machine, "even the *smallest* stores can afford to have as accurate information as the *largest* stores."

Retail advisers were less unanimous in recommending that small stores imitate mass merchandisers by doing away with services than they were about adopting record-keeping systems. Large stores publicized their services. "In Olden Times the Customer Came to the Store," the Joseph R. Peebles' Sons Company, a major Cincinnati wholesale and retail grocer, wrote in a 1901 headline for its delivery schedule. "Now we Come to the Customer, either in Person or by Telephone." The store delivered up to three times a day in the city, and had regular routes to surrounding Ohio and Kentucky towns. "Your wishes, as given over the Telephone, will receive just as careful and considerate attention as if you 'pick' the articles out," Peebles promised. "Our efforts are to please you and to hold your business." One 1913 text warned, however, that delivery service could be a small retailer's undoing, especially with customers who had telephones and might pick up the phone two or three times a day to order one cake of soap or can of beans. Other advisers maintained instead that excellent delivery services

Cover for *Stopping Store Leaks,* from the System Service Bureau operated by the Burroughs Adding Machine Company.

would help distinguish stores from their competitors; one such article described a druggist who replaced his delivery bicycles with motorcycles.

Delivery drivers did not handle money, so stores that delivered necessarily gave credit, another service about which retail advisers disagreed. Although cash business was undoubtedly attractive to small retailers and conducive to their success, credit

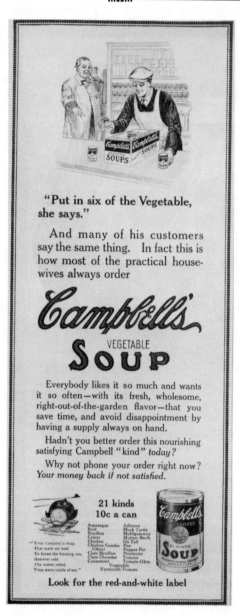

"Put in six of the Vegetable, she says."

And many of his customers say the same thing. In fact this is how most of the practical house-wives always order

Campbell's
VEGETABLE
Soup

Everybody likes it so much and wants it so often—with its fresh, wholesome, right-out-of-the-garden flavor—that you save time, and avoid disappointment by having a supply always on hand.

Hadn't you better order this nourishing satisfying Campbell "kind" *today?*

Why not phone your order right now? *Your money back if not satisfied.*

21 kinds
10c a can

Look for the red-and-white label

Some stores competed by offering services, such as telephone ordering, shown in this Campbell's ad from the *Saturday Evening Post,* 1913.

distinguished their service from that of the mail-order houses and consolidated their position in their communities. Trade journals and other sources of retail guidance sometimes attacked credit as unbusinesslike and old-fashioned, like bargaining an indication of a failure to treat customers uniformly or to take money seriously enough. Many put imprudent credit at the top of their list of subjects about which retailers were ignorant. In small towns and urban neighborhoods, however, retailers granted credit to people with whom they had many daily interactions and complex relationships. Their financial well-being depended not on abolishing credit but on granting it judiciously.

Butler Brothers, with a clear financial interest in its retail customers' survival, told them unambiguously not to give credit. "One of the great advantages of a Variety business is that it is a cash business," the wholesaler claimed. This was true in cities, where chains dominated variety-store trade practices, but it could hardly be said of the rural general stores that patronized Butler Brothers for their variety merchandise. Even here, the company took a firm stand: "In spite of the current belief, it is not necessary to do a credit business in a farming community." Other services, such as hitching rails or rest rooms for the "women folks," would suffice to keep the farmer's business. Butler Brothers even argued that the mail-order houses owed their success to rural retail credit because the farmer "would send his ready cash to Chicago rather than meet his creditor."

Retail advisers less directly dependent on their readers' financial success more often acknowledged the importance of credit. The American Sales Book Company's *Where Have My Profits Gone?* listed eight arguments in favor of charge business, even suggesting that credit was a moneymaker because it would create customer tolerance. "Charge customers will put up with more of your shortcomings (if you have any) than will a cash customer," a speaker pointed out at a meeting of the Philadelphia Retail Grocers' Association, extolling the "feeling of friendliness that cannot be had from a floating cash trade." Credit offered retail proprietors the opportunity to establish good reputations and "to grow into the esteem of the community."

For retailers ready to risk giving up credit, a new kind of business emerged that would sell them bait to lure customers into their stores: trading stamps and other premium systems. Retail premiums themselves were not new. The A & P had offered them almost from its beginnings in the 1860s, and many other retailers gave small gifts or additional merchandise in return for customers' coupons, cash-register receipts, or cards that were punched with each purchase. In 1896, Sperry and Hutchinson began operations in Bridgeport, Connecticut; it was the first trading-stamp company to operate as an independent business, offering its product to a limited number of retailers who would give the stamps to customers buying with cash. Its success, Thomas Sperry's widow recalled at the company's silver anniversary party in 1921, "immediately justified the employment of more men and the opening of additional branches. To specify city by city and town by town would be to infringe upon the functions of a geography. It is sufficient to say that the plan spread like a prairie fire."

Within eight years, the country had stamp fever. Other companies competed with S & H, issuing stamps in all colors. Large retailers offered their own trading stamps and sold them to smaller stores interested in converting their trade to cash. Montgomery Ward issued its own stamps, and Sears tried a premium plan. Manufacturers announced that they would redeem package fronts for stamps. Consumers responded enthusiastically to nearly all of the plans, which apparently did offer something for nothing more than the time expended in pasting the stamps into the books. In 1905, when the Benedict and MacFarlane Company, makers of "Blue Trading Stamps," closed its offices in New York after a financial collapse, women hoping to cash in their blue stamps rioted, damaging the store and each other's clothing, and bringing on the police. Artemas Ward's magazine *Fame* saw the incident as the "beginning of the end" for "the trading stamp craze."

Retailers' organizations opposed the stamps. Consumers

This S & H advertisement appeared in *Everybody's Magazine* in 1904, the year the trading-stamp craze was at its height.

might get something for nothing, but storekeepers paid to participate in the plans, and if every merchant gave stamps of one color or another, none of them gained any advantage over competitors and only the stamp companies benefitted. Labor unions joined the near-unanimous protest of the retail organizations. Together they urged state legislatures to consider antistamp bills because, like other kinds of premiums, the plans were con-

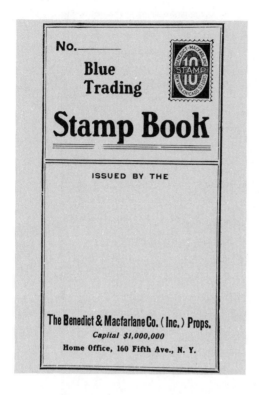

Front cover from an unused Blue Trading Stamp Book, Benedict and MacFarlane.

sistently victorious in the courts. But despite the almost unanimous opposition of their organizations, retailers joined the stamp plans in the belief that customers wanted stamps. The Philadelphia Retail Grocers' Association, which had long opposed stamps and refused to admit stamp-users to membership, rescinded the rules in 1904 because it could not keep members in line, but it stayed on record as opposed.

By 1910, the craze was over but the stamp system was well established. "Laws have been passed, a constant fight carried on against their use and yet they are more generally used than ever before," wrote the *American Grocer*. "The people want them. That settles that in spite of laws or prejudice." The A & P gave S & H green stamps; department stores that bought stamps at quantity prices gave double stamps on certain days. S & H en-

hanced its position by consolidating the redemption of a variety
of coupons, boxtops, and other stamps. Its 1910 stamp book
listed hundreds of products whose labels and coupons the company would accept. In addition, S & H took the popular "Library
Slips" issued with Armour products, H-O cereals, Prophylactic
toothbrushes, and 3-in-1 oil, and the coupons of the United
Cigar Stores. Protests, court cases, and legislative battles continued until the 1916 Supreme Court decision that upheld the
right of the states to regulate premiums and stamps. In 1921,
25,000 stores offered S & H green stamps, which could be re-

Although this 1904 cartoon originally published in *Puck* censures the retailer, the *Grocers' Review* reprinted it, with an editorial commenting that it
would "bear close study. . . . Trading Stamps delude two classes; the consumer who expects something for nothing and the storekeeper who imag-
ines that he secures trade at the expense of his competitor. The only person
who is not deceived is the seller of the stamps who reaps a golden harvest
of dollars."

The Fox.—I knew those hens would be attracted by my advertisement promising Tinted Trading Stamps.
From "Puck" January 20th. 1904. Copyrighted by Keppler and Schwarzmann.

deemed at 600 redemption centers. Retailers attempting to switch their customers to cash could also buy other premium systems from a number of firms.

Trading stamps provided retailers with a form of promotion that required little creativity. For storekeepers who wished to be more innovative, retailers' trade journals and books were full of ideas for stimulating sluggish trade. A collection of 333 sales plans reprinted from the *Merchants' Record and Show Window* in 1906 described successful promotions from all over the country: Curme's shoe store in Richmond, Indiana, held a Cinderella slipper contest; Pettee's hardware store in Oklahoma City gave large amounts of free ice with every icebox it sold; a Kentucky grocer used his newspaper advertising space for a recipe contest. Two chapters record the genesis of Christmas as a retail holiday, one describing the "perfected advertising machinery running full blast" at the big department stores, the other offering adaptations for smaller establishments.

Most advisers recommended sprucing up the store. The "very first thing" to do when the "syndicate" five-and-ten moves into town, Butler Brothers told the proprietors of established variety and general stores, is to "modernize your store room, fixtures and front. Unless your store compares favorably in appearance with the syndicate's, you will be badly handicapped from the start." Chaotic stores increased sales costs because it took clerks more time to find and retrieve the goods, and slow service could alienate customers. The Harvard Bureau of Business Research lamented in 1919 that too few retail grocers had put any effort into systematizing store layout. Some even purposely devised inconvenient arrangements, on the theory that customers who passed by more merchandise would buy more.

Mass-merchandising principles and the new relationships they engendered mandated new designs. Stores divided into departments that corresponded with those described in bookkeeping systems could be inventoried more easily. Butler Brothers recommended that every store set up a bargain basement, the innovation that had brought "the laboring man's wife" into

SODA FOUNTAIN, RICHARD F. BRUNE CO.

FRESH MEAT AND FRUIT DISPLAYS, RICHARD F. BRUNE CO.

Two pictures showing model store layouts in one of Richard F. Brune's stores in Sawtelle, California, published in *Grocers' Magazine* in 1912. The soda fountain was unusual. "The drug stores are grabbing our profitable tea, spice and extract business," Brune wrote. "Why should not we wake up and retaliate by getting our rightful share of the soda fountain trade?"

Marshall Field's and that provided a place for marked-down merchandise. The 1910 edition of *Success in Retailing* instructed readers in laying drain tile, cinders, cement, and wood over dirt cellar floors and installing stairs from the main part of the store. Department stores also contributed models for fixtures and display. "In the department store," writes historian Susan Porter Benson, explaining that they depended for their success on their expensive downtown locations, "space was money." After 1910, the big stores redesigned displays with special racks, holders, and hangers that enabled customers to see the array of goods and clerks to retrieve them easily.

"The ideal," wrote Marshall J. Bailey, who composed treatises on store fixtures for *System*, "is a fixture from which the customer can select goods without assistance, pay the cashier and leave the store." A few other early writers shared this goal; in recommending price marks in 1909, the *American Grocer* maintained that customers "like to be at liberty to inspect the goods, find the price and make a decision as to purchase without being interfered with by a clerk." Some Southern California grocery stores tried partial self-service in response to labor shortages during World War I, but the idea is generally credited to Clarence Saunders, who opened his first Piggly Wiggly store in Memphis, Tennessee, in 1916 and received a patent on the design the next year. Saunders, too, believed that customers who saw more would buy more, and arranged a maze of aisles that exposed them to all the merchandise. They walked through with baskets and exited at check-out stands. The Piggly Wiggly chain ultimately had 2,660 stores, and Saunders franchised his self-service design.

Self-service would eventually offer two important solutions to the problems that beset early-twentieth-century retail trade. It would cut costs by eliminating delivery and by using as few workers as possible. And it would mitigate the problem that for so long stood between manufacturers and retailers: with no clerk, there could be no substitution to the customer who wanted a particular brand. By 1926 each Piggly Wiggly sold merchandise worth well over twice that sold by the average A & P, but Saunders's stores never reached the size of the later supermarkets, which brought these advantages to fruition. Instituted during the 1930s by imaginative entrepreneurs who understood the new conditions of a population accustomed to branded goods, equipped with automobiles, and looking for low prices as the Depression deepened, supermarkets were built on cheap land outside major urban areas. In large spaces, manufacturers could mount the big displays that made self-service an effective selling technique for packaged goods. Supermarkets' large parking lots could serve customers from miles away. Supermarket shoppers, not constrained by the amount they could carry, could buy in great quantities, contributing to the high volume and fast turnover.

Few of the retail advisers during the first two decades of the twentieth century had urged stores to grow in so many words, but that idea had pervaded their lessons. Better methods alone would not save small businesses from mass-merchandising competition. Inventory control and complicated bookkeeping systems were not much help to the small retailer who chose to remain small. The trade journals and dealer helps consistently compared such men with the "wide-awake merchant" and the "progressive" storekeeper, whose striving for turnover made for larger businesses that could handle the output of mass production. Retail trade was not simply a community service; it was part of the capitalist system, interdependent with manufacturing firms whose managers sought new production technologies and marketing techniques because they understood that capitalism mandated growth.

By themselves, small retailers could in the long run do little to fight mass-retailer competition. They could rearrange their stores, set up bookkeeping systems, and give trading stamps, but they would still be undersold by the chains, department stores, and mail-order houses whose advantages lay in volume and turnover. They could attempt to respond to the mass merchandisers' low prices by substituting private brands or brands

Two views of a Piggly Wiggly store, 1918. This chain, which began in Memphis in 1916, is generally credited with introducing self-service.

with better margins. But more and more of their customers asked for Ivory soap and Baker's cocoa; national advertisers were training them to "refuse all substitutes." Against these brands—and against the systematic methods that gave the mass retailers so much power—independent merchants stood little chance. As one Brooklyn retail tobacconist put it, "The cemetery of the independent tobacconists is as large as the country."

CHAPTER 8

||||⊏)||||||||||||⊏)||||||||||||⊏)||||

THE
POLITICS
OF
PACKAGED
PRODUCTS

THE TURN-OF-THE-CENTURY DECADES WERE MARKED BY PROFOUND
political ferment. Matters once construed as belonging to the
province of private initiative became topics of public debate.
Previously unorganized individuals joined groups formed to influence public policy; highly articulate reformers campaigned
on behalf of people shut out of the political process and victim-
ized by industrial development. The rich and the powerful, by
no means unanimous on the solutions to the political issues
raised by the increasing success of large corporations, debated
in trade organizations and other forums of their own and also
in contests involving broader constituencies. Nearly every social
and economic development had its political expressions. So,
too, did the changes brought about by the upheaval in production and distribution, the advent of mass-produced branded
goods, and the intensive development in marketing strategy.
Muckraking journalists and well-known reformers challenged
the prerogatives of corporations in hiring workers, buying raw
materials, making and selling products, and collaborating with
other business enterprises, and they issued calls for regulation
by federal, state, and local governments.

McClure's, Collier's, and other inexpensive popular magazines—the media of the new advertising—were also the media of reform. The *Ladies' Home Journal* spearheaded the campaign for pure food and drugs that produced federal legislation in 1906; in 1913, the *Journal* introduced columns by muckraking journalist Ida Tarbell and social feminist Jane Addams, who explained women's suffrage, child labor, strikes, and working women's wages to the "home-sheltered" women who read the magazine. No irony attached to the juxtaposition of articles exposing the atrocities of industrialization with advertisements for standardized products produced in factories. Both the products and the reform campaigns were manifestations of industrial progress as turn-of-the-century Americans understood it.

As a political label the term "progressive," still new in 1911, can only be applied conclusively to Theodore Roosevelt's Progressive party of 1912. But the word went well beyond electoral politics. People literally believed in progress; the philosophical conviction that world history proceeded from worse to better pervaded American thought, with roots in the European industrial and political revolutions of the late eighteenth and early nineteenth centuries. Confidence in the future permeated even the thinking of Americans who did not consciously base their ideas on European philosophy. They flocked to world's fairs that celebrated modern technology and industrial progress; their labor organizations promised members a better future; they bought goods promoted as examples of progress. The business community customarily used "progressive" as a term of praise to commend both small merchants and big industrialists who understood changing trends and knew how to adapt their businesses to them.

Historians have recently challenged the existence of "Progressivism" or of a "Progressive movement," pointing out the many inconsistent ideas, incompatible agendas, and varieties of reform that were once lumped together under these umbrellas. But the concept has persisted because most of the participants in the political conflicts understood that genuinely new trends— corporate organization, mass production, mass distribution, and the national market—required new strategies, "progres-sive" thinking. They operated in the context of much broader reform movements and genuine public controversy about the rights of capital and the nature of the public interest. That controversy was confused and contradictory in part because it *was* broad, challenging the manifestations of the new corporate power in many aspects of daily life, and in part because it *was* "progressive," celebrating the technology and the rational orga-nization that were fruits of that same power.

Business efforts to influence both public opinion and legisla-tion on the political issues of the marketplace were coordinated by the many organizations that amounted to a vast and general movement among businessmen towards political organization. As national markets formed in groceries, drugs, hardware, and other consumer goods, manufacturers, wholesalers, and retail-ers faced national problems, issues involving federal legislation and ones concerning standardization of trade practices among states and regions. By the turn of the century they had formed national organizations capable of sophisticated lobbying efforts as well as the local and regional organizations that provided more direct services to members. In all of the consumer-goods lines, manufacturers, wholesalers, and retailers shared interests in combatting mass distribution. As they became organized, therefore, officers of their associations routinely attended and addressed each other's conventions and only occasionally com-plained from the podium.

These organizations had to respond not only to new condi-tions in the trade but to public agitation: branded, packaged goods had become political matters. Reformers challenged politicians to require manufacturers to take responsibility for the contents of their packages—the healthfulness of food and drugs and the accuracy of weights and measures. Others, con-cerned about consumers hoodwinked by fancy labels, made the packaging itself into a public issue. Regulations were debated and enacted on local, state, and federal levels. Another pro-tracted controversy, carried on in both political and legal arenas, concerned the manufacturers' rights in marketing the packages. This dispute involved resale price maintenance, the attempt by manufacturers to dictate the conditions of sale for their trade-marked products, setting not only the wholesale but also the retail prices.

Agitating for many decades, the movement for pure food consisted of a multitude of organizations; articles supporting the pure-food cause appeared in periodicals of all kinds, and long before the federal Pure Food and Drug Act of 1906, regulations were debated and enacted on state and local levels. Adulterated food had been a subject for public complaint and legislative lobbying since well before the Civil War. As cities grew, as factories and commercial farms supplanted home production, and as food stores became more distant from food sources—geographically and in the number of middlemen—local salespeople could not be held fully accountable for products they sold. Distant manufacturing enterprises proved themselves not merely unaccountable but often untrustworthy. "We buy everything, and have no idea of the processes by which articles are produced, and have no means of knowing beforehand what the quality may be," explained Ellen Richards, one of the central figures of the home economics movement, in *Food Materials and Their Adulteration,* published in 1885. "Relatively we are in a state of barbarous innocence, as compared with our grandmothers, about the common articles of daily use."

Over the next twenty years, Richards's explanation became even more powerful, as the new techniques of mass production and mass distribution definitively eclipsed home production. Food and drug reformers concerned themselves with two major issues: fraud and poison. Without regulations demanding truthful product labeling, manufacturers substituted colored and flavored cane sugar for maple sugar; they extended flour, mustard, and ground coffee with cheap fillers, including sawdust and chalk. Patent-medicine manufacturers made exaggerated claims about their products' effects, and formulated them with cocaine, opium, and alcohol. At the end of the century, a new kind of adulteration joined these rather traditional fraudulent practices. Manufacturers seeking national markets, concerned about shelf life, promoted the development of chemical preservatives; new chemical technologies provided them also with artificial colorings and flavorings. Company laboratories tested the chemicals' efficacy but not their safety.

Reformers called for legislation that would establish the principle that the ownership of sufficient capital to build a factory did not give individuals or corporations the right to sell poison and call it food or medicine. Responding to this issue and to public-health concerns about spoilage and fraud in urban milk and meat supplies, state legislatures began to pass laws regulating food and drugs during the 1880s. The federal government regulated food imports and exports, but had no jurisdiction over domestic food supplies until the Pure Food and Drug Act of 1906. That law regulated labeling and established testing under the Agriculture Department's Chemistry Division.

Harvey W. Wiley, the division's chief, had written the bill. Outspoken and determined, Wiley was known for uncompromising public advocacy from 1887, when he began to issue bulletins on food adulteration, until his death in 1930. He both led and represented a virtual crusade. Congress considered 190 pure-food bills between 1879 and 1906, in response to an immense number of petitions and letters; it conducted hearings on many of those bills, gathering testimony and generating extensive newspaper publicity. In 1903, the *Ladies' Home Journal* conducted a huge campaign against what editor Edward Bok called the American people's "accursed passion for self-doctoring" with patent medicines. Home economists publicized pure-food concerns in their classes; state agencies mounted displays at food expositions. The campaign heated up even more in October 1905, when *Collier's* began a series on patent medicines. Upton Sinclair's book *The Jungle* brought attention to the horrors of the meat-packing industry in February 1906, and on June 30, Theodore Roosevelt signed both the food and drug bill and the meat-inspection bill into law.

The pure-food reformers challenged the fundamental claims of the manufacturers' brands. "What is Ariosa Coffee?" a reader asked in the *New York Analyst* in 1885; this magazine published recipes, household hints, and the results of its own chemical tests. "It is roasted and glazed coffee, put up by a firm in Brooklyn, probably a Java," the magazine replied. "The fact that it is glazed makes it suspicious. Glazing is not put on for the benefit of the *consumer,* nor to hide desirable qualities." Writing in *Everybody's Magazine* a month before the bills passed, Upton Sinclair listed the numerous Armour products ruled illegal by state authorities—Armour's Shield leaf lard in Minnesota, Armour's Veribest potted ham in Pennsylvania, Armour's Star sausage in Kentucky, and Armour's Gold Brand bacon in North Dakota, among many others. Quoting a former Armour superintendent who disclosed outrageous practices at the company's plants, Sinclair demonstrated that the brand that identified the manufacturer did not necessarily guarantee purity or quality.

Led by H. J. Heinz and Frederick Pabst, many of the major branded-food manufacturers came out in favor of the legislation. Pure-food laws helped branded, packaged goods; in 1904, for example, the *Grocers' Review* commented that after some Philadelphia grocers had been arrested for selling syrup as bulk molasses, others would handle only the canned product. As Mrs. Julian Heath, the founder of the Housewives' League, explained in the *New York Times,* "All our pure food laws insist that the label is the thing. . . . Bulk goods bear no label." Furthermore, plagued by regulations that varied from state to state, manufacturers with national markets wanted a uniform federal law. And regulation of all kinds had the potential to destroy the national manufacturers' marginal competitors: small businesses with fewer resources found compliance a greater burden than did bigger ones.

Probably no aspect of Progressivism has been as thoroughly explored by historians—or as thoroughly exposed—as government regulation of business. Since the late 1960s, historical work has demonstrated the broad extent of business cooperation in and control of its own regulation during the period and the existence of a new consensus that accepted some regulation as better than none. At the same time, there was considerable conflict over the specific nature of regulation and regulatory agencies that involved arguments among groups of business-men. Opinions were divided in trade associations and in such intertrade business organizations as the National Association of Manufacturers over the relation of various kinds of regulation to foreign-market expansion, trade unionism, and banking and currency reform. "Indeed," writes historian Martin J. Sklar, "such differences divided capitalists within one and the same firm, corporation, bank, or investment banking house."

Manufacturers were hardly unanimous in the case of the Pure Food and Drug Act, or in their lobbying efforts to influence its definition. Some dairy farmers, for example, opposed the sale of oleomargarine, wanting it outlawed or labeled "imitation"; oth-ers demanded only "truth in labeling" laws that would prevent margarine from being sold as butter. Margarine manufacturers were also divided, some willing to accept accurate labeling of ingredients and others believing that it would destroy their product's ability to compete. Many manufacturers gave nominal support to the bill but opposed its specifics because they used preservatives and colorings. Some trade organizations passed resolutions; the National Wholesale Liquor Dealers' Associa-tion, the Proprietary Association of America (which represented the patent-medicine interests), and the National Food Manufac-turers' Association all went on record as opposed. The National Association of Manufacturers was divided. Its Pure Food Com-mittee lobbied for the legislation and received overwhelming support on the floor of the 1906 convention. But the organiza-tion's leadership opposed the bill, and NAM lobbyists worked to weaken it.

Even within the boundaries of the Pure Food and Drug Act as passed, there were endless obstacles to its administration. Har-vey Wiley's fate is a case in point. He continued to receive support from some pure-food reformers, who continued to agi-tate, pointing to the flaws in the act, which regulated false claims on labels but not in advertising, and which affected manufacturers but not middlemen. But manufacturers, too, continued their political activity. They lobbied his office and those of his superiors in favor of particular chemicals, complaining that an approved color made soda pop bitter or that the exclusion of oil-soluble chemicals would force them to use less effective vegetable dyes to color butter and margarine. He finally faced presidential power when he spoke out against saccharin, which Theodore Roosevelt used and wanted to defend: the president instructed the secretary of agriculture to appoint a committee of eminent chemists to review Wiley's work. The Referee Board of Consulting Scientific Experts, headed by Ira Remsen of Johns Hopkins, had only investigational and advisory powers. Nonetheless, opponents of the pure-food law challenged the board's authority, and although it was not terminated until 1915, it was

––––––––––––––––––––––––IIICIIII––––––––––––––––––––––––

Many manufacturers printed guarantees in the wake of the 1906 Pure Food and Drug Act. This one from Arbuckle, which packaged Ariosa and later Yuban coffee, made an explicit statement of the manufacturers' defense against reformers.

largely ignored, as when it too banned saccharin.

After years of fighting with his superiors, Wiley resigned in 1912, and over the following months issued public statements describing the impossibilities of administering the law. Under both the Roosevelt and the Taft administrations, the *New York Times* editorialized, "he was hampered and restrained in his efforts to save us from adulterators and poisoners. Sometimes the antagonism was active, sometimes passive, and always the pressure was kept up that finally drove him from his place." The *Grocers' Review* also sympathized: "None will regret the retirement of Dr. Wiley as much as will the retail grocers, whose interests he always guarded."

Many people would have been surprised to read of grocery trade support for Wiley and the pure-food movement because so much publicity blamed grocers for bad food practices. For decades, packaged-food manufacturers had depicted them as backward and dirty; they were said to swindle by substituting and by giving short weight, and they were accused of endangering the health of their customers by allowing bulk food to get dirty. Packaged foods, according to this line of argument, offered consumer protection, and no honest grocer who believed in pure food would sell bulk goods. Actually, few grocers who carried Uneeda Biscuits and Quaker Oats got rid of their cracker tins and oat barrels; most handled both bulk and packaged goods. Moreover, the trade eventually tired of the allegations. A 1913 *Printers' Ink* article described an advertising campaign that backfired, when the Acme Hominy Company (a pseudonym for a real packaged-food company) attempted "to create in the public's mind a clean-cut division between the sheep and the goats in the grocery business, the clean, package-hominy sheep, and the dirty, bulk-hominy goats." Enraged grocers' associations and grocery trade papers organized meetings with the manufacturer and the advertising agent, insisting that the division was not so clear.

Packages did protect food from dirt, but without stringent labeling laws they did not protect consumers from another problem. Deception in the matter of weights and measures could be perpetrated by the manufacturer who sold large boxes full of air as well as by the grocer who rested his thumb on the scale as he weighed out raisins or sugar, and reformers called for regulation of both kinds. The federal government had a constitutional responsibility to regulate weights and measures, but until the turn of the century this was interpreted as a question of creating standards—authorized models of the pound or the pint that were distributed to the states. The related consumer issues were regulated sporadically, by states and especially by cities, which maintained some control over weights and measures in public markets. In 1905, the new United States Bureau of Standards established an annual conference that brought state weights-

---

The swindling grocer as he appeared on the first page of a lithographed pamphlet, *A Tale of the Rising Sun Stove Polish.* In the ensuing three pages, Mrs. Smith goes home and gives her maid Dinah the "swindling compound," which prevents Dinah from accomplishing anything else. Fortunately a wise neighbor steps in to recommend a better product,

THE CRAFTY SHOPKEEPER.

" It's just as good !" the shopman said—he was a vile deceiver,
And Mrs. Smith, unused to guile, alas, was a believer,
And on the rascal's oily words and lying tongue depended,
And bought the swindling compound that that shopman recommended.

DONALDSON BROTHERS. FIVE POINTS. NEW YORK.

See his thumb at the scales. The old rogue thinks he's clever,
But he'll find to his cost he's been foolish,
And wish, oh, so much! when his trade throws him o'er,
He'd sold BUFFALO SOAP and been honest.

Another swindling grocer, from a trade card for Buffalo Soap.

and-measures officials together to discuss enforcement, but for the most part the matter remained a local one.

Activists in the weights-and-measures battles were inspired by and allied with pure-food advocates. At the food expositions and state and county fairs, they erected displays that showed measuring devices with false bottoms and compared correct and incorrect sizes of milk bottles and bushel baskets. Some exhibits pointed the finger at the storekeeper. A booth at the 1910 Domestic Science and Pure Food Exposition at Madison Square Garden invited fairgoers to inform on their retailers by placing comments in a box. "If you are suspicious of your tradesman," read the sign, "write your complaint and drop it here." In some localities, weights-and-measures officers carried out dramatic raids on grocery stores and stalls in public markets.

In a few places, city officials construed their charge as protecting both consumers and small retailers from violations by packaged-foods manufacturers who operated factories or sold products within their jurisdictions. These crusaders encountered in the manufacturer a more powerful obstacle than small grocers with bad scales. Speaking at the 1910 Bureau of Standards conference, a Chicago city official recounted his battle for city legislation to require packaged food to carry net weights. "I lost that bill," he told the audience. "Capital was too big. I could not stand up against the pressure. However we gave them a fight for three long years." Five years later, an officer of the Philadelphia Bureau of Weights and Measures continued to take this stance, urging a 1915 meeting of Pennsylvania weights-and-measures officials not only to inspect weights and measures, but to act "in the capacity of a detective and look to it that the purchasing public is not defrauded when they are buying package goods, or anything else."

Whether local or federal, and whether focused on retailers or manufacturers, the controversies over weights and measures and pure food raised few genuinely new issues. Mass production and the creation of national markets had increased the proportion of things people used daily that came from the realm of trade rather than from home production, and had removed the sale of the new products farther from their sources. But throughout the history of trade, sellers and buyers had argued over the quality of merchandise (especially the purity of food) and the accuracy and fairness of the seller. The pure-food and weights-and-measures movements were public versions of this ages-old contest between buyer and seller.

Controversies about branding and packaging per se, on the other hand, raised new issues. In dealing with bulk goods, the arguments over quality and fairness still took place much as they always had, between merchants and customers in public market stands or at the corner grocery, between wholesalers' salesmen and the merchants, and between the manufacturers and wholesalers. But, reformers now maintained, branded products had ended the contest, pronouncing automatic victory for the manufacturer, who by prevailing upon consumers to accept only Ivory or Campbell's could set the terms of the bargain, and who did so at high prices.

One such controversy developed around an educational campaign sponsored by the New York Mayor's Committee on Food Supply. Working with the Board of Education, this group issued more than 800,000 copies of a new circular every day beginning

IIICIIII

Seattle weights-and-measures officers pose with confiscated scales, 1917.

on October 1, 1914, to be used in every school in the city as the text for the day's talks about food. The pamphlets followed a tradition of material that home economists prepared for the poor, based on the theory that educated consumers could combat high prices. They contained detailed information about food purchasing, nutrition, weights and measures, and the expense of delivery and telephone orders; they recommended recipes for preparing cheap cuts of meat and gave instructions for reducing waste.

The January 18, 1915 circular, headed "BUY IN BULK—NOT IN PACKAGE," compared bulk and package prices for seventeen common articles. "The package looks pretty, appeals to the eye, and makes the food seem more appetizing," the text read. "Most of the packages are air-tight and dustproof, and for sanitary reasons a great many people prefer food that is done up in packages. As a matter of fact, it is possible for your grocer to keep on hand, in bulk, exactly the same foods as the packages contain, and it is also possible for him to keep them in bulk in a perfectly sanitary manner, so that dust and dirt cannot reach them. . . . Break yourself of the package habit," the pamphlet urged; "pass these pointers on to your neighbors."

Ten days later, *Printers' Ink* reprinted the pamphlet and solicited responses from the leading lights of the advertising world. Earnest Elmo Calkins addressed an open letter to the Food Supply Committee's chairman, using vinegar as an illustration. "The reason that such vinegar costs more than the bulk vinegar is not entirely due to the package, although, of course, the cost of the package must be considered," he wrote, "but it is more largely due to the fact that it is a much better vinegar and is the only vinegar fit for human consumption." Shredded Wheat's Truman A. DeWeese protested the committee's right "to injure or destroy any legitimate industry through the medium of public schools." Praising sanitary packages, he acclaimed the virtues of his company's product, a processed food that housewives could not make at home. Nathan Musher of the Pompeian olive oil company articulated the advertising industry's primary defense, insisting that because advertising increased production volumes it reduced costs, and that therefore consumers paid less for advertised products, not more.

Printers' Ink also published a response from Mrs. Julian Heath, whose Housewives' League had passed a resolution protesting the Food Supply Committee's recommendation of bulk goods. Mrs. Heath, at one time the chair of the Jacob Riis Settlement House and of the New York City Federation of Women's Clubs' home economics department, had started the Housewives' League three years before, in December 1911. The league's "principal object," the *New York Times* reported when it began, "is to have enforced the health laws regarding sanitary conditions, the pure food laws, and the giving of fair weight. This is to be accomplished not so much by appealing to the departments charged with enforcing the law but by making every woman an inspector." Members would meet in neighborhood groups to compare conditions at nearby stores.

A month later, in the first of three long interviews published in the Sunday *Times* during the league's lifetime, Mrs. Heath took the side of the buyer against sellers of all kinds. She complained that grocers handled bulk foods badly, by overcharging, failing to give fair weight, and allowing open bins to collect dirt and insects. "It would be impossible to estimate the number of good lives which have been destroyed by grocers' dirty hands; by the fingers of the candy store girl who keeps her pencil in her hair and handles candies with the fingers which write checks with it," she declared. At the same time, Mrs. Heath came out against packaged goods for their high cost. She had weighed one breakfast cereal, for example, and discovered that it cost as much as meat. "But, you see," she told the *Times* reporter, "we women have not been buying that cereal by the pound; we have bought it by the package. That was a clever scheme the manufacturers and retailers learned long ago. They can give us short weight without any kind of danger that we'll criticise them if they put it in a fancy box, paste a red label on it, and sell it by the package, not the pound."

During the ensuing three years, Mrs. Heath retreated from this position. An article she published in the *Ladies' Home Journal* in February 1913 stressed private action, not public policy, and bore a title—"How Housewives Waste Money"—that suggested home economics more than consumer advocacy and that blamed consumers themselves for high prices. Here Mrs. Heath urged women not to waste meat trimmings and to buy in quantity. She warned them against grocers using false weights and measures and decried telephone ordering, delivery, and charge accounts. But now she was silent on the subject of bulk and packaged goods. Addressing a professional audience in the American Academy of Political and Social Science's *Annals*, she blamed consumers even for adulterated foods: they provided a market.

In November of 1914, the Sunday *Times* published another long interview, in which Mrs. Heath claimed 750,000 members and described the league's new headquarters and its plan for its own pier in Atlantic City. Much of the membership came from the league's alliances with other groups that joined en masse; the money for the headquarters came from fees paid by a new class of member, the manufacturers. Mrs. Heath justified this policy change by echoing Ellen Richards's historical argument about the trend away from home production, but adding a new twist. "The wonderful thing to me," she told the interviewer, "has been the frankness with which women have admitted that they no longer are competent housewives and the energy with which they have set to work to remedy the fault. In three years they have achieved the closest and most salutary touch with the manufacturers who have taken their places as providers for the family table." Tradesmen and manufacturers had been forced to work with the league, but were coming to understand the benefits of doing so. Cooperation would wipe out misunderstandings. "We housewives are learning," Mrs. Heath asserted, "that we don't have to fight the manufacturers of or dealers in impure food. That was destructive. The constructive and far more effective course is to co-operate."

Here and in the long interview that appeared in the Sunday *New York Times Magazine* about three months later, where Mrs. Heath responded to the Mayor's Food Supply Committee, she described her change of mind. "I, too, talked scornfully of the modern housewife and her 'package habit,' " she acknowledged. "I said women were . . . paying principally for fancy labels and patent cans, and getting a very little nutriment thrown in. I thought I was perfectly right. I felt myself to be embarking on a holy war." Over the years, however, she had come to believe that the only way women could be certain of what they bought was to buy package goods. The trademark, she now proclaimed, was the guarantee of the housewife's protection.

The extent of Mrs. Heath's cooperation with manufacturers was revealed a year later, when dissident league members brought legal charges against her, disputing her membership claims, asking for financial statements, and challenging the organizational structure for perpetuating a "dynasty" of leaders. The legal proceedings further questioned the organization's policies about product endorsement through advertisements in the league magazine and through manufacturers' displays, which paid the rent on the new headquarters. At the state attorney general's hearings, representatives from the Diamond Match Company and the Southern Cottonseed Oil Company testified about their business relationships with the league; those from the Royal Baking Powder Company and the Franco-American Food and Soup companies refused to testify, as did Mrs. Heath and the other league officers. In May 1916, the attorney general's office concluded the hearings with a severe criticism of the league's management but dismissed the legal charges. It reopened the investigation two years later, however, and ordered Mrs. Heath to resign; she refused to do so, and the state did not pursue the matter. In 1919, the city's commissioner of markets responded to an attack from Mrs. Heath by calling the Housewives' League "a dead organization, existing only on paper."

The Housewives' League cooperated with manufacturers in

political affairs at least as early as February 1914, when it sent Christine Frederick to Washington to testify in favor of retail price maintenance, an issue of paramount importance to the manufacturers of branded goods. A consulting editor of the *Ladies' Home Journal,* Frederick promoted the use of branded products throughout her career as the principal theorist of household efficiency. She was married to J. George Frederick, then the editor of *Advertising and Selling,* and she had founded the League of Advertising Women in 1912. "I am here as a consumer," she nonetheless told the House Judiciary Committee's hearings on trust legislation, "and hold no brief for either dealer or manufacturer."

Retail price maintenance, the policy Frederick supported, was a logical expression of the power that brands gave manufacturers. The bargain over price, too, was as old as trade itself, but under time-honored conditions of trade, the producer who sold to a middleman gave up not only title to the goods but any right to govern the sale that the middleman made to a third party. With the ascendancy of branded goods, however, the manufacturers—who invested not only in the equipment to produce Uneeda Biscuits or Kodak cameras but also in the apparatus for marketing them—had an intense interest in what happened to their goods after they sold them. Calling it "fair trade," manufacturers adopted price maintenance, a policy of setting prices not only to their own customers, the wholesalers, but also to retailers and consumers, sometimes by printing a price on the package.

Retail price maintenance established pricing not as the outcome of a series of bargains and negotiations—between customer and merchant, merchant and wholesaler, wholesaler and producer—but as part of the marketing process. Manufacturers would set prices, and the most sophisticated ones would do so with respect to targeted market segments, creating lines of competing but differently priced products, like Ivory and Star or Yuban and Ariosa. The price of Kellogg's corn flakes would not be determined simply by the costs of production or by bargains between Kellogg and its wholesaler customers, but by marketing decisions about the product's status with respect to its other products and those of its competitors. Those decisions could be undermined by price-cutters: low prices on Ivory soap at the chain drug store could suggest to consumers that the product was not worth the price that other merchants charged.

Manufacturers therefore used retail price maintenance as a weapon in the war against the mass retailers. Their opponents regarded it as an unfair weapon and called it "price-fixing"; this term had been in common use for some time, applied to railroad rates and the prices of industrial commodities that were fixed by trusts, monopolies, conspiracies, and the specific kinds of combinations made illegal by the Sherman Antitrust Act of 1890. The legal battle over retail price maintenance took the form of a series of cases between manufacturers and distributors that addressed questions about the rights attaching to the ownership of specific assets: patents and trademarks. The political battle joined issues that went far beyond those assets and even beyond retail trade, raising the more general Progressive Era issues about big business, the rights of capital ownership, and the nature of competition. During the decades after the Sherman Act, few people denied that unfair competition should be outlawed; by 1909, many agreed that the act did not effectively do so. There was, however, considerable controversy about what was unfair. Over the next five years, retail price maintenance, like other business policies that contributed to that controversy, became the subject of numerous bills in Congress and sundry congressional hearings.

At one time, Christine Frederick explained at one of those hearings, "I thought that the best way to do my family marketing was to ask the dealer his price and then Jew him down. That, I am told, was the attitude of all consumers in this country 50 years ago. This condition existed because at that time all dealers and merchants overpriced their articles, and the shrewd buyer was the only one who could get the best trade or bargain, after hours of talk and discussion." These "Asiatic methods" had been replaced by the one-price plan and by branded merchandise, for which manufacturers set fair prices with fair profits, she declared. Price-cutting, not retail price maintenance, created unfair competition. "When a dealer offers me three cans of Campbell's tomato soup for a quarter," Frederick told the legislators, "I know at once that it is simply a bait to lure or induce me to enter the store not only to buy the three cans of Campbell's tomato soup, but other untrademarked and unstandardized articles which that store sells." Department stores and chains, she sneered, needed "other reputations than their own to draw a crowd."

Frederick extolled the importance of small dealers, claiming that between 90 and 98 percent of them favored price maintenance. Indeed, many retailers' organizations—and presumably many of their members—did support the policy, which had become a central aspect of the alliance between manufacturers and small retailers. Unless a bar of Ivory soap or a box of Kellogg's corn flakes cost the same at the corner store as at the A & P, the personal service that small retailers offered was threatened. "Staples like bread, sugar, tea, thread, elastic, tape, pins, buttons, etc., must be bought every day," Frederick explained. "To whom can we turn for instant service, for considerate and personal service, but to the small dealer around the corner to whom our trade means a great deal?" She chided the folly "of hundreds of women who spend half a day, 6,000 calories of energy, and 10 cents in car fare to run down town to take advantage of a cut price—such as a 25-cent toothbrush selling for 19 cents. Here is economic waste for you."

Such attempts to describe retail price maintenance as a consumer position never worked. The lower-priced cans of soup were indeed bait, but nobody could explain why not to take them, precisely because Campbell's and other manufacturers had standardized their products, making every can of tomato soup exactly like every other one. "The cost to the consumer," Harvard's Paul Cherington wrote, "is the one argument which still resists the logic and the skill of the fixed-price advocates."

Perhaps consumers could be persuaded otherwise, he suggested, but most were "very apt to feel that if the price cutter
is so clever that he can profitably deliver the goods at a lower
price, or so stupid that he is willing to sell them at a loss, the
result to him, as a consumer, is much the same. And thoughtful,
indeed, is the consumer who turns his back on these savings,
taxing himself, by that much, to save his less able, or less foolish,
local storekeeper from annihilation." As historian Daniel Pope
writes, "It was quite difficult, if not impossible, to persuade
consumers that merchants needed to be protected by law from
offering them lower prices."

Testifying to the Judiciary Committee in the middle of a federal case testing the Kellogg Toasted Corn Flake Company's
price-maintenance plan, W. K. Kellogg explained the manufacturers' point of view: "We consider it is no hardship to any one
to pay, we will say, 10 cents for a package of our product, for
the reason if he does not want our kind there are many others
that can be had at less money." His company sold only to wholesalers and it set both the price they were to charge retailers and
the ultimate consumer price. Neither policy had eliminated
competition, Kellogg maintained, in response to the fundamental charge that price maintenance was "price-fixing," operating
in restraint of free trade. Competition had always been brisk in
the corn-flake business, he declared, comprising 107 other
brands over the years.

By this time, the Kellogg company was a leading participant
in the price-maintenance controversy. Five years before, in
1909, it had announced a new set of terms for its relationships
with the grocery trade, which it called the "Square Deal," a term
familiar since the 1904 presidential campaign as a description of
Theodore Roosevelt's trustbusting policies. The company's advertisement in the July *American Grocer* revealed its intent: "The
average grocer buys on just as favorable terms as Department
Stores, Chain Stores, Buying Exchanges, Mail-order Houses,
etc." Kellogg would sell every case at the same price, whether
the purchaser bought one case or many. It would offer neither

Four Points

of the

Square Deal Policy

**BEST SELLER
ON THE MARKET**

**PROFITS SURE
AND CONTINUOUS**

W. K. Kellogg

Kellogg Toasted Corn Flake Co.

Battle Creek, Mich.

Kellogg's advertisement in the *Grocers' Review,* November 1909.

price-promotion deals to jobbers and retailers, nor premiums to their customers. "Any factor in the trade not willing to observe this scale of prices is requested not to handle the goods," the company declared in its price announcement. Any merchant accused of violating the company's terms would be asked to provide "a certificate, to be verified by his oath and the oath of the salesman making the sale"; Kellogg would construe refusal to swear to its policies as reason to decline further orders.

However old-fashioned its insistence on oaths, Kellogg was a new company in the new and highly profitable breakfast-food industry, not constrained by old relationships or ways of doing business. It had grown fast since incorporating in 1906, and by 1909 could make demands on the trade and offer itself as a powerful ally to small retailers concerned about competition from mass merchandisers. Over the next six years, Kellogg's legal defense of its policies would establish its leadership among manufacturers defending the traditional distribution system. Those manufacturers arranged a truce with retailers and wholesalers. The manufacturers would refuse to sell advertised goods to price-cutters and would lead both the legal and political struggles against the mass distributors. In exchange, the retailers and wholesalers would stop practicing substitution and pushing private brands.

Kellogg had some unspoken reasons for the new policy. Its packaging had not been perfected; the company had to instruct consumers to "heat for a moment in an open oven to restore crispness." Large stocks had to be avoided, and without quantity prices, premiums, or free deals, neither wholesalers nor retailers would have an incentive to build them up. Although it relied on wholesalers ("because they work cheap," Kellogg's sales manager Andrew Ross explained in testimony to the United States Bureau of Corporations), the company operated its own warehouses around the country to facilitate deliveries and keep corn flakes fresh.

Companies whose reputations relied less on keeping fresh stock had less reason for such stringent policies. Few manufacturers went as far as Kellogg in battling mass distributors; most continued to give quantity prices, rebates, and free deals even if they tried to fix retail prices. "There is a strong feeling abroad in the trade that the quantity price will prevail, and that Kellogg's fixed price policy is unnatural," a *Printers' Ink* writer maintained in 1910, the year after the Square Deal went into effect. The Diamond Match Company sold through jobbers and insisted on price maintenance, but gave free cases when a certain quantity was ordered. Babbitt Soap charged different prices for orders of different sizes. The N. K. Fairbank soap company gave quantity prices but not on more than a carload, while Kellogg's competitor Post gave rebates, but not on orders totaling more than twenty-five cases.

Similarly, manufacturer opinion differed on retail price main-

W. K. Kellogg's Corner

Message No. 3.

Backing Up the Dealer

THE manufacturer who has built his business on merit, has the confidence of consumer and dealer alike.

To maintain the popularity of his brand he must not only keep up the quality but he must give a *square deal* to both the trade and the public.

In maintaining the highest quality at a fair price he is giving full value to the consumer—he must give equal opportunities to each individual—big or little—in the trade.

No special favorites—no schemes or rebates—no premiums to burden the grocer and deceive the public. These are features of the Kellogg policy that have given Kellogg's Toasted Corn Flakes equal popularity with dealer and consumer and the largest sale of any cereal in the world.

The Genuine has this Signature

W. K. Kellogg

Kellogg's TOASTED CORN FLAKES
NONE GENUINE WITHOUT THIS SIGNATURE
W. K. Kellogg
KELLOGG TOASTED CORN FLAKE CO.
BATTLE CREEK, MICH.
The sweet heart of the corn

Kellogg described its trade policies to consumers in a series of 1910 advertisements. This one was published in the *Saturday Evening Post*.

‑IIICƆIII‑

KELLOGG'S SQUARE DEALER

Touching Every Base ¹¹

SCORE is tied. The bases are full and two men are out.

The pinch hitter comes to bat. Breathless silence reigns in the grand stand.

From the coaching line comes the raucous call of the manager:

"Don't forget to touch every base!"

We are all infielders in the Big League of Business, where the score is always close, and the world is in the grand stand looking on.

Nemesis is umpire, and the manufacturer, wholesaler, and retailer, respectively, hold down first, sec‑

One company explanation of the Square Deal employed the metaphor of another square, the baseball diamond. In the "Big League of Business," according to the house organ *Kellogg's Square Dealer,* 1912, "every product entered in the game is striving . . . to reach the consumer and the home plate." The manufacturers played first base, the wholesaler (here wearing the capitalist top hat) played second, and the retailer played third. The rules required runners to touch all the bases, but some players cut corners. Many products died at third. And the whole game suffered from bad teamwork in the infield: players attempted to play two or more positions at the same time. The company claimed that its policies allowed all of them to play their own positions. "Quit Scrapping—Play Ball!" the *Square Dealer* urged.

‑IIICƆIII‑

tenance. Franco-American, Royal Baking Powder, Onyx Hosiery, Eberhard Faber, and Yale Lock did not maintain prices; Beech-Nut, Jap-a-lac Varnish, Smith and Wesson, and Eastman Kodak did. As in so many issues of trade policy during a period of rapid change, opinion differed among executives for these manufacturers. Those who supported price maintenance believed that pricing was an essential part of marketing and that they could maintain their power with respect to the mass distributors by preventing price-cutting. They wanted to be able to control the conditions under which the products they made, the products that bore their trademarks, would be sold to consumers—despite the fact that they usually gave up ownership of the goods by selling them to wholesalers. Those who sold their products without insisting on setting the retail price believed that such control was superfluous or too difficult to enforce.

The legal question revolved around whether retail price maintenance constituted unfair competition and restraint of trade. By 1910, the courts established the principle that patent holders like the Ingersoll watch company and the Victor Talking Machine Company could dictate some of the conditions of sale of their goods. "Uncle Sam, while a bitter enemy of monopoly in general, is a hefty friend of the holder of a patent," a *Printers' Ink* writer explained. Like manufacturers of copyrighted computer software seventy-five years later, patent holders attempted to protect their goods with licenses stating that they were sold subject to certain conditions. Gillette, for example, used the license plan to obtain injunctions against price-cutters, including dealers who bought razors with United Cigar Stores coupons to sell at a cut price. Even the package of razor blades bore a license that set the price, stated that the blades could be used only with Gillette razors, and insisted that they not be resharpened. (The company could enforce the price provisions, but millions of people got blades resharpened through druggists and hardware dealers.)

Then, by a 7 to 1 decision in 1911, the Supreme Court ruled retail price maintenance illegal in *Dr. Miles Medical Co. v. John D.*

Park & Sons Co. Dr. Miles sold its trademarked elixir through 400 wholesalers and 25,000 retailers. It required jobbers to sell on consignment to a stated list of agents, and demanded that both jobbers and retailers sign contracts stating that they would not undersell the company's fixed price. "The agreements are designed to maintain prices," the Court explained in its ruling against the plan, "after the complainant [Dr. Miles] has parted with the title to the articles, and to prevent competition among those who trade in them." In effect, then, the contracts created a combination to prevent competition. Dr. Miles "having sold its product at prices satisfactory to itself, the public is entitled to whatever advantage may be derived from competition in the subsequent traffic." As *Printers' Ink* had warned in a discussion of the case a year before the decision, the *Dr. Miles* case sounded "a death knell" for retail price maintenance for manufacturers using jobbers. The magazine had predicted that such a decision would exacerbate the tendency of manufacturers to deal directly with retailers instead.

The *American Grocer* reported that W. K. Kellogg was unconcerned about the *Miles* decision. "It is my understanding that any manufacturer has an absolute right to sell goods to whomsoever he chooses, and on whatever terms he may choose," he responded. Insisting that price maintenance was still legal, he announced that he would be willing to make Kellogg's a test case. Other manufacturers of unpatented goods had invented ingenious ways to maintain prices: Colgate used spies to find price-cutters' sources; Procter and Gamble gave an extra discount to dealers who maintained the fixed price on Ivory. Now Kellogg instituted a plan that one *Printers' Ink* writer called the "most ingenious of all."

Following a 1912 Supreme Court case that upheld the A. B. Dick Company's right to govern the sales of its patented mimeograph machines and supplies by posting a notice on the machine, Kellogg began to print a notice on the corn-flakes box. It stated that the package was patented and that retailing it at less than ten cents would infringe on Kellogg's patent rights and

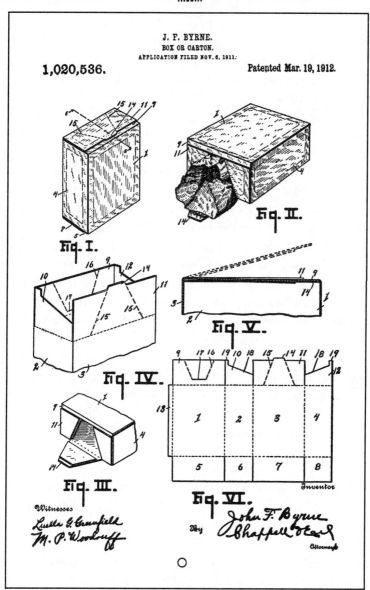

Kellogg claimed to be able to set retail prices as a patent holder, on the basis of this carton. The patent, obtained by J. F. Byrne of Battle Creek, was assigned to the company.

"render the vendor liable to prosecution." A few months later, the company secured an injunction against a price-cutting Michigan grocer. "The Kellogg Company are deserving of warm praise for the energy and good sense they are displaying in pioneering this matter," wrote the *Grocers' Magazine* in its report on the injunction.

Before the year was out, the government sued Kellogg, claiming in court on December 26, 1912, that the patented carton could offer the product no legal protection. "The case is regarded by the Government as of vast importance," the *New York Times* reported. "Said carton was not in fact patentable," read the complaint; all of its features had long been in use. People bought the product, not the carton, the government maintained, the "purchase of the carton being a mere incident in the contract of sale." Kellogg parted with title to the goods and the legal power to set prices when it sold cartons and their contents to jobbers. The company was using the carton, the government concluded, "as a mere subterfuge and device" to get around the law.

W. K. Kellogg, about to embark on an ocean voyage, issued a statement expressing surprise that the government had brought suit, and got on the boat. "The things we aimed to accomplish by our selling plan," he declared, "are the very things for which we understood the Sherman and other conspiracy laws were designed—the protection of the consumer and small dealer in the same condition of opportunity enjoyed by 'trusts' and big buyers." In the pages of *Printers' Ink,* the vice-president of the George Batten advertising agency expressed surprise as well. He reported that the Justice Department had contacted Kellogg three months earlier about a test case but the company had declined. Kellogg, he explained, provided a good test of price maintenance under the Sherman Act because there was no conspiracy and no collusion. The company did not even make jobbers and retailers sign legal contracts, though they had made them take oaths.

Within three weeks, the company sent a letter to its wholesalers, using the suit as an occasion to sell more cereal. "Here we are confronted with a Government suit," the letter read. "If we fight it means a big expense; if we lose, we will be no worse off than if we hadn't fought at all—than if we yielded gracefully without contest. If we win, we will get a lot of glory, but will we sell any more corn flakes?" The jobbers could show their support for Kellogg's defense of traditional distribution by doing just that. Kellogg asked them to send sales-boosting letters to their salesmen and enclosed the text of a suggested one that urged salesmen to push the product to retailers.

R. O. Eastman, the editor of *Kellogg's Square Dealer,* the company house organ, appealed to the advertising trade in *Printers' Ink.* National advertising itself was on trial, he claimed. The issue was not "price-fixing," he stressed, but *"price maintenance."* The whole question had arisen out of a new order of merchandising, itself the result of the new force of national advertising. "The national advertiser to-day in actuality—not merely in effect—sells his goods by means of the printed message direct to the consumer," Eastman maintained, "and as the *seller* of the goods he has and must have the natural prerogative of establishing the price."

The Supreme Court continued to sound the death knell for retail price maintenance. In 1913, in *Bauer v. O'Donnell* (called the Sanatogen case, after the medicine involved), the Court denied manufacturers the right to set resale prices on patented goods as well as on those that were simply trademarked. Manufacturers responded by moving out of the legal arena and into the political one. They mobilized small retailers and their organizations into active support for legislation that would make price maintenance legal, in what historian Thomas K. McCraw (who describes the movement as a retailers' fight) has called "one of the longest, most relentless, and best organized business lobbying efforts in American history." The American Fair Trade League, controlled by manufacturers of branded, advertised products, led the legislative battle. Legislation permitting price maintenance was first introduced in Congress in 1914; the

House Committee on Interstate and Foreign Commerce held hearings for the next three years, with testimony from a variety of organizations and experts.

National manufacturers stayed in the background of the supporting forces, while mass retailers led the attacks on the legislation. Some critics understood the fight to be between one kind of big business and another; Congressman Alben Barkley of Kentucky, for example, echoed merchants' fears that they would become "simply the agent of the manufacturer to do what the manufacturer tells [them] to do" and would be able to sell only on the manufacturer's terms. But retailers' trade journals uniformly endorsed retail price maintenance, and their organizations passed resolutions asking manufacturers to fix prices. As a result, the Fair Trade League's secretary told the 1915 annual meeting: "We have been able to carry it so far as a retailers' fight and you won't hear in Washington a suggestion that this is a manufacturers' fight. The retailers have been in evidence and they are doing the obvious work, the work that is on the surface." Manufacturers like Eastman Kodak, Waterman, Kellogg, and the Hamilton Watch Company packed questionnaires into cases of their goods and polled their dealers to determine overwhelming support for the manufacturers' leadership, at least among those who sent in responses.

Louis Brandeis, the famous "People's Lawyer," spearheaded the public relations campaign. Publishing in *Harper's Weekly* and other popular magazines, Brandeis set the issue historically, arguing for the progress represented by trademarked goods in one-price stores. Like Christine Frederick, he explained that cut prices were bait—"misleaders," he said they should be called, instead of "leaders." An ardent opponent of bigness, Brandeis preferred to support the manufacturers, many of which were still relatively small, rather than "capitalistic combinations," the mass distributors like Sears and Woolworth's. "Already the displacement of the small independent business man by the huge corporation with its myriad of employees, its absentee ownership, and its financier control, presents a grave danger to our democracy," he wrote. By cutting prices, "far-seeing organized capital secures . . . the cooperation of the short-sighted unorganized consumer to his own undoing. Thoughtless or weak, he yields to the temptation of trifling immediate gain; and selling his birthright for a mess of pottage, becomes himself an instrument of monopoly." Brandeis echoed the sentiments of muckrakers like Charles Edward Russell, whose 1908 attack on the Tobacco Trust had focused in part on the United Cigar Stores and the demise of the independent tobacconist.

Brandeis served as Woodrow Wilson's adviser during the debates surrounding the drafting of the 1914 Clayton Antitrust Act, which amended the Sherman Act. Section 2 of the new law specifically permitted quantity prices but said nothing about retail price maintenance, leaving the question in the courts. The first price-maintenance case to be decided under the Clayton Act was the suit brought by the A & P against Cream of Wheat for refusing to fill its orders because the chain cut prices. The federal district court ruled for Cream of Wheat, stressing that the company did not manufacture a unique substance called Cream of Wheat but bought a commodity, wheat middlings, and packaged it with its trademark. The company might like to fix prices, the court maintained, but it had no power of enforcement, since anybody else could buy and sell wheat middlings. Cream of Wheat could only refuse to sell, and that refusal was perfectly legal. Judge Lacombe of the circuit court of appeals agreed. Neither the Sherman Act nor the Clayton Act nor any Supreme Court decision up to that time, he explained, had changed "the law that a trader might reject the offer of a proposing buyer for any reason that appealed to him; it might be because he did not like the other's business methods, or because he had some personal difference with him political, racial or social."

In the Kellogg case, the question at issue was not whether Kellogg could refuse to sell to a chain store, but whether it could govern its jobber customers' sales of its product to a third party, the retailer, and that party's sales to a fourth party, the consumer, on the basis of its patented package. In April 1915, the United States Circuit Court of Appeals in Detroit found in favor of the government. The company began an appeal, but withdrew its opposition in October. "The history of the case and the arguments show that the Kellogg Company considered it hopeless to contend that it was not a conspirator in restraint of trade," the *New York Times* explained in an editorial sympathetic to Kellogg. "This is a burning question. There are bills upon it pending in Congress, one of them making it a felony to cut prices and another making it legal to fix prices. . . . The opinions of traders are as divided as those of the courts. . . . What is the principle to simplify the tangle?"

No principle was ever conclusively established. "If the standardization of prices and maintenance of resale prices is sound economically it will survive and the law will ultimately conform to the economic necessity, because law is nothing but crystallizing public opinion," a Chicago patent lawyer wrote in 1914. But public opinion did not crystallize. The Miller-Tydings Act of 1937 gave federal sanction to price maintenance, but it was repealed in 1976, and the series of court cases that began before *Dr. Miles* had not ended in 1988, when a Supreme Court decision concerning a manufacturer refusing to sell to a discounter involved not Cream of Wheat but Sharp Electronics, not the A & P but a Houston discount electronics retailer.

Likewise, the battle over quantity discounts to mass merchandisers continues; now independent bookstores fight B. Dalton and Crown Books in court, charging that publishers give the chains volume discounts and allow them to influence publishing decisions. Wholesalers, for the most part, have lost their clout, as so many observers believed they would; like Heinz and Swift then, most manufacturers now either have their own selling forces or use brokers who provide them direct services. Chain-store systems have continued to grow, and merchandising based on high turnover characterizes K-Mart as it did the cash-and-carry A & P. Meanwhile, the enduring power struggles and political issues result from conflicts inherent in a system where manufacturers create relationships with consumers through branding and advertising but sell their products through wholesalers and retailers.

Although the struggle between manufacturers and mass retailers continues, and although a handful of the largest retailers still stand with the major consumer-goods manufacturers on the lists of the biggest American corporations, the manufacturers may be said to have won the turn-of-the-century battle. Even beyond the financial resources that enabled them to engage in extended court cases in defense of their policies, they held the power in their industries by virtue of their advertised trademarks. Over the course of the twentieth century, those trademarks have become even more powerful; now, in department stores and discount houses as in supermarkets, brand-name goods act as drawing cards. And beyond those forms of influence, the manufacturers and their marketing consultants have triumphed by creating the cultural definition of progress. At the turn of the century, they offered Americans their versions of a society that proceeded from worse to better—from bulk goods to packaged ones, from the "dip, dip, dip" of the steel pen to the take-anywhere fountain pen, from the barbershop and the photography studio to the Gillette and the Kodak. Progress would be characterized by an abundance of consumer goods, as up-to-date as tomorrow.

CHAPTER 9

EPILOGUE

THE MARKETING TECHNIQUES DEVELOPED FOR CRISCO, SAPOLIO, and other turn-of-the-century products are universal today. Airline frequent-flyer programs echo Quaker Oats premium promotions; like spoons and china packed in the cereal boxes, the "miles" that travelers "earn" are intended to induce brand loyalty. Manufacturers from Maytag to Maxwell House produce more than one brand of their products and segment their markets by class, as Arbuckle did with Ariosa and Yuban. Companies in many industries have adopted the techniques of branded distribution that create direct relationships with consumers. Airline flight attendants, franchised day-care operators, and employees of temporary-help agencies offer branded services, their personal demeanor advertised as part of the company image. Brand-named fresh chicken and mushrooms have joined branded bacon and lemons. Now displayed even on our bodies, the brand has become a statement about consumers themselves, a representation of tastes and life-styles, of status in the market.

Few consumers are familiar with either production or distribution processes; few consider their consumption choices as matters of cultural or political importance. The marketplace is an arena of everyday life that most people accept uncritically—

though perhaps sardonically—and think about as little as possible. Consumption is work; the people who do it want to shop in attractive and comfortable surroundings. They do not want to stand in line at the cash register. Juggling the demands of jobs, families, social life, and household management is hard enough; we want to save time and to reduce the incessant planning that getting through the day seems to demand. Decisions in the store require another kind of juggling, a constant attempt to strike balances among attributes of the products and of our lives: prices and budgets; durability and safety; convenience; styles, colors, flavors, and scents; and our hopes of pleasing other household members who will use the things we buy.

Comparing products in the aisles of supermarkets and discount stores, modern consumers stand apart from the social relationships that structure the shopping environment. Store managers negotiate end-of-aisle displays with manufacturers' salesmen; sales forces get pep talks from their managers and bring information back from the stores; industry-wide trade conventions bring competing manufacturers' representatives together; hierarchical management structures and project-oriented working teams explore product ideas. Consumers buy what is on the shelves. We get our credit from the bank, not the merchant. A favorite cashier may enliven the day, but when she talks about products and prices she does so as a fellow consumer, not as a link in the chain of distribution. We live, in other words, in the world of goods created by the historical processes described in this book.

Manufacturers have for a century worked to produce merchandise that guarantees satisfaction; people who like products will buy them again and recommend them to their friends. Few of those products have been completely useless goods foisted upon an unwilling populace. Successful products have offered benefits that people were willing to pay for: many saved considerable labor and time in household tasks, extended the range of people's activities and knowledge beyond their immediate neighborhoods, or filled their newly found leisure time with amusement or pleasure. Consumer preference—while hardly the sole component of market-making in a system of production by private firms motivated by profit—does play its part.

Some of the satisfactions that consumer products offer, however, are limited, even trivial. With extensive testing, manufacturers develop laundry-detergent perfumes that people like; they bring change and variety to household work by introducing new colors of dishwashing liquid. In a culture pervaded by product images—amalgams of feelings derived from products, from other products like them, from the market segments they are directed to, from advertisements and label design—particular purchases actually do contribute to individuals' self-esteem. Advertisements suggest that while individuality is to be assembled from standardized goods, people who buy the same car or deodorant are the same kind of people, and consumers must therefore attune themselves to the connotations of the goods they buy and use. In this context the color of dishwashing detergent and the packaging of toothpaste become important matters. Unlike the issues that arise in the perplexing realms of personal and political life, these are easy to solve: buy the green one, buy the white one.

Since Vance Packard published *The Hidden Persuaders* in 1957, Americans have become curiously comfortable with the idea that advertising manipulates them. Packard's book, an attack on the field of motivational research, raised explicitly moral issues about the means and ends of that manipulation: encouraging impulsive buying, wasting natural resources, exploiting secret desires and sexual sensitivities for commercial purposes, and extending commercial models for control to political situations. His moral tone now seems old-fashioned.

The manipulation issue diverts attention from far more serious questions of power. Marketers are not Svengalis on Madison Avenue; they achieve influence by perceiving cultural change as much as by attempting to create it. Many successful products attest to their ability to influence consumer behavior; many failures attest to their inability to control it. More important, although twentieth-century rhetoric has conflated democracy with an abundance of consumer goods, the fundamental decisions about production are made on a one dollar–one vote basis. Poor people are disenfranchised; in a culture of individuals who define themselves through products and product images, they hardly rate as people. Wealthy investors and managers make decisions directly; as consumers, their choices influence production out of proportion to their numbers because they have more purchasing power.

In neoclassical economic theory, decisions about what and how much to produce are made by the market, which operates—by definition—for the benefit of the consumer. In reality, those decisions are made by managers who ask a number of questions for the benefit of their companies. Is there a market, or can one be created? Can the product generate profits that can be returned to investors at rates competitive with the other things they can do with their money? Will it sell enough to take a share of the market from the competition? Markets, in the words of sociologist Harrison White, "are tangible cliques of producers observing each other. Pressure from the buyer side creates a mirror in which producers see themselves, not consumers." Looking in that mirror, managers imagine markets as pies cut up into shares, not as historically evolving sets of relationships between producers and consumers.

At the end of the twentieth century, the fundamental concepts of manufacturer-created demand and marketing-driven production that underlie most production decisions face an unprecedented challenge. During the years it took to research and write this book, industrial catastrophes in the Rhine River and at Chernobyl and Bhopal, a garbage-laden barge roaming American waterways in search of a dumping ground, ocean beaches covered with medical waste, and the persistent everyday destruction of the rain forests, the ozone layer, and other major elements of the planetary ecosystem have called into question the central ideas underlying production decisions. In the broadest sense, these issues test an economy and a culture founded

on the rights of individual corporations and consumers to make
and buy things without regard to long-term implications.

Like King Gillette, urged by the bottle-cap inventor to make
his fortune by creating a disposable product, modern manufacturers concentrate on the growth and profitability of their firms.
On a systemic level, economic growth through marketing-driven
production is fueled by waste: extravagant packaging, disposa-
bles, planned obsolescence and styling changes that create markets for replacement products. When corporate researchers
develop ways to expand the volume of paper towels or corn
flakes so they will take up more shelf space and increase market
share, the distribution process uses more packaging materials,
more trucks, more petroleum, more supermarket and warehouse space and labor, and more shopping bags, and it creates
more road congestion and more air pollution. The overall goal
of the marketing process remains to "grow the market," however that may be done: with new products or new packaging, by
expanding the market geographically or by getting people to
use more of an existing product. Prodded by regulators or irate
citizen groups, some individual manufacturers may alleviate industrial pollution. But the sources of crisis go well beyond the
need for pollution controls.

The significance of the historical process of market creation
described in this book lies in its location at the intersection of
public and private life. The ecological consequences of unlim-
ited market creation demand a public discourse about matters
generally considered private: the things people buy and use
every day, the ways they spend their time, the ways they perceive
their needs. Although personal, our buying habits are not
wholly private: they have public sources and public consequences. Indeed, their privacy is a recent historical construct;
neighborhood retailers once knew their customers very well and
influenced their consumption choices.

The mythology of consumption—expounded by writers from
Adam Smith to David Ogilvy and Daniel Boorstin—insists that
consumers are kings and queens, that industry exists to serve us.

Indeed, humble people do exercise choices and enjoy comforts available only to royalty in previous centuries. Freed from the backbreaking and unending toil of staying warm and clean and fed, we have reason to celebrate human ingenuity at the end of the twentieth century as at its beginning. But a belief in progress is more difficult to sustain in the face of environmental destruction, of market segmentation that codifies increasing class distinctions, and of a consumer culture that itself breeds constant discontent, depending always on individuals wanting more. Despite shopping malls full of things to buy, we are denied satisfactions that we identify—and romanticize—in our own past and in the activities of other human cultures: a sense of community, meaningful work, and time not consumed by getting and spending.

In advertisements, in the cultural attitudes they represent and stimulate, and in the habits of daily life, consumer products have embodied progress and promised convenient solutions to problems throughout the twentieth century. They have provided satisfactions and pastimes that have diverted people from the political arena. But there are no convenient solutions to the environmental challenge. These issues require new kinds of planning of matters that should not be left to private industrial firms to settle in their own interests, and new policies and strategies for everybody—consumers, factory managers, and governments around the world. Those new strategies must come, not from the sum of individual choices in the marketplace, but from a political process that addresses inherent conflicts and competing interests. The new public discourse that creates and accompanies that political process must be based in a revived and renewed concept of public interest that comprehends issues not confined to "environmentalists" or "consumer advocates." And it must challenge the fundamental "privacy" of our buying habits, recognizing that production and consumption—the concerns of economic activity and the intimate habits of daily life—are and always have been intertwined aspects of human cultures.

NOTES

||||||||||||⟨⟩||||||||||||

ABBREVIATIONS

A&S *Advertising and Selling*

ABF Paul Terry Cherington, *Advertising as a Business Force: A Compilation of Experience Records* (New York: Doubleday, Page, for Associated Advertising Clubs of America, 1913)

AG *American Grocer*

CAH Collection of Advertising History, Archives Center, National Museum of American History, Smithsonian Institution

FAB Paul Terry Cherington, *The First Advertising Book* (New York: Doubleday, Page, for Associated Advertising Clubs of the World, 1916)

GM *Grocers' Magazine*

GR *Grocers' Review*

HBR *Harvard Business Review*

LHJ *Ladies' Home Journal*

NYT *The New York Times*

PI *Printers' Ink*

SC *The Sample Case*

CHAPTER 1. AMERICAN PIE

PAGE 3 First Crisco ad: "An Absolutely New Product," *LHJ*, January 1912, p. 45.

PAGE 4 Cottonseed oil market: Oscar Schisgall, *Eyes on Tomorrow: The Evolution of Procter & Gamble* (Chicago: J. G. Ferguson, 1981), p. 66; Victor S. Clark,

History of Manufactures in the United States, Vol. 3 (New York: McGraw-Hill, 1929), p. 284.

PAGE 6   Production quantities: Calculated from Edwin Frickey, *Production in the United States, 1860–1914* (Cambridge: Harvard University Press, 1947), pp. 8–15; 1879 and 1909 figures used for paper.

Continuous-process production: David A. Hounshell, *From the American System to Mass Production, 1800–1932: The Development of Manufacturing Technology in the United States* (Baltimore: Johns Hopkins University Press, 1984), pp. 240–45; Alfred D. Chandler, Jr., *The Visible Hand: The Managerial Revolution in American Business* (Cambridge: Harvard University Press, 1977), pp. 249ff.

PAGE 7   Ivory development and marketing: Schisgall, *Eyes on Tomorrow,* pp. 27–28, 33–35.

PAGE 8   Crisco and the Cottolene failure: See Stanley Resor, Stockholder's Affidavit, March 19, 1924, p. 63, J. Walter Thompson Archives.

PAGE 9   Crisco naming: Vote in Memo of Resolution, in Crisco 50th anniversary booklet, typescript (FP 3A-a 5/22/61), between pp. 13 and 14. Three drafts of this booklet, dated 5/14, 5/15, and 5/22, may be found in P&G Archives, Brands, Foods, box 2, Crisco—History. Prior claim: Crisco booklet (5/14), p. 2.

PAGE 10   "Answer questions": Helen Resor, Stockholder's Affidavit, March 19, 1924, p. 68, J. Walter Thompson Archives.

Adoptions: See Crisco booklet (5/22), p. 14, P&G Archives.

Altering the formula: J. George Frederick, "Efficient Planning Before Advertising," *PI,* January 9, 1913, p. 6.

Promotion plans: Frederick, "Efficient Planning," p. 3.

"We want you to have Crisco": Quoted in R. Bigelow Lockwood, *A&S,* May 1912, reprinted in *ABF,* p. 130.

PAGE 11   "Through the length and breadth": "Here it is," Crisco ad in *Saturday Evening Post,* December 18, 1915, CAH, Food.

Dallas 1913 form letter: Reproduced in Crisco booklet (5/22), between pp. 17 and 18, P&G Archives. Rochester 1912 letter: CAH, Direct Mail, box 1.

Fort Smith demonstration: "Mrs. Vaughn Is a 'Perfect Dear,' " *Southwest American,* June 24, 1913, reproduced in Crisco booklet (5/22), between pp. 22 and 23, P&G Archives.

PAGE 12   "For, if women believed": Newspaper publisher prospectus quoted in Crisco booklet (5/22), p. 23, P&G Archives.

Tested Crisco Recipes: Offered in "What Women Ask About Crisco," *Good Housekeeping,* June 1912, p. 15; "Crisco Foods Everywhere," *Saturday Evening Post,* July 26, 1913, p. 2; "Crisco Doughnuts, Wholesome and Delicious," *Saturday Evening Post,* September 6, 1913, p. 2.

New book offers: "Give the Youngsters Crisco Foods," *Saturday Evening Post,* October 11, 1913, p. 2.

Railroad container: Crisco booklet (5/22), p. 14, P&G Archives.

PAGE 14   Kosher packaging: Crisco booklet (5/15), p. 15, P&G Archives; *The Story of Crisco,* p. 15, CAH, Cookbooks, box 2.

Home economists and Americanization: See Susan Strasser, *Never Done: A History of American Housework* (New York: Pantheon Books, 1982), p. 206; Harvey A. Levenstein, *Revolution at the Table: The Transformation of the American Diet* (New York: Oxford University Press, 1988).

"Instead of filling the earth": Frederick, "Efficient Planning," p. 6.

PAGE 17 "Quantity-production of customers": Thorstein Veblen, *Absentee Ownership and Business Enterprise in Recent Times* (New York: Viking, 1923), p. 305.

Akutaq: Personal correspondence with Cristy Willer Tilden, an anthropologist at the University of Alaska, September 2, 1987.

PAGE 18 "Although men tended to cling": Ralph M. Hower, "Urban Retailing 100 Years Ago," *Bulletin of the Business Historical Society* 12 (December 1938): 100.

PAGE 19 Integration of mass production and distribution: Chandler, *Visible Hand,* pp. 285–314.

PAGE 21 Hjermstad story: Lockwood, in *ABF,* pp. 129–34.

PAGE 23 Track statistics: U.S. Bureau of the Census, *Historical Statistics of the United States, Colonial Times to 1970* (Washington: Government Printing Office, 1975), ser. Q288, p. 728.

Western Union: John G. Glover and William B. Cornell, *The Development of American Industries* (New York: Prentice-Hall, 1936), p. 700.

PAGE 24 Storekeepers pay carfares: Thomas A. Bird, *Sales Plans* (Chicago: Merchants Record Co., 1906), pp. 91–92.

PAGE 25 Bell system: Glover and Cornell, *Development of American Industries,* pp. 723, 726–27.

Early corporations: James W. Hurst, *The Legitimacy of the Business Corporation in the Law of the United States, 1780–1970* (Charlottesville: University Press of Virginia, 1970).

"The basic instrument": Peter Dobkin Hall, *The Organization of American Culture, 1700–1900: Private Institutions, Elites, and the Origins of American Nationality* (New York: New York University Press, 1984), p. 96.

Changes in corporation law: Martin J. Sklar, "The Corporate Reconstruction of American Society, 1896–1914: The Market and the Law" (Ph.D. diss., University of Rochester, 1982), pp. 29–31; John R. Commons, *Legal Foundations of Capitalism* (1924; reprint ed., Madison: University of Wisconsin Press, 1968), pp. 11–21.

PAGE 27 Nashville Ad Club speaker: W. R. Hotchkin, "The Sales Possibilities of the Unknown Want," *PI,* March 16, 1916, p. 25.

CHAPTER 2. THE NAME ON THE LABEL

PAGE 29 "It is wonderful": "Package Advertising," *Fame,* 1900, reprinted in *PI,* August 15, 1910, p. 30.

PAGE 30 Singer and McCormick marketing techniques: See Hounshell, *From the American System,* pp. 89, 185–86.

PAGE 31   Packaging: Alec Davis, *Package and Print: The Development of Container and Label Design* (New York: Clarkson Potter, 1967), pp. 33, 47, 57, 66, 73, 77–78; Daniel J. Boorstin, *The Americans: The Democratic Experience* (New York: Vintage Books, 1973), pp. 434–38. Can factory: Chandler, *Visible Hand*, p. 253.

PAGE 32   Colgate toothpaste: See W. P. Werheim, in *PI,* January 5, 1911, reprinted in *ABF,* p. 59.

"An integral part": Gerald B. Wadsworth, 'Principles and Practice of Advertising," *A&S,* January 1913, p. 55.

PAGE 34   In-Er-Seal and National Biscuit: William Cahn, *Out of the Cracker Barrel: The Nabisco Story from Animal Crackers to Zuzus* (New York: Simon & Schuster, 1969), pp. 79–85, 104, 108; James H. Collins, "National Biscuit," *PI,* April 18, 1906, p. 3.

PAGE 35   Grocers' magazine on packaged food: "Why Not Have a Demonstration of Your Own?" *GR,* December 1912. "Afraid of canned goods": p. 624; "The difficulty": p. 622.

Bulk and package crackers: W. H. S. Stevens, "Marketing Biscuits and Crackers," *HBR* 6 (October 1927): 21.

PAGE 37   Schilling plan: A. Schilling & Co., *Advice to Traveling Salesmen Introducing Perfection Canned Teas* (San Francisco, 1884), pp. 16–17, 18–19, 23, 38, 53. *"The can is simply":* p. 43; "so arrange matters": pp. 42–43; "The label has nothing to do": p. 47.

PAGE 43   Goodwill history: Commons, *Legal Foundations of Capitalism,* pp. 263–64. Justice Story quotation: pp. 269–70.

PAGE 44   Supreme Court and property definition: Commons, *Legal Foundations,* 11–17; Sklar, "Corporate Reconstruction," pp. 30–31.

Court reversals: Frank I. Schechter, *The Historical Foundations of the Law Relating to Trade-Marks* (New York: Columbia University Press, 1925), pp. 153–67.

Trademark societies: "The Organization of the United States Trade-Mark Association," *Bulletin of the United States Trade-Mark Association,* n.s., 6 (January 1910): 1–35. See also "International Industrial Mark Protective Association" letter, April 15, 1893, CAH, Trademarks.

PAGE 45   1905 trademark law: John T. Robb, "Some Impressions of New Trade-Mark Laws," *PI,* December 30, 1908, p. 4; Orson D. Munn, *Trade Marks, Trade Names, and Unfair Competition in Trade* (New York: Munn & Co., 1915), pp. 31–35.

Ten thousand new marks: *Dictionary of American History* (1976), vol. 7, p. 93.

Legal marks: Arthur E. Goddard, "Trade Marks—What They Mean in the Eyes of the Business Man and the Law," *System,* May 1911, reprinted in *ABF,* pp. 345–46.

PAGE 46   Standard typewriters: "Advertising That Truly Creates," *PI,* April 25, 1906, p. 9.

"The Word 'Pianola' ": *McClure's,* August 1905, p. 64a.

PAGE 47   Kodak ads: *Review of Reviews,* March 1898, p. 61; *The Century,* January 1899, p. 35.

Trademark values: Waldon Fawcett, "Trade-marks That Have Been Denied Registration," *PI*, May 2, 1912, reprinted in *ABF*, p. 351.

Rogers: Edward S. Rogers, *Good Will, Trade-Marks and Unfair Trading* (Chicago: A. W. Shaw Co., 1914), pp. 28, 30.

PAGE 48 Iwanta case: National Biscuit Company, *Trade Mark Litigation: Opinions, Orders, Injunctions and Decrees Relating to Unfair Competition and Infringement of Trade Marks*, 5th ed. (New York, 1915), pp. 13–14; 233.

PAGE 50 Espo-Cola case: Southern District of New York 2 T.M.R. 234, cited in Coca-Cola Company, *Opinions, Orders, Injunctions, and Decrees Relating to Unfair Competition and Infringement of Trade-Mark* (Atlanta, 1923), p. 157.

Citro-Cola case: "The Name Citro-Cola Not an Infringement," *Soda Fountain*, November 1909, p. 52.

Camels: Nannie M. Tilley, *The R. J. Reynolds Tobacco Company* (Chapel Hill: University of North Carolina Press, 1985), pp. 216–17.

PAGE 51 Trademark advice: Compare Munn and Company, *Trade Marks, Trade Names: For the Business Man* (New York, 1912), with Munn, *Trade Marks* (1915); J. Walter Thompson Company, *Things to Know About Trade-Marks: A Manual of Trade-Mark Information* (New York, 1911).

"What constitutes a good trademark?": Glen Buck, *Trademark Power: An Expedition into an Unprobed and Inviting Wilderness* (Chicago: Munroe & Southworth, 1916), p. 70.

Trademark "is being served": Buck, *Trademark Power*, pp. 5–6.

Campbell bill: H.R. 16844, 62nd Cong., 2nd sess., sent to Committee on Interstate and Foreign Commerce, January 4, 1912. "The bill is along the same lines": Quoted in "Name on the Label Bill Introduced in Congress," *Kellogg's Square Dealer*, April 1912, p. 6, CAH, Cereals.

PAGE 52 Swift annual report: "The Broad Policy of Swift & Co. in Public Relations," *PI*, February 23, 1910, p. 9.

Journal of Applied Psychology: L. R. Geissler, "Association-Reactions Applied to Ideas of Commercial Brands of Familiar Articles," *Journal of Applied Psychology* 1 (September 1917): 278.

Chicago grocers: *Chicago Tribune*, "Baked Bean and Soup Investigation," typescript (1922), Baker Library, Harvard Graduate School of Business Administration.

NYU researchers: George Burton Hotchkiss and Richard B. Franken, *The Leadership of Advertised Brands: A Study of 100 Representative Commodities Showing the Names and Brands That Are Most Familiar to the Public* (New York: Doubleday, Page & Co. for Associated Advertising Clubs of the World, 1923), pp. 113–14.

PAGE 53 Domino sugar: American Sugar Refining Company, circular letter no. 58 (January 20, 1920), in "Circular Letters, etc." (looseleaf binder), Baker Library, Harvard Graduate School of Business Administration.

Munsingwear: Marcia G. Anderson, "Munsingwear: An Underwear for America," *Minnesota History* 50 (Winter 1986): 156.

Fundamental transformation: See Chandler, *Visible Hand*, p. 298 and *passim*.

"I will say": Quoted in article by Lynn G. Wright, *PI,* December 22, 1910, reprinted in *ABF,* p. 260.

PAGE 56   "Corn flake pit-falls": Kellogg ad reproduced in P. R. Barney, "The Private Brand Pitfall," *PI,* August 4, 1910, p. 8.

Kellogg accuses Quaker: " 'Name on the Label' and Mail Order Trade," *Kellogg's Square Dealer,* April 1912, pp. 3–4, CAH, Cereals.

"What interests every manufacturer": V. B. Brown, "A 'Private Brand' Manufacturer Hits Back," *PI,* November 15, 1910, p. 17.

PAGE 57   Branding and price stability: Naomi R. Lamoreaux, *The Great Merger Movement in American Business, 1895–1904* (Cambridge: Cambridge University Press, 1985), pp. 16–19.

Woodbury advertising manager: "That Ivory Soap Dent," *PI,* March 17, 1909, p. 20. See also other *PI* articles on the Ivory million-dollar controversy: January 6, 1909; February 3, 1909, pp. 12–13; February 17, 1909, p. 20.

CHAPTER 3. THE CHAIN OF DISTRIBUTION

PAGE 58   Scott Paper Company: Arthur H. Scott, *PI,* June 30, 1912, reprinted in *ABF.* "Each year the jobbers' claims": p. 245; "not, like the jobber's sales-man": p. 247; "the jobbers will welcome": pp. 247–48.

PAGE 59   Changing roles of wholesalers: See Chandler, *Visible Hand,* pp. 215–24, 236–37, and *passim;* Harold Barger, *Distribution's Place in the American Economy Since 1869* (Princeton: Princeton University Press for National Bureau of Economic Research, 1955), pp. 14, 69ff., table B-5; Glenn Porter and Harold C. Livesay, *Merchants and Manufacturers: Studies in the Changing Structure of Nineteenth Century Marketing* (Baltimore: Johns Hopkins University Press, 1971), esp. pp. 214–31.

Terms for middlemen: See William H. Becker, "American Wholesale Hardware Trade Associations, 1870–1900," *Business History Review* 45 (Summer 1971): 180n.; Porter and Livesay, *Merchants and Manufacturers,* p. 5; Chandler, *Visible Hand,* pp. 25–26.

PAGE 60   Omaha wholesaling: Penelope Chatfield Sodhi, "The 'Old Market': Omaha's Wholesale Jobbing Development, 1880–1895," *Heritage of the Great Plains* 15 (Fall 1982): 1–10.

PAGE 61   Bobsleds: Robert W. Twyman, *History of Marshall Field and Co., 1852–1906* (Philadelphia: University of Pennsylvania Press, 1954), p. 94.

PAGE 62   Salesman and collector personalities: J. O. Goodpasture, "Selling and Collecting," *SC,* September 1915, p. 225; see also A. M. Grigg, "Some Observations on Credits," *SC,* November 1915, pp. 381–83.

Commercial Travelers' Magazine reminiscence: Rev. Henry H. Morrill, "Drummers Old and New," *Commercial Travelers' Magazine,* September 1910, p. 321.

Salesman personality: See Susan Strasser, "The Smile That Pays: The Culture of Traveling Salesmen, 1880–1930," in R. Jackson Wilson, ed., *Essays in American Culture and Society* (Belmont, Calif.: Wadsworth, 1991).

PAGE 64   Major retailing innovations: Godfrey M. Lebhar, *Chain Stores in Amer-*

ica, 1859–1959 (New York: Chain Store Publishing Corp., 1959), pp. 25, 34; Boris Emmet and John E. Jeuck, *Catalogues and Counters: A History of Sears, Roebuck and Company* (Chicago: University of Chicago Press, 1950), pp. 19, 22.

Urban retail specialization: Ralph M. Hower, *History of Macy's of New York, 1858–1919: Chapters in the Evolution of the Department Store* (Cambridge: Harvard University Press, 1943), pp. 82ff.

Massachusetts census: Calculated from *Census of the Commonwealth of Massachusetts, 1905,* vol. 3, *Manufactures and Trade* (Boston: Wright & Potter, 1908), p. 197.

PAGE 65 Johnstown immigrants: Ewa Morawska, *For Bread with Butter: The Life-Worlds of East Central Europeans in Johnstown, Pennsylvania, 1890–1940* (Cambridge: Cambridge University Press, 1985), p. 153.

1923 "mom-and-pop" stores: Paul H. Nystrom, "An Estimate of the Volume of Retail Business in the United States," *HBR* 3 (January 1925), reprinted in Daniel Bloomfield, *Selected Articles on Trends in Retail Distribution* (New York: H. W. Wilson, 1930), pp. 68–69.

PAGE 66 Women shopkeepers: See Alan M. Kraut, "The Butcher, the Baker, the Pushcart Peddler: Jewish Foodways and Entrepreneurial Opportunity in the East European Immigrant Community, 1880–1940," *Journal of American Culture* 6 (Winter 1983): 75.

PAGE 67 "Wrote and translated letters": John J. Bukowczyk, "The Transformation of Working-Class Ethnicity: Corporate Control, Americanization, and the Polish Immigrant Middle Class in Bayonne, New Jersey, 1915–1925," *Labor History* 25 (Winter 1984): 59–60.

PAGE 68 Credit in Ada, Minnesota: Louis Dwight Harvell Weld, *Social and Economic Survey of a Community in the Red River Valley,* University of Minnesota Research Publications, Current Problems Series, no. 4 (Minneapolis, January 1915), pp. 56, 63, 70–73.

Credit in Homestead, Pennsylvania: Margaret Byington, *Homestead: The Households of a Mill Town* (1910; reprint ed., Pittsburgh: University Center for International Studies, 1974), pp. 75, 98–100. "Grocers knew their customers": pp. 99–100.

PAGE 69 "In the other stores": Quoted in Laura Anker Schwartz, "Immigrant Voices from Home, Work, and Community: Women and Family in the Migration Process, 1890–1938" (Ph.D. diss., State University of New York, Stony Brook, 1983), p. 371; see also p. 376.

Harvard Bureau of Business Research: Harvard University Bureau of Business Research, *Management Problems in Retail Grocery Stores,* Bulletin No. 13 (Cambridge: Harvard University Press, 1919), p. 24.

"That's the way": Quoted in Schwartz, "Immigrant Voices," p. 377.

"Credit Is Lending": *GR,* November 1904, p. 454.

PAGE 70 "If they are true friends": "Facts to Be Remembered," *GR,* November 1904, p. 456.

Poughkeepsie study: Ruth Gillette Hutchinson, Arthur R. Hutchinson, and Mabel Newcomer, "A Study in Business Mortality: Length of Life of Business

Enterprises in Poughkeepsie, New York, 1843–1936," *American Economic Review* 28 (September 1938): 512.

Oshkosh business failures: Calculated from Paul H. Nystrom, *The Economics of Retailing* (New York: Ronald Press, 1915), p. 307.

PAGE 71 "Always give us a full report": Iten Biscuit Company, "Instructions to Salesmen" (1916), p. 8, Baker Library, Harvard Graduate School of Business Administration.

"It is safe to say": Weld, *Social and Economic Survey,* p. 56.

PAGE 72 " 'Anybody can keep store' ": Nystrom, *Economics of Retailing,* p. 311.

"With a continual influx": Melvin Thomas Copeland, *Principles of Merchandising* (Chicago: A. W. Shaw Co., 1924), p. 42.

"When I get ready": " 'Grocers Are the Poorest of Business Men,' Says Price," *GR,* June 1921, pp. 205–7.

"The majority of retail merchants": Introductory letter from Edward N. Herley, chairman, in Federal Trade Commission, *A System of Accounts for Retail Merchants* (Washington: Government Printing Office, 1916), p. 3.

"A surprisingly large proportion": Harvard Bureau of Business Research, *Management Problems,* p. 16.

"What's the use?": Quoted in Charles W. Hurd and M. M. Zimmerman, "How Accounting Helps the Chains Outbattle the Independents, XIII," *PI,* December 10, 1914, p. 20.

PAGE 73 Income tax exemption: John F. Witte, *The Politics and Development of the Federal Income Tax* (Madison: University of Wisconsin Press, 1985), p. 77.

"Every dealer": Artemas Ward, *The Grocers' Hand-Book and Directory for 1883* (Philadelphia: Philadelphia Grocer Publishing Co., 1882), pp. 18–21.

"Depend upon it": "Advantages of a Bank Account," *GR,* April 1912, pp. 109–11.

"Have a bank account": Butler Brothers, *Success in Retailing: The Variety Business. A Text Book on Merchandising* (New York, 1920), p. 86.

"Country dealers": Ward, *Grocer's Hand-Book,* p. 22.

Harvard study: Harvard Bureau of Business Research, *Management Problems,* pp. 47–48.

PAGE 74 Grandmother's bargaining routine: Richard Gambino, *Blood of My Blood* (Garden City, N.Y.: Doubleday, 1974), p. 167, quoted in Elizabeth Ewen, *Immigrant Women in the Land of Dollars: Life and Culture on the Lower East Side, 1890–1925* (New York: Monthly Review Press, 1985), p. 169. See also Schwartz, "Immigrant Voices," pp. 377–78.

Secret price marks: System Company, *The Business Man's Brain Partners, including The Business Man's Encyclopedia,* 6th rev. ed. (Chicago, 1911), p. 69; R. R. Williams, ed., *Hardware Store Business Methods,* new and enlarged ed. (New York: David Williams, 1901), pp. 89, 153–54.

Bargaining with salesmen: Williams, *Hardware Store Business Methods,* pp. 24–26. "More than this": p. 24; "authority to quote": p. 25; "Salesmen seldom name": p. 26; "solicit further concessions": p. 25.

PAGE 75 "The Tactics of Selling": Arthur Frederick Sheldon, *The Art of Selling,* *for Business College, High Schools of Commerce, Y.M.C.A. Classes and Private Students* (Chicago: Sheldon School, 1911), pp. 85–86.

"Converse freely": Williams, *Hardware Store Business Methods,* p. 25.

PAGE 76 "The young man would be told": Twyman, *History of Marshall Field,* p. 95.

PAGE 77 Marshall Field manufacturing: Twyman, *History,* pp. 98, 102.

Continuous-flow principles in distribution: See Chandler, *Visible Hand,* pp. 231–32.

Steero: Charles W. Hurd, in *PI,* January 25, 1912, reprinted in *ABF,* pp. 232ff.

"We recall the time here": Major Price, quoted in Ward, *Grocers' Hand-Book,* p. 107.

PAGE 78 Lines among trades: For a celebration of these changes, see Henry S. Bunting, *Added Lines in Modern Merchandising* (Chicago: Bunting Publications, 1918).

Singer network: Hotchkiss and Franken, *Leadership of Advertised Brands,* p. 53.

Ingersoll: "General Publicity Sells Ingersolls," *PI,* June 13, 1906, p. 6.

PAGE 79 Munsingwear individual items: " 'Munsingwear's' Successful Cultivation of Dealer-Agents," *PI,* April 30, 1914, p. 6.

Heinz: Roland Cole, "How Heinz Advertises Idea Behind Plant and Product," *Printers' Ink Monthly,* July 1922, p. 94.

PAGE 80 Hotpoint: R. E. Dildine, "How 'Hotpoint' Has Made 'Big' Competition Step Lively," *PI,* July 1, 1915, p. 6.

Wrigley Spearmint introduction: James H. Collins, "The Story of 'Spearmint' Gum," *PI,* January 5, 1910, p. 4.

Functional middlemen: Arch W. Shaw, "Some Problems in Market Distribution," *Quarterly Journal of Economics* 26 (August 1912): 731–33. On Shaw, see Paul T. Converse, *The Beginning of Marketing Thought in the United States, with Reminiscences of Some of the Pioneer Marketing Scholars* (Austin: University of Texas Bureau of Business Research, 1959), pp. 38–42.

"The application of the corporate form": Shaw, "Some Problems in Market Distribution," p. 733.

PAGE 81 Express companies: Boorstin, *The Americans,* p. 134.

"To the manufacturer who advertises": Earnest Elmo Calkins, "Eliminating the Jobber," *PI,* May 31, 1905, p. 8.

Companies selling directly: J. George Frederick, "Why Selling Direct to Retailer Is Becoming Popular," *PI,* February 13, 1913, p. 17.

P & G distribution: Schisgall, *Eyes on Tomorrow,* pp. 76–77, 88ff.

PAGE 82 "The jobber has no particular interest": Schilling, *Advice to Traveling Salesmen,* p. 49.

"The wisdom of adopting": Raymond W. Gage, "The Mix-Up Centering About the Jobber," *PI,* September 22, 1910, p. 30.

Arguments for the jobber: See "The Jobber a Necessity," *AG,* January 25, 1911, p. 6; " 'Looking Backward' upon the U.S. Without a Jobber in 1925,"

PI, July 28, 1910, pp. 56–61; "Why the Wholesaler Is a Fixture," *A&S,* December 1912, pp. 24ff.

PAGE 83   Harvard study: Harvard Bureau of Business Research, *Management Problems,* pp. 27–30.

Uneeda, etc., margins: V. B. Brown, "A 'Private Brand' Manufacturer Hits Back," *PI,* November 15, 1910, pp. 17–18.

Ivory and Crisco margins: L. Bigelow Lockwood, in *A&S,* May 1912, reprinted in *ABF,* pp. 130–31.

"Don't sell 'em": "The Cereal Problem Solved," *Anco Special,* July 1903, CAH.

PAGE 84   *System* article: George L. Louis, in *System,* June 1912, reprinted in *ABF,* pp. 40–41.

"Drop that attitude": Louis Henry Martin, "Interesting the Small Retailer," *PI,* July 21, 1910, p. 49.

PAGE 86   Hires advertisement: *Soda Fountain,* November 1909, p. 4, CAH, Beverages, Hires folder.

Grocers' magazine defense of substitution: "The Merchant Grocer," *GM,* April 1912, p. 8.

N. C. Jensen: *Chicago Tribune,* "Baked Bean and Soup Investigation," typescript (1922), p. 28, Baker Library, Harvard Graduate School of Business Administration.

Sapolio ad: *Cottage Hearth* (Boston), April 1888, n.p., CAH.

PAGE 87   Gillette ads: See 1907 ads in CAH, Barbering.

Standard ad: *McClure's,* August 1905, p. 75.

PAGE 88   "Friendly intimacy": O. J. Gude Co. advertisement, *A&S,* January 1913, p. 49.

CHAPTER 4. NEW PRODUCTS, NEW HABITS

PAGE 89   "Consumption starts": Mary Douglas and Baron Isherwood, *The World of Goods: Towards an Anthropology of Consumption* (New York: W. W. Norton, 1979), p. 57.

PAGE 90   Magazine and newspaper advertising: Frank Presbrey, *The History and Development of Advertising* (Garden City, N.Y.: Doubleday, Doran, 1929), pp. 468–70, 479–81, 352–55.

PAGE 91   Billboard controversies: See Quentin J. Schultze, "Legislating Morality: The Progressive Response to American Outdoor Advertising, 1900–1917," *Journal of Popular Culture* 17 (Spring 1984): 37–44; Kristin Szylvian Bailey, "Fighting 'Civic Smallpox': The Civic Club of Allegheny County's Campaign for Billboard Regulation, 1896–1917," *Western Pennsylvania Historical Magazine,* January 1987, pp. 3–28.

PAGE 93   Ward and Sapolio: Presbrey, *History and Development of Advertising,* pp. 512–19.

"New hub": "New Hub of the Advertising Universe," *PI,* April 4, 1906, pp. 3–7.

Advertising organizations: Presbrey, *History and Development of Advertising*, pp. 541–55; Daniel Pope, *The Making of Modern Advertising* (New York: Basic Books, 1983), *passim*.

Military language: J. W. Schwartz, "A Scheme of Magnitude in Soap Publicity," *PI*, January 29, 1902, p. 10; James H. Collins, "National Biscuit," *PI*, April 18, 1906, pp. 6, 8; "A $100,000 Newspaper Campaign Starts for Shredded Wheat," *PI*, March 17, 1909, p. 14.

PAGE 95   "Symptom blank": John Irving Romer, "The Written Plan of Campaign," *PI*, September 30, 1908, p. 4.

Calkins and Holden: Converse, *Beginning of Marketing Thought*, p. 30.

Campbell's advertising policy: Hotchkiss and Franken, *Leadership of Advertised Brands*, pp. 55–56.

Prophylactic advertising policy: Hotchkiss and Franken, *Leadership*, p. 71.

Colgate advertising policy: Hotchkiss and Franken, *Leadership*, pp. 74–76.

PAGE 97   *ABC of the Teeth:* Colgate & Co., New York, n.d. (c. 1900), CAH, Dental, box 2, Dentrifice folder.

Hapgoods ad: In James H. Collins, "The Safety Razor," *PI*, February 20, 1907, p. 4.

Gillette advertising: Quotations not from ad reproduced are from "You Ought to Shave" ad in *Town and Country*, November 20, 1909, CAH, Barbering.

King Gillette: Russell B. Adams, Jr., *King C. Gillette: The Man and His Wonderful Shaving Device* (Boston: Little, Brown, 1978); James Gilbert, *Designing the Industrial State* (Chicago: Quadrangle Books, 1972); Kenneth M. Roemer, "Technology, Corporation, and Utopia: Gillette's Unity Regained," *Technology and Culture* 26 (July 1985): 560–70.

PAGE 100   Gillette pricing decision: Adams, *King Gillette*, p. 44.

PAGE 101   Dozens of manufacturers: Collins, "Safety Razor," p. 3.

Sterling razor: James H. Collins, "Selling Talk and Big Space," *PI*, May 30, 1906, pp. 3, 6.

"The idea of producing a blade": Gillette, quoted in Adams, *King Gillette*, p. 49.

Gillette's biographer: Adams, *King Gillette*, p. 18.

PAGE 102   United Cigar Stores premiums: United Cigar Stores Company, "Profit Sharing List," 1908–1909, CAH, Premiums, box 1.

Streetcars and billboards: Hotchkiss and Franken, *Leadership of Advertised Brands*, p. 48.

"No Game Laws": "Hunt with Kodak," CAH, Photography, box 6.

"The big idea behind the selling": C. B. Larrabee, "How Kodak Chooses Its Advertising Illustrations," *Printers' Ink Monthly*, July 1922, p. 30.

PAGE 107   "Men often get married": *Waterman Ideal Salesmanship: Being an Illustrated Series of Twenty Lessons on the Best Methods of Salesmanship of Waterman's Ideal Fountain Pen* (New York, 1902), p. 26.

"Simple conditions": *Waterman Ideal Salesmanship*, p. 30.

"That no one would have a suspicion": *Waterman Ideal Salesmanship*, p. 50.

PAGE 108   Waterman extra advertising: Hotchkiss and Franken, *Leadership of Advertised Brands,* pp. 61–63.

PAGE 109   Waterman Christmas price lists: See examples in CAH, Pens, box 1.

"Plan now": "The One Thing Needful," *Town and Country,* June 3, 1911, CAH, Pens, box 1.

PAGE 110   Historians on modernity in 1920s advertising: See especially Roland Marchand, *Advertising the American Dream: Making Way for Modernity, 1920–1940* (Berkeley: University of California Press, 1985); Stuart Ewen, *Captains of Consciousness: Advertising and the Social Roots of the Consumer Culture* (New York: McGraw-Hill, 1976).

PAGE 112   "Shipped in Train Loads": Quaker ad, *Munsey's,* April 1895, CAH, Cereal.

Wrigley's freight car: "ONLY A FREIGHT CAR," 1905 dealer's leaflet, CAH, Chewing Gum.

PAGE 113   "A Million a Year" campaign: A. Rowden King, "The Factory and Its Relation to the Advertising Department," *PI,* September 15, 1910, pp. 34–35.

"An idea of stability": King, "Factory and Its Relation," p. 30.

Shredded Wheat: 100,000 figure in "For Every Age in Every Season" advertisement, 1907, and in 1914 pamphlet *The Wonders of Niagara.* Other figures from "Interesting Data About the Natural Food Conservatory," 1903; 1915 souvenir postcard for 2 million biscuits. All in CAH, Cereals, Natural Food Company.

PAGE 117   Campbell Kids dolls: Advertising card, CAH, Food.

Sunny Jim: *Through Foreign Lands* is advertised on a card; the recipes and philosophy are in *The Gentle Art of using* FORCE (Buffalo, N.Y., 1903). Both in CAH, Cereals, H-O Company.

PAGE 118   "Everybody talked": Helen Woodward, *Through Many Windows* (New York: Harper, 1926), p. 359. See also Earnest Elmo Calkins and Ralph Holden, *Modern Advertising* (New York: D. Appleton, 1905), p. 274.

PAGE 119   "Aunt Em'ly": "Aunt Em'ly and Pie," *LHJ,* May 1912.

PAGE 121   Heinz factory tour and Ocean Pier: Robert C. Alberts, *The Good Provider: H. J. Heinz and His 57 Varieties* (Boston: Houghton Mifflin, 1973), pp. 125, 131–33; "Our 'Light at the Seaboard,' " *Pickles,* April 1901, p. 1.

Average tenure in canneries: Elizabeth Beardsley Butler, *Women and the Trades, Pittsburgh, 1907–1908* (New York: Charities Publication Committee, 1909), pp. 41–42.

CHAPTER 5. DESIGNING MARKETS

PAGE 124   Market as a concept: This discussion follows Jean-Christophe Agnew's pathbreaking article, "The Threshold of Exchange: Speculations on the Market," *Radical History Review* 21 (Fall 1979): 99–118, and its later version, chap. 1 of *Worlds Apart: The Market and the Theater in Anglo-American Thought, 1550–1750* (Cambridge: Cambridge University Press, 1986), pp. 17–56. "Suspicion and apprehension": *Worlds Apart,* p. 20.

Ancient Greeks: Agnew, *Worlds Apart,* pp. 18–19.

Eighteenth–twentieth-century meanings: *Oxford English Dictionary,* 2nd ed., vol. 9, pp. 384–86.

PAGE 126 "If your grocer hasn't them": Van Camp advertisement in *McClure's,* August 1905, p. 76.

Flexo ad: *McClure's,* August 1905, p. 64d.

Carnation: James H. Collins, "From Local to National Distribution," *PI,* January 5, 1910, pp. 20–22; A. Rowden King, in *A&S,* May 1912, reprinted in *ABF,* pp. 80–87. "When advertising methods": Collins, "From Local to National," p. 22.

PAGE 128 Pompeian olive oil: "Changing a Luxury into a Household Utility," *PI,* April 9, 1914, pp. 3–13. "So firm": p. 13.

PAGE 129 "One dreadful malady": James H. Collins, "Remarkable Proprietary Beverage," *PI,* November 4, 1908, pp. 3–4.

"A profound ambiguity": Pat Watters, *Coca-Cola: An Illustrated History* (Garden City, N.Y.: Doubleday, 1978), p. 18.

Bubble party: Suggestion may be found in a collection of advertisements, "What a Cake of Soap Will Do," CAH, Soap, Procter & Gamble.

PAGE 131 Swan and lily pad booklet: "It Floats," CAH, Soap, Procter & Gamble.

Hints for Housewives: CAH, Soap, Cudahy.

How to Use California Lemons: CAH, Food, box 25, California.

Vital Question Cookbook: CAH, Cereals, Natural Food Co.

Baker recipe book: Editions and copies listed on the books, in box K1, Baker papers, manuscript division, Baker Library, Harvard Graduate School of Business Administration.

Jell-O contest: Genesee Pure Food Co. leaflet "$200.00 a Month in Cash," n.d. (about 1902), CAH, Food, box 13.

PAGE 133 "When I first started": Collins, "Remarkable Proprietary Beverage," p. 6.

Domino Golden Syrup: American Sugar Refining Company, "Circular Letters, etc." (looseleaf binder), Baker Library, Harvard Graduate School of Business Administration. Year-round supply: no. 41 (March 24, 1919); "Our belief": no. 49 (June 25, 1919); Nut Sundae: no. 71 (May 14, 1920); exhortation: no. 66 (March 23, 1920).

PAGE 134 Sapolio history: Donald S. Tull, "A Re-Examination of the Causes of the Decline in Sales of Sapolio," *Journal of Business* 28 (1955): 128–30.

"The series has been parodied": "The History of 'Spotless Town,'" *PI,* February 19, 1902, p. 8.

Ye Booke of Spotless Town: 1909 ed., CAH, Soap.

"Allusions to Spotless Town": Presbrey, *History and Development of Advertising,* p. 378.

PAGE 135 "Perhaps the most persistent": "Advertising by Sample," *PI*, March 3, 1909, p. 22.

"Get a cleanser": Quoted in Tull, "Re-Examination," p. 131.

PAGE 136 Sales figures: Calculated from Tull, "Re-Examination," table 1, p. 132.

Bon Ami contest: *PI*, April 8, 1915, reprinted in *FAB*, p. 346; Roy W. Johnson, "When a Consumer Contest Is Profitable and When It Isn't," *PI*, August 10, 1916, pp. 4–5.

"Development of a new product": Tull, "Re-Examination," p. 131.

"A salesman can talk": *PI*, April 20, 1911, reprinted in *ABF*, p. 339.

Line and franchise extensions: Edward M. Tauber, "Brand Franchise Extension: New Product Benefits from Existing Brand Names," *Business Horizons* 24 (March–April 1981): 36–41.

PAGE 138 Edison line: "Edison Phonograph's Thorough-Going Newspaper Campaign," *PI*, February 16, 1910, pp. 6–10.

Hunt canned fruit brands: "The Hunt Brothers' Advertising and Pure-Food Stir," *PI*, March 9, 1910, p. 22.

PAGE 139 "The private coffee": Stanley Resor, Stockholder's Affidavit, March 19, 1924, p. 64, J. Walter Thompson Archives.

Yuban and Ariosa markets: Memoranda, reel 195, J. Walter Thompson Archives.

Ingersoll: "General Publicity sells Ingersolls," *PI*, June 13, 1906, p. 8.

PAGE 142 Wrigley: James H. Collins, "The Story of 'Spearmint' Gum," *PI*, January 5, 1910, pp. 3–8; "Wrigley Strongly Pushing an Old Brand," *PI*, November 2, 1916, pp. 87–88.

PAGE 143 *"The loud pedal"*: Frank T. Hill, "Fitting National Copy to Sectional Variations," *PI*, September 22, 1910, p. 42.

International Harvester poster: James H. Collins, "The Advertising of a $120,000 Corporation," *PI*, June 29, 1904, p. 6.

Armour: E. B. Merritt, "How Armour & Co. Are Solving Their Vast Selling Problem," *PI*, January 23, 1913. *"Made from little girls!"*: p. 8; product line: pp. 3–4; *"cumulative publicity"*: p. 8.

PAGE 144 Hotpoint: R. E. Dildine, "How 'Hotpoint' Has Made 'Big' Competition Step Lively," *PI*, July 1, 1915, pp. 4, 117.

Ralston: "The Grocer and the Miller," *Checkerboard Monthly,* May 1903, pp. 2–3.

PAGE 146 Colgate 225 products: H. L. Allen, *PI*, June 30, 1910, reprinted in *ABF*, p. 343.

Advertising and Selling article: A. Rowden King, "Advertising a Family of Products in Rotation: The Story of Libby, McNeill & Libby," *A&S*, November 1912, p. 24.

Schilling estimate: Schilling, *Advice to Traveling Salesmen*, pp. 10–11.

PAGE 147 Keyed responses: Calkins and Holden, *Modern Advertising*, pp. 263ff.

"The present-day tendency": Calkins and Holden, *Modern Advertising*, p. 261.

PAGE 148   Scott: Edmund C. Lynch, "Walter Dill Scott: Pioneer Industrial Psychologist," *Business History Review* 42 (Summer 1968): 149–70.

Harlow Gale: Converse, *Beginning of Marketing Thought*, pp. 10–12.

Market studies: Calkins and Holden, *Modern Advertising*, pp. 291ff., 296ff.

PAGE 149   Call for statistical work: Calkins and Holden, *Modern Advertising*, p. 285.

Mahin research: "Making the Copy Fit the Plan," *PI*, June 27, 1904, pp. 3–4. "Just the surface": p. 3.

PAGE 150   "The difference between advertising then and now": Earnest Elmo Calkins, *The Business of Advertising* (New York: D. Appleton, 1915), p. viii.

"Anyone with a food product problem": J. Walter Thompson weekly newsletter, July 18, 1916, J. Walter Thompson Archives.

Winning a Great Market on Facts: Chicago Tribune, *Winning a Great Market on Facts* (Chicago, 1916). Salad dressing manufacturer: p. 25.

PAGE 153   "What should this quota be": J. Walter Thompson Company, *Population and Its Distribution: Compiled from the United States Census Figures of 1910* (New York, 1912), introduction.

J. Walter Thompson library: J. Walter Thompson weekly newsletter, no. 20, October 17, 1916, p. 5, J. Walter Thompson Archives.

Second edition: J. Walter Thompson Company, *Population and Its Distribution: Compiled from the United States Bureau of Census Figures,* 2nd ed., rev. and enlarged (New York, 1918).

PAGE 154   "It puts New England": Eastern Advertising Company, *Advertisers Hand Book of New England* (New York, n.d. [Baker Library copy stamped 1915]), p. 3.

Nabisco questions: James H. Collins, "National Biscuit," *PI*, April 18, 1906, p. 4.

PAGE 155   Eastman: Lawrence C. Lockley, "Notes on the History of Marketing Research," *Journal of Marketing* 14 (April 1950): 734.

Parlin in *Printers' Ink:* Charles Coolidge Parlin, "Why and How a Manufacturer Should Make Trade Investigations," *PI*, October 22, 1914, p. 4.

"Reports of salesmen": Calkins, *Business of Advertising*, p. 156.

Agate Club dinner: Lynch, "Walter Dill Scott," p. 151.

Watson: Kerry W. Buckley, "The Selling of a Psychologist: John Broadus Watson and the Application of Behavioral Techniques to Advertising," *Journal of the History of the Behavioral Sciences* 18 (July 1982): 209–11. "Chickens or cabbages," p. 211.

PAGE 156   Biographical information: Lockley, "Notes on the History of Marketing Research"; Converse, *Beginning of Marketing Thought*, pp. 25ff.; *Who's Who in Advertising* (Detroit: Business Service Corp., 1916).

PAGE 157   "The engineer does not choose": Arch W. Shaw, "Some Problems in Market Distribution," *Quarterly Journal of Economics* 26 (August 1912): 757.

Scientific management in housekeeping and education: See Strasser, *Never Done*, and Raymond Callahan, *Education and the Cult of Efficiency* (Chicago: University of Chicago Press, 1962).

Steamboat vs. railroad towns: J. Walter Thompson, *Population and Its Distribution* (1912), introduction.

" 'Popular Opinion' ": John E. Kennedy, "Epistles on Advertising," *A&S*, August 1912, p. 7.

PAGE 158   "The book contains nothing": Review of Scott, *Theory of Advertising*, *PI*, December 9, 1903, p. 34.

"The average business executive": J. George Frederick, *Business Research and Statistics* (New York: D. Appleton, 1920), p. v.

Human nature: Merle Curti, "The Changing Concept of 'Human Nature' in the Literature of American Advertising," *Business History Review* 41 (Winter 1967): 337-45.

PAGE 159   Psychological studies: See David P. Kuna, "The Concept of Suggestion in the Early History of Advertising Psychology," *Journal of the History of the Behavioral Sciences* 12 (October 1976): 347-53; Neil H. Borden, *Determination of Confusion in Trade-Mark Conflict Cases*, Harvard University Business Research Studies, no. 16 (vol. 23, no. 8) (Cambridge, December, 1936), pp. 3-4; *FAB*, pp. 11-18; Harry L. Hollingworth, *Advertising and Selling: Principles of Appeal and Response* (New York: D. Appleton for Advertising Men's League of New York City, 1913).

Everybody's contest: Francis Bellamy, ed., *Effective Magazine Advertising* (New York: Mitchell Kennerley, 1909), contains about 500 of the essays.

Colgate contest: *LHJ*, October 1909, back cover; for responses, "The Colgate Prize Contest," *LHJ*, February 1910, p. 29.

"The demand for candles": Ralph Starr Butler, "Marketing Methods," part 1 of *Marketing Methods and Salesmanship* (New York: Alexander Hamilton Institute, 1914), p. 172.

PAGE 161   "The far-seeing manufacturer": Ralph Starr Butler, "Investigating the Market—Factors to Be Considered," *PI*, December 12, 1918, p. 10.

CHAPTER 6. SALES AND PROMOTIONS

PAGE 163   Quaker train promotion: Arthur F. Marquette, *Brands, Trademarks and Good Will: The Story of the Quaker Oats Company* (New York: McGraw-Hill, 1967), pp. 62-64.

St. Louis fair: Marquette, *Brands, Trademarks*, p. 102.

PAGE 164   American Cereal advertising expenditures: Pope, *Making of Modern Advertising*, pp. 55, 43-44.

Trade cards: Robert Jay, *The Trade Card in Nineteenth-Century America* (Columbia: University of Missouri Press, 1987), esp. pp. 39-40, 99-100. Arbuckle cards: p. 93. Singer cards: CAH, Sewing Machines, Singer.

PAGE 165   Patent medicine booklets: James Harvey Young, *The Toadstool Millionaires: A Social History of Patent Medicines in America Before Federal Regulation* (Princeton: Princeton University Press, 1961), pp. 168-69.

Non-food-company cookbooks: See, for example, Metropolitan Life Insurance Company, *Metropolitan Cook Book* (New York, n.d. [before 1900]).

One 1905 magazine: *McClure's,* August 1905. Ostermoor: p. 17; Cuticura: p. 48; Nestlé's: p. 64c; Eaton's: p. 64m.

PAGE 166   Promotions to children: Jay, *Trade Card,* pp. 91, 95–96; James H. Collins, "The Story of 'Spearmint' Gum," *PI,* January 5, 1910, p. 8. Nursery rhyme booklets: *Wrigley's Mother Goose* (1915), CAH, Chewing Gum; *Quaker Nursery Rhymes,* CAH, Cereal; Colgate's *Foot Up and Other Mother Goose Melodies* (1913), CAH, Dental, box 2. Kellogg's *Funny Jungleland:* Horace B. Powell, *The Original Has This Signature—W. K. Kellogg* (Englewood Cliffs, N.J.: Prentice-Hall, 1956), p. 139.

PAGE 167   Specialty advertising: See Henry S. Bunting, *Specialty Advertising—The New Way to Build Business* (Chicago: Novelty News Press, 1910). Shredded Wheat bookmark: CAH, Cereals, Natural Food Co. Welch corkscrew: "Welch's Grape Juice" (1901), CAH, Food, box 20. Karo: Paul Findlay, "Karo and the Premium Idea," *PI,* March 9, 1916, pp. 57–58.

PAGE 168   American Cereal premiums: Pettijohn's slides and coupons in CAH, Cereal, box 42. See also Marquette, *Brands, Trademarks,* pp. 46, 81.

One contemporary observer: I. M. Rubinow, "Premiums in Retail Trade," *Journal of Political Economy* 13 (September 1905): 576.

Ivory sentimental pictures: See examples in CAH, Soap.

PAGE 170   Knox drawing: CAH, Food, box 12.

Dunham's: Dunham Manufacturing Company, *1893 Premium Catalogue, Illustrating many Useful and Valuable Articles Given Away* (New York, 1893), CAH, Premiums, box 1.

PAGE 171   Colgate and H-O premium programs: Octagon wrapper: CAH, Soap. Library slip on reverse of Kinderbeast puzzle: CAH, Cereals. H-O 1914–1915 premium catalogue: CAH, Cereals. *The Right Way to Wash Clothes:* CAH, Soap.

"Wherever possible": United Cigar Stores Company, *Profit-Sharing List, Season 1908–1909* (New York, 1907), p. 3, CAH, Premiums, box 1. See similar statements from other years.

United Profit Sharing Corporation: Leverett S. Lyon and Helen May Wheeler, *The Economics of Free Deals* (Washington: Brookings Institution, 1933), p. 32. List of cities on 1915–16 catalogue: CAH, Premiums, box 1. List of products on Economy Canvas Gloves flyer: CAH, Premiums, box 1.

PAGE 172   Duke advertising budget: Richard B. Tennant, *The American Cigarette Industry: A Study in Economic Analysis and Public Policy* (New Haven: Yale University Press, 1950), pp. 24, 42.

Floradora: *Presents,* Floradora Tag Company catalogue (St. Louis, 1904), CAH, Premiums, box 2. Baseball: p. 8; wagons: p. 24.

PAGE 173   R. J. Reynolds premiums: Tillie, *R. J. Reynolds,* p. 141.

Liggett and Myers: Curt A. Wessel, "Merchandising Work That Turned a Losing into a Banner Year," *PI,* reprinted in American Sunday Magazine, *The Selling Problem* (New York, n.d. [1914]), p. 69.

Camels: Tillie, *R. J. Reynolds,* pp. 212–15; Tennant, *American Cigarette Industry,* pp. 77–78, 83–84.

PAGE 174   Ariosa premiums: Memo to Arbuckle re 1915 Ariosa campaign, p. 2, reel 195, J. Walter Thompson Archives.

PAGE 175   Procter and Gamble premiums: S. C. Lambert, "How Procter & Gamble Base Sales Policies on Actual Market Conditions," *PI,* April 27, 1916, pp. 4, 8. "Poorer class of stores": p. 8.

PAGE 176   "Go to a class of people": Quoted in "A Flank Movement on the Profit-Sharing Coupon System," *Current Opinion,* June 15, 1915, p. 40.

"Scarcely a middle-class": Rubinow, "Premiums," p. 574.

"Premium Mad": *GR,* January 1905, p. 584. For resolutions from organizations, see pp. 574, 576.

Dingley tariff: Tennant, *American Cigarette Industry,* p. 42.

Opposition to premiums: "Flank Movement," p. 439; C. S. Duncan, "The Economics and Legality of Premium Giving," *Journal of Political Economy* 24 (December 1916): 928.

"It is not evident": Rubinow, "Premiums," p. 577.

Arguments for and against premiums: See Duncan, "Economics and Legality," pp. 927–31. See also Henry S. Bunting, *The Premium System of Forcing Sales: Its Principles, Laws, and Uses* (Chicago: Novelty News Press, 1913).

Olean, New York association: *GR,* January 1905, p. 576.

PAGE 177   Chicago manufacturer: "Flank Movement," p. 442.

State laws: Lyon and Wheeler, *Economics of Free Deals,* pp. 34–37.

PAGE 178   "Advertising is mere identification": Quoted in Duncan, "Economics and Legality," p. 947.

"After all": Duncan, "Economics and Legality," p. 948.

PAGE 180   Old Dutch Cleanser: "Advertising by Sample," *PI,* March 3, 1909, p. 22.

Samples and free trials: These examples are from *Harper's,* November 1888, and *McClure's,* August 1905.

Mellin's Food: Rima D. Apple, " 'Advertised by our loving friends': The Infant Formula Industry and the Creation of New Pharmaceutical Markets, 1870–1910," *Journal of the History of Medicine and Allied Sciences* 41 (1986): 15–16.

Printers' Ink warning: "Advertising by Sample," pp. 22–23.

Heinz in Buffalo: "Pan-American Exhibits," *Pickles,* April 1901, p. 8, CAH.

PAGE 181   Lavish exhibits: Expenditures and American Radiator example in Russell Lewis, "Everything Under One Roof: World's Fairs and Department Stores in Paris and Chicago," *Chicago History* 12 (Fall 1983): 45–46.

PAGE 182   Rydell: Robert W. Rydell, *All the World's a Fair: Visions of Empire at American International Expositions, 1876–1916* (Chicago: University of Chicago Press, 1984).

Singer at Columbian Exposition: Booklet in CAH, Sewing Machines.

Aunt Jemima: Rydell, *All the World's a Fair,* p. 119; Marquette, *Brands, Trademarks,* pp. 144–48.

PAGE 183   Recycled booths: See "The Food of the World," *New England Kitchen Magazine,* September 1894, p. 280; "World's Food Fair," *New England Kitchen Magazine,* October 1894, p. 5.

PAGE 184   Madison Square Garden show: Peter Edward Samson, "The Emergence of a Consumer Interest in America, 1870–1930" (Ph.D. diss., University of Chicago, 1980), p. 67.

Boston food fairs: Advertisement in *AG*, July 10, 1901, p. 12.

"One could make quite a satisfactory luncheon": "World's Food Fair," p. 5.

Brooklyn food exposition: "The Food Exposition," *PI*, February 22, 1893, pp. 290–91.

Sarah Tyson Rorer: "Mrs. Rorer on Samples," *PI*, April 11, 1900, p. 11.

Antipeddling statutes: See Powell, *Original Has This Signature*, p. 132, and "Kellogg Toasted Corn Flake Co. Wins," *AG*, December 8, 1909, p. 18.

PAGE 185   Coca-Cola coupons: Sam E. Whitmire, "Coco-Cola [*sic*]," *PI*, August 29, 1900, pp. 3–5. See also *Coca-Cola News*, May 15, 1898, CAH, Drugs, box 10.

PAGE 186   Van Camp's sampling: "Advertising by Sample," pp. 20–23. "Enormously extravagant": p. 20.

Quaker coupons: "21,071,199 Free Coupons," *GR*, April 1912, p. 118.

Star sampling and coupons: Lambert, "How Procter and Gamble," pp. 6–8. "A sizable proportion": p. 8.

PAGE 187   Chase and Sanborn retailer premiums: Paul M. Angle, "My Father's Grocery Store," *American Heritage*, August 1963, p. 35. Colgate barbers' premium catalogue: *Colgate's Barbers' Premium List*, CAH, Soap. Wrigley premiums: see cards offering premiums in CAH, Chewing Gum. Knox contest: Charles B. Knox, *Anaconda, the Fastest Race Horse in the World* (Johnstown, N.Y., 1903), CAH, Food.

PAGE 188   "For a valuable (?) premium": *GR*, January 1905, p. 574.

"Dealer helps": Cherington definition: *ABF*, p. 127. For a six-day diary of the dealer literature received by a New Jersey druggist, see the article from *PI*, November 9, 1911, reprinted in *ABF*, pp. 135–40.

PAGE 189   *Dutch Boy Painter:* R. Bigelow Lockwood, in *A&S*, February 1911, reprinted in *ABF*, p. 302.

Standard Sanitary Manufacturing Company: "Advertising That Truly Creates," *PI*, April 25, 1906, pp. 9–10.

Department store windows: See Susan Porter Benson, *Counter Cultures: Saleswomen, Managers, and Customers in American Department Stores, 1890–1940* (Urbana: University of Illinois Press, 1986), pp. 18, 102; William R. Leach, "Transformations in a Culture of Consumption: Women and Department Stores, 1890–1925," *Journal of American History* 71 (September 1984): 322, 325.

Window trimmers' organizations: Leonard S. Marcus, *The American Store Window* (New York: Whitney Library of Design, 1978), pp. 12, 16.

Manufacturers' window displays: Victor Talking Machine: Ellis Hansen, in *PI*, January 19, 1911, reprinted in *ABF*, pp. 141–43. Shredded Wheat: Charles W. Hurd, "Color Display in the Dealer's Window and How It Pays," *PI*, May 28, 1914, pp. 23–26. Karo: Findlay, "Karo and the Premium Idea," p. 61.

PAGE 190   Display materials: Ingersoll: "General Publicity Sells Ingersolls,"

PI, June 13, 1906, p. 6. Bissell: "Special Easter Offer—Season 1903," CAH, Carpet Cleaners.

PAGE 191   Hoosier kitchen cabinets: Louis Henry Martin, "Interesting the Small Retailer," *PI,* July 21, 1910, pp. 47–48.

Iowa clothing-store owner: *PI,* November 26, 1914, reprinted in *FAB,* p. 110.

PAGE 193   "Is literally swamped": C. E. Wright, "Manufacturer's Advertising Matter from Retail View," *PI,* July 21, 1910, p. 30.

"Just as your bundle": Martin, "Interesting the Small Retailer," p. 48.

"Backward, unprogressive store": John Allen Underwood, "Building Sales Through Dealers' Selling Helps," *PI,* May 28, 1914, p. 4.

"Advertising and the Unappreciative Retailer": C. L. Greene, *PI,* July 14, 1910, pp. 24–25.

Retailer hostility: J. Walter Thompson weekly newsletter no. 18 (October 3, 1916), p. 5, J. Walter Thompson Archives. See also "Winning Over the Balky Dealer," *PI,* April 9, 1914, pp. 40–44.

"Bare faced attempts": "Rambler's Column," *GR,* March 1904, pp. 54–55.

PAGE 194   Display deterioration and smaller electros: American Sugar Refining Company, circular letters no. 52 (August 28, 1919) and no. 68 (April 27, 1920), in "Circular Letters, etc." (looseleaf binder), Baker Library, Harvard Graduate School of Business Administration.

Courting clerks: Morton: Morton Salt Company, *The Sales Manual,* from Morton Annual Convention, Chicago, January 1915, pp. 44–45. Heinz and Johnson & Johnson: Cameron McPherson, "What Advertisers Are Doing This Fall to Educate Dealers' Clerks," *PI,* November 2, 1916, pp. 95, 100. On booklets for clerks, see also "Advertisers' Endeavors to Improve Retail Salesmanship," *PI,* January 5, 1910, pp. 16–18.

PAGE 195   Heinz: Frederick W. Nash, in *PI,* November 23, 1911, reprinted in *ABF,* p. 308.

Rochester stove works: Arthur N. Day, "A Square Deal for the Retailers," *PI,* January 12, 1910, p. 8.

Morton sample dialogue: *Sales Manual,* pp. 31–32.

Coca-Cola workshops: James H. Collins, "Remarkable Proprietary Beverage," *PI,* November 4, 1908, p. 6.

Heinz workshops and stock work: Nash, reprinted in *ABF,* p. 308; G. D. Crain, Jr., "How the H. J. Heinz Company Links Up Advertising with Selling," *PI,* November 25, 1915, pp. 3, 5.

PAGE 196   Demonstrations: Heinz: Nash, reprinted in *ABF,* p. 308; "Demonstration, The Sale Clincher," *PI,* March 6, 1913, p. 4. Morton: *Sales Manual,* pp. 29–30. Domino: American Sugar Refining Company, circular letters no. 63 (March 2, 1920) and no. 93 (October 29, 1920), in "Circular Letters, etc." (looseleaf binder), Baker Library, Harvard Graduate School of Business Administration.

NCR training: See Roy W. Johnson and Russell W. Lynch, *The Sales Strategy of John H. Patterson, Founder of the National Cash Register Company,* Dartnell Corporation Sales Leaders Series (Chicago, 1932), pp. 142, 230–35, 257; "The National Cash Register Company," *PI*, February 14, 1900, p. 3.

Contests and conventions: See Walter H. Cottingham, "Using Contests to Spur on Salesmen," in A. W. Shaw Company, *Salesmanship and Sales Management*, Library of Sales and Advertising, vol. 1 (Chicago, 1914), pp. 93–108; Herbert F. DeBower and John G. Jones, "Sales Management," part 3 of *Marketing Methods and Salesmanship*, Modern Business, vol. 3 (New York: Alexander Hamilton Institute, 1914), pp. 492–99, 502–8; Charles Wilson Hoyt, *Scientific Sales Management* (New York: George B. Woolson, 1912), pp. 115–30, 89–94; W. C. Holman, "Making a Sales Convention Pay," in Shaw, *Salesmanship and Sales Management*, pp. 116–27. On general issues of salesman morale, see Susan Strasser, "The Smile That Pays: The Culture of Traveling Salesmen, 1880–1920," in R. Jackson Wilson, ed., *Essays in American Culture and Society* (Belmont, Calif.: Wadsworth, 1991).

PAGE 197   Heinz convention: *Pickles*, International Convention Number (February 1902), CAH, Foods. "Only enough men": p. 5; "there was more enthusiasm": p. 7.

PAGE 198   One manual on sales management: DeBower and Jones, "Sales Management," p. 509.

"To form habits and tastes": Johnson and Lynch, *Sales Strategy*, 69–70; see also Samuel Crowther, *John H. Patterson: Pioneer in Industrial Welfare* (Garden City, N.Y.: Garden City Publishing Co., 1926), pp. 234–35.

Expense accounts: See Wilbur Elijah Castelow, *Only a Drummer: A Short History of the Commercial Travelling Salesman's Life* (n.p.: privately published, 1903), pp. 24–25; Hoyt, *Scientific Sales Management*, pp. 157–62; W. A. Waterbury, "Points to Watch in the Expense Account," in Shaw, *Salesmanship and Sales Management*, pp. 109–15.

PAGE 199   "The most wonderful merchandising machine": E. B. Merritt, "How Armour & Co. Are Solving Their Vast Selling Problem," *PI*, January 23, 1913, p. 4; see also "Reasons Back of Armour's Selling Policies," *PI*, February 27, 1913, p. 6.

Sales force size: See "Should the Credit Man Travel—a Reply," *SC*, December 1909, pp. 383–84.

Reports and surveillance systems: See W. A. Waterbury, "Guiding Salesmen by Map and Tack," in A. W. Shaw Company, *Selling Methods*, Library of Sales and Advertising, vol. 4 (Chicago, 1914), pp. 137–46; B. C. Bean, "What Your Salesmen Should Report," *ibid.*, pp. 153–59; Debower and Jones, "Sales Management," pp. 473–79.

"Usually the ruction is started": Roy B. Simpson, "Who Shall Be the Advertising Boss?" *PI*, August 25, 1910, p. 3.

"Ninety-nine per cent": F. Manning, "Why Sales and Advertising Managerships Should Be One," *PI*, September 29, 1910, p. 6.

Advertising and Selling writer: Herbert Mildrum, "Unity of Effort in Selling and Advertising," *A&S*, February 1913, pp. 58, 54, 56.

DeWeese: Truman A. DeWeese, "The Advertising Manager," *PI,* July 14, 1910, p. 141.

PAGE 200   Calkins: Earnest Elmo Calkins, "Eliminating the Jobber," *PI,* May 31, 1905, p. 11.

"The Old Idea": R. M. Nicholson, "How Advertising Helps the Salesman," *SC,* March 1909, p. 146.

"Different modes": Arch W. Shaw, "Some Problems in Market Distribution," *Quarterly Journal of Economics* 26 (August 1912): 741.

Chalmers: Hugh Chalmers, "Relation of Salesmanship to Advertising," *SC,* December 1909, p. 369.

PAGE 201   Advertising agents and conventions: James H. Collins, "Advertising and the Sales Plan," *PI,* January 19, 1910, p. 4. See also Charles Wilson Hoyt, "Practical Team Work with Salesmen," *PI,* July 14, 1910, pp. 26–29; J. Walter Thompson weekly newsletter no. 23 (November 6, 1916), J. Walter Thompson Archives.

"Advertising increases the importance": N. W. Ayer and Son, *Advertising and the Salesman"* (Philadelphia, n.d. [distributed to Domino salesmen in 1920]), last page.

Local advertising and national campaigns: Dan A. Carroll, "Distribution and Selling Cost," *A&S,* July 1912, p. 18.

CHAPTER 7. THE NEW RETAILING

PAGE 203   Edison: "Edison on Selling and Advertising Patent Goods," *PI,* September 8, 1910, pp. 3–4.

PAGE 204   *Printers' Ink* writers: Charles W. Hurd and M. Zimmerman, "Why Advertisers Must Give Chain-Store Growth Their Serious Attention, I," *PI,* September 10, 1914, p. 3.

"The old dicker and bargain policy": Nystrom, *Economics of Retailing,* p. 192.

PAGE 206   A. T. Stewart: Harry E. Resseguie, "Alexander Turney Stewart and the Development of the Department Store, 1823–1876," *Business History Review* 39 (Autumn 1965): 301–22. See also Deborah S. Gardner, " 'A Paradise of Fashion': A. T. Stewart's Department Store, 1862–1875," in Joan M. Jensen and Sue Davidson, eds., *A Needle, a Bobbin, a Strike: Women Needleworkers in America* (Philadelphia: Temple University Press, 1985), pp. 60–80. "Although I realize": quoted in Resseguie, p. 308. "Not one of them has his discretion": quoted in Resseguie, p. 314.

PAGE 207   Macy's: Hower, *History of Macy's,* pp. 50, 100, 105–6.

Departments: See Nystrom, *Economics of Retailing,* p. 205.

Macy's mail order: Emmet and Jeuck, *Catalogues and Counters,* pp. 22, 164–67.

Centralization: Benson, *Counter Cultures,* pp. 16–17.

"Mass encounters": Neil Harris, "Museums, Merchandising, and Popular Taste: The Struggle for Influence," in Ian M. G. Quimby, *Material Culture and the Study of American Life* (New York: W. W. Norton, 1978), p. 149.

PAGE 209   Lighting and display: William R. Leach, "Transformations in a

Culture of Consumption: Women and Department Stores, 1890–1925," *Journal of American History* 71 (September 1984): 19.

New services: Benson, *Counter Cultures*, p. 20; Leach, "Transformations," pp. 329–30; Nystrom, *Economics of Retailing*, p. 199.

PAGE 210   Telephone service: Alphonsus P. Haire, "The Telephone in Retail Business," *PI*, November 27, 1907, p. 8.

Department store size: Susan Porter Benson, "Palace of Consumption and Machine for Selling: The American Department Store, 1880–1940," *Radical History Review* 21 (Fall 1979): 200–201.

Women workers: Benson, *Counter Cultures*, pp. 23–24.

"A wonderful business mechanism": Nystrom, *Economics of Retailing*, p. 208.

Four thousand stores: *ABF*, p. 158.

"Specific, concrete presentation": Nystrom, *Economics of Retailing*, p. 201.

Advertising allowances: F. Beale, Jr., "What I Would Do as a Manufacturer if I Were Seeking Department-Store Co-operation," *PI*, January 22, 1915, p. 54. For examples of cooperative advertising in the early 1920s, see American Sugar Refining Company, "Circular Letters, etc." (looseleaf binder), Baker Library, Harvard Graduate School of Business Administration.

PAGE 211   One large store: Beale, "What I Would Do," p. 58.

PAGE 212   "Here was an organization": Edna Ferber, *Fanny Herself* (New York: Frederick A. Stokes Co., 1917), p. 115.

"Our business": Montgomery Ward and Company, *Catalogue and Buyers Guide No. 56* (Fall and Winter 1894–95), p. 1.

Montgomery Ward history: Emmet and Jeuck, *Catalogues and Counters*, pp. 20–21.

PAGE 213   Sears's early history: Emmet and Jeuck, *Catalogues*, pp. 36–37, 47.

"Nearly everything in merchandise": Fred L. Israel, ed., *1897 Sears Roebuck Catalogue* (New York: Chelsea House, 1968), p. 786.

Sears determined to "Iowa-ize": Emmet and Jeuck, *Catalogues and Counters*, p. 92–96.

Sears's manufacturing plants: Emmet and Jeuck, *Catalogues*, pp. 119, 241–42.

PAGE 214   New plant: "A Great Mail-Order Plant," *PI*, April 18, 1906, pp. 20–23.

Scheduling system: Emmet and Jeuck, *Catalogues and Counters*, pp. 132–36.

Customer classification: Emmet and Jeuck, *Catalogues*, pp. 461–64.

Mail-order card files: T. H. Price, *The Outlook*, January 26, 1916, quoted in C. S. Duncan, *Commercial Research: An Outline of Working Principles* (New York: Macmillan Co., 1920), p. 165.

PAGE 215   Mailing lists: See advertisement from Rapid Addressing Machine Company, *AG*, January 13, 1892, p. 29.

Spiegel and Larkin: Emmet and Jeuck, *Catalogues and Counters*, pp. 22, 274.

Larkin: See "Larkin's Latest Mail Order Scheme," *GM*, March 1912, p. 9; Larkin materials: CAH, Premiums, and CAH, Food.

Opposition to department stores: Hower, *History of Macy's,* p. 156; Chandler, *Visible Hand,* p. 229.

Sears and Ward catalogue copy: Emmet and Jeuck, *Catalogues and Counters,* p. 160

PAGE 216 " 'Tainted' dry goods": "William Allen White on the Mail Order House," *SC,* November 1909, p. 319.

"Many people object": Joseph J. Schroeder, Jr., ed., *Sears, Roebuck & Co., 1908 Catalogue No. 117, The Great Price Maker* (Chicago: Follett, 1969), p. 8; see also Stanley C. Hollander, *History of Labels* (New York: Allen Hollander Co., 1956), p. 36.

PAGE 217 Parcel-post legislation: Wayne E. Fuller, *RFD: The Changing Face of Rural America* (Bloomington: Indiana University Press, 1964), pp. 199–227. "Likely to change fundamentally": Quoted in Boorstin, *The Americans,* p. 134. "Severe blow": "Relating to Merchandise Parcel Post," *Iron Age,* reprinted in *SC,* March 1909, p. 149.

Protests against mail-order trade: Larkin in "Fight Premium House," *GR,* January 1910, p. 634; Cedar Falls in "A Mail Order Bonfire," *GM,* April 1912, p. 8; Peabody, Kansas, in "Some Live Wire Retailers," *GM,* May 1912, p. 26. See also Emmet and Jeuck, *Catalogues and Counters,* p. 151.

PAGE 219 Ada, Minnesota: Weld, *Social and Economic Survey,* pp. 65–66.

New Haven, Connecticut: L. D. H. Weld, *Marketing Survey of New Haven, Conducted for the Town and City Improvement Committee of the New Haven Chamber of Commerce* (New Haven, n.d. [1917]), p. 47.

"From the perspective": Emmet and Jeuck, *Catalogues and Counters,* p. 150.

PAGE 221 "Rearguard actions": Boorstin, *The Americans,* p. 111.

Opposition to chain stores: See F. J. Harper, " 'A New Battle on Evolution': The Anti-Chain Store Trade-at-Home Agitation of 1929–1930," *Journal of American Studies* 16 (December 1982): 407–26; Carl G. Ryant, "The South and the Movement Against Chain Stores," *Journal of Southern History* 39 (May 1973): 207–22; Ryant, "Kentucky and the Movement to Regulate Chain Stores, 1925–1945," *Filson Club History Quarterly* 57 (July 1983): 270–85; Emmet and Jeuck, *Catalogues and Counters,* pp. 606–21; Lebhar, *Chain Stores,* pp. 159–60.

Henderson: Harper, " 'A New Battle on Evolution,' " pp. 413–18.

PAGE 222 "Elaborately casual publicity program": M. A. Adelman, *A&P: A Study in Price-Cost Behavior and Public Policy* (Cambridge: Harvard University Press, 1966), p. 80. See also Lebhar, *Chain Stores,* p. 169; Joseph Cornwall Palamountain, Jr., *The Politics of Distribution* (Cambridge: Harvard University Press, 1955), pp. 172–73; Richard S. Tedlow, *Keeping the Corporate Image: Public Relations and Business, 1900–1950* (Greenwich, Conn.: JAI Press, 1979), pp. 91–96.

Chain statistics: Harper, " 'A New Battle on Evolution,' " p. 407; Federal Trade Commission, *Chain Stores: Final Report on the Chain-Store Investigation* (Washington: Government Printing Office, 1935), pp. 4, 5. These figures are more conservative than those in M. M. Zimmerman, *The Challenge of Chain Store Distribution* (New York: Harper, 1931), pp. 10, 12.

A & P history: Roy J. Bullock, "The Early History of the Great Atlantic & Pacific Tea Company," *HBR* 11 (April 1933): 298; Bullock, "A History of the Great Atlantic & Pacific Tea Company Since 1878," *HBR* 12 (October 1933): 59–69. See also Lebhar, *Chain Stores,* chap. 2, "The Birth of the System."

Kroger and Woolworth's: Lebhar, *Chain Stores,* pp. 25, 35.

PAGE 223   Wall Street interests: Charles W. Hurd and M. M. Zimmerman, "Chain Store Advantages in Organization and Financing, VII," *PI,* October 29, 1914, p. 78.

PAGE 224   Freericks testimony: V. T. Robinson, "What Are We Advertising For Anyhow?" *GR,* May 1912, pp. 141–52. Freericks quotations: p. 141; Robinson response: p. 152. See also excerpts from Freericks's testimony in "Methods of the Great Retail Combines," *GM,* May 1912, pp. 17–18.

Traveling system: Charles W. Hurd, "How Shall the Advertiser Regard the Newly Forming Chains?" *PI,* December 28, 1916, pp. 88–89; see also Bullock, "Great Atlantic & Pacific Tea Company Since 1878," p. 62.

McDonald's: McDonald's had about 7,500 American stores in 1988, according to a company spokesperson interviewed by Ernestine Kimbro of The Evergreen State College library, May 11, 1988.

Other chains abolish credit and delivery: Hurd, "How Shall the Advertiser," pp. 88–101.

Chain numbers and fields: Charles W. Hurd and M. M. Zimmerman, "Taking the Chains by Fields and Their Number in Each, V," *PI,* October 15, 1914, pp. 71, 76, 78, 82; Hurd and Zimmerman, "How the Chains Are Taking Over the Retail Field, IV," *PI,* October 8, 1914, p. 35. See also Hurd and Zimmerman, "Chains Picking Up the Best Sites in Retail Field, IX," *PI,* November 12, 1914, p. 61.

PAGE 225   Low-cost labor: Charles W. Hurd and M. M. Zimmerman, "How Big Retailers' Chains Outsell Independent Competitors, XI," *PI,* November 26, 1914, pp. 73–74.

High stock turn: Hurd and Zimmerman, "How Big Retailers' Chains, XI," pp. 66–68.

PAGE 226   Chain locations: Hurd and Zimmerman, "Chains Picking Up the Best Sites, IX," *PI,* November 12, 1914, pp. 58–62; Childs: p. 58; United Cigars: pp. 62, 58; Hurd and Zimmerman, "How Big Retailers' Chains, XI," p. 76.

Vertical integration: United Drug Company: Hurd and Zimmerman, "Taking the Chains, V," p. 80; Sears: Emmet and Jeuck, *Catalogues and Counters,* p. 76; Kroger: Hurd and Zimmerman, "How the Chains, IV," pp. 38, 41.

PAGE 227   Discounts and payments: Charles W. Hurd and M. M. Zimmerman, "Chains Outclass Individual Dealers in Buying Advantages, X," *PI,* November 19, 1914, p. 64.

Cream of Wheat charges: Bullock, "Great Atlantic & Pacific Tea Company Since 1878," p. 66.

Price cutting: Hurd and Zimmerman, "How the Chains, IV," p. 37, and

"How Big Retailers' Chains, XI," pp. 70, 72. "Pronounced price cutters": Hurd and Zimmerman, "Taking the Chains, V," p. 79.

PAGE 228 "Commercial debauchery": R. E. Shanamon, "The Bissell Sweeper Success at Maintaining Price," *PI,* January 19, 1910, p. 30.

PAGE 229 Heinz: G. D. Crain, Jr., "How the H.J. Heinz Company Links Up Advertising with Selling," *PI,* November 25, 1915, p. 8.

H. H. Good and Bon Ami representative: Charles W. Hurd and M. M. Zimmerman, "Why Advertisers and Dealers See Danger in Chain Stores, II," *PI,* September 17, 1914, pp. 72–73.

"Nothing less than 'revolution' ": Charles W. Hurd and M. M. Zimmerman, "Why Advertisers and Dealers See Danger in Chain Stores, III," *PI,* September 24, 1914, p. 22.

Jobbers' chains: Hurd and Zimmerman, "Taking the Chains, V," p. 76; Nystrom, *Economics of Retailing,* pp. 220–21.

1919 chain statistics: Harper, " 'A New Battle on Evolution,' " p. 407.

PAGE 230 1923 chain statistics: Paul H. Nystrom, "An Estimate of the Volume of Retail Business in the United States," *HBR* 3 (January 1925), reprinted in Bloomfield, *Trends in Retail Distribution,* pp. 68–69.

"A price attached to every article": "Is a Price Mark Desirable?" *AG,* July 28, 1909, p. 8.

"Air of prosperity": "The Growing Use of Price-Cards," *GM,* July 1912.

Price-placard photograph: Butler Brothers, *Success in Retailing: The Variety Business. A Handbook for Earnest Beginners in Merchandising* (New York, 1910), p. 196; Butler Brothers, *Success in Retailing* (1920), p. 180.

Secret price marks: Butler Brothers, *Success in Retailing* (1910), p. 132; (1920), pp. 122–23.

PAGE 231 Stock-turn advice: Butler Brothers, *The Butler Way System Book* (New York, 1916), p. 166; "Chart Eight—How to Make Money," in Brown Shoe Company, *Manual for Salesmen* (St. Louis, 1917), p. 11. Life Savers: Hotchkiss and Franken, *Leadership of Advertised Brands,* p. 88.

Stock records difficulties: Harvard University Bureau of Business Research, *Expenses in Operating Retail Grocery Stores,* Bulletin no. 5 (Cambridge: Harvard University Press, 1915), p. 14.

Commercial manuals: See Eugene Herz, *Controlling Profits: Simplified Efficiency Methods in Store Record Keeping* (Chicago: Laird & Lee, 1917), pp. 13ff.; System Company, *Business Man's Brain Partners,* pp. 132–34.

PAGE 232 Sales slips: Herz, *Controlling Profits,* pp. 5, 27. See also J. C. Walker, *Retail Accounting and Store Management,* Twentieth Century Bookkeeping Series (Cincinnati: South-Western Publishing, 1916), p. 45.

Abell speech: W. T. Abell, "Address to the Retail Grocers' Association of Philadelphia," *GR,* October 1912. "To make claims": p. 538; "every hour . . . every few minutes": pp. 536–37; "habit hard to form": p. 536.

Ingersoll and FTC accounting systems: *PI,* December 17, 1914, reprinted in *FAB,* p. 161; FTC, *System of Accounts.*

"This Course is not for John Wanamaker": A. W. Shaw Company, *A Course in Retail Merchandising* (Chicago, 1916), vol. 1, lecture 5, "Cash Records That Safeguard the Cash," p. 1.

PAGE 233   "A concrete method": Shaw, *Course in Retail Merchandising*, vol. 1, lecture 1, "Starting a System of Store Records," p. 5.

"Banks are paying more and more attention": FTC, *System of Accounts*, p. 5.

Insurance: Butler Brothers, *System Book*, pp. 100, 106; Herz, *Controlling Profits*, p. 40; Walker, *Retail Accounting*, p. 2.

PAGE 235   Credit rating: Butler Brothers, *System Book*, pp. 97–98.

"Just as soon as you start into business": Butler Brothers, *Success in Retailing* (1910), p. 114; (1920), p. 107.

"Sharks": T. C. Henry, *Tricks of the Cash Register Trust* (Winchester, Ky.: privately printed, 1913), p. 17.

Price of expensive models: Henry, *Tricks*, p. 37; Butler Brothers, *Success in Retailing* (1910), p. 115; (1920), p. 107.

McCann essay: E. C. McCann, "Meeting the Price Argument," in Beech-Nut Packing Company, *Bring Home the Beech-Nut* (Canajoharie, N.Y., 1923), pp. 11, 15.

PAGE 236   Patterson's "Don'ts": Crowther, *John H. Patterson*, p. 116.

"System department": Henry, *Tricks*, p. 9.

PAGE 237   Clerks' rebellion: Johnson and Lynch, *Sales Strategy of John H. Patterson*, pp. 83–87, 99, 101.

Where Have My Profits Gone?: Abell, "Address to the Retail Grocers' Association," p. 541.

PAGE 238   Burroughs: Burroughs Adding Machine Company, System Service Bureau, *The Retail Field*, reprinted from sales bulletin of August 4, 1913; *Applying Mechanical Methods to Store Accounting*, n.d. These and other materials are described or contained in binder in Baker Library, Harvard Graduate School of Business Administration.

Joseph R. Peebles: *Peebles Every Month*, March 1901, p. iii, CAH, Food.

One 1913 text: James Edward Hagerty, *Mercantile Credit* (New York: Henry Holt, 1913), p. 82.

Delivery services: W. W. Loomis, "How Quicker Deliveries Met Competition," in Shaw, *Selling Methods*, pp. 121–28.

PAGE 239   Credit: See, for example, "Credit Is Lending" and "Facts to be Remembered," *GR*, November 1904, pp. 454–56; "Making Better Customers by Making Better Dealers," *PI*, May 21, 1914, p. 10.

PAGE 241   Butler Brothers on credit: "One of the great advantages": *Success in Retailing* (1910), p. 137; (1920), p. 128. "In spite of the current belief": (1910), p. 159; (1920), p. 149. "Would send his ready cash": (1910), p. 139; (1920), p. 129.

Where Have My Profits Gone?: Described in Abell, "Address to the Retail Grocers' Association," p. 542.

Abell on credit: Abell, "Address," p. 542.

PAGE 242   Early store premiums and trading stamps: See Harvey L. Veedenburg, *Trading Stamps,* Indiana University School of Business, Bureau of Business Research, Indiana Business Report no. 21 (Bloomington, 1956).

Thomas Sperry's widow: Sperry and Hutchinson Company, *Twenty-Fifth Anniversary* (New York, n.d. [1921]), p. 13.

Sears and Ward premiums: Emmet and Jeuck, *Catalogues and Counters,* pp. 77–78.

Blue stamp riot: "The Bursting of the Bubble," *Fame,* May 1905, p. 100; see also "Collapse After Women Stamp Holders' Run," *NYT,* April 21, 1905, p. 1.

Opposition to stamps: See S. Westerfeld, "The Trading Stamp Evil as Affecting Both Retailer and Consumer," *GR,* May 1904, pp. 138–44; R. F. Cook, "Is the Retail Merchant Responsible for the Continued Existence of the Trading Stamp?" *GR,* November 1904, pp. 470–74.

PAGE 243   Union protests: "Unions Join Merchants," *GR,* March 1904, p. 19; notes on New York City and Scranton Central Labor Council resolutions in *GR,* May 1904, pp. 125–26.

PAGE 244   Philadelphia Retail Grocers' Association: "In Re: Trading Stamps," *GR,* May 1904, pp. 152–54.

"Laws have been passed": "The Manufacturing Jobber," *AG,* December 7, 1910, p. 6.

Department stores: I. M. Rubinow, "Premiums in Retail Trade," *Journal of Political Economy* 13 (September 1905): 584; see also S & H, *Twenty-Fifth Anniversary, passim.*

PAGE 245   S & H 1910 stamp book: CAH, Trading Stamps.

S&H in 1921: S & H, *Twenty-Fifth Anniversary,* p. 39.

PAGE 246   *Merchants' Record and Show Window:* Bird, *Sales Plans,* pp. 265, 133, 216. "Perfected advertising machinery": p. 74; Christmas chapters: pp. 74–86.

The "very first thing": Butler Brothers, *Success in Retailing* (1910), p. 157; (1920), p. 147.

Harvard Bureau of Business Research: Harvard Bureau of Business Research, *Management Problems,* p. 37.

PAGE 248   *Success in Retailing* on basements: Butler Brothers, *Success in Retailing* (1910), pp. 151–52.

Department store space and display: Benson, "Palace of Consumption," pp. 200–201, 215–16.

Bailey on store fixtures: Marshall J. Bailey, "Making Store Fixtures Sell," in Shaw, *Selling Methods,* p. 120.

American Grocer on customers' liberty: "Is a Price Mark Desirable?" p. 8.

Piggly Wiggly: M. M. Zimmerman, *The Supermarket: A Revolution in Distribution* (New York: McGraw-Hill, 1955), pp. 21–24; David B. Sicilia, "The Origins of the Supermarket, 1930–1945," unpublished manuscript, p. 7; Lebhar, *Chain Stores,* p. 31n.

PAGE 251   "The cemetery of the independent tobacconists": Hurd and Zimmerman, "Why Advertisers and Dealers, III," p. 26.

CHAPTER 8. THE POLITICS OF PACKAGED PRODUCTS

PAGE 253   Addams and Tarbell: See *LHJ*, January 1913, pp. 24–25, for the inauguration of their columns.

Progress and Progressivism: Daniel T. Rodgers, "In Search of Progressivism," *Reviews in American History* 10 (December 1982): 127n.; Clark Chambers, "The Belief in Progress in Twentieth-Century America," *Journal of the History of Ideas* 19 (April 1958): 197–204; Raymond Williams, *Keywords: A Vocabulary of Culture and Society,* rev. ed. (New York: Oxford University Press, 1983), pp. 146–47, 243–45.

PAGE 254   Early state food and drug regulation: See Mitchell Okun, *Fair Play in the Marketplace: The First Battle for Pure Food and Drugs* (Dekalb: Northern Illinois University Press, 1986).

PAGE 255   Ellen Richards: Quoted in Peter Edward Samson, "The Emergence of a Consumer Interest in America, 1870–1930" (Ph.D. diss., University of Chicago, 1980), p. 38.

PAGE 256   Wiley: See Oscar E. Anderson, Jr., *The Health of a Nation: Harvey W. Wiley and the Fight for Pure Food* (Chicago: University of Chicago Press, 1958).

Bills before the 1906 law: For a description of federal legislative efforts, see Gustavus A. Weber, *The Food, Drug, and Insecticide Administration: Its History, Activities, and Organization,* Institute for Government Research Service Monographs of the U.S. Government, no. 50 (Baltimore: Johns Hopkins University Press, 1928), pp. 7–10.

"Accursed passion": Donna J. Wood, "The Strategic Use of Public Policy: Business Support for the 1906 Food and Drug Act," *Business History Review* 59 (Autumn 1985): 409.

PAGE 257   "What is Ariosa Coffee?": *New York Analyst,* June 15, 1885, quoted in Samson, "Emergence of a Consumer Interest," p. 56.

Sinclair: Upton Sinclair, "The Condemned-Meat Industry: A Reply to Mr. J. Ogden Armour," reprinted in Harvey Swados, *Years of Conscience: The Muckrakers* (New York: World Publishing, 1962), pp. 255, 247–49.

Philadelphia grocers: "Rambler's Column," *GR*, March 1904, p. 54.

"All our pure food laws": Edward Marshall, "Modern Women vs. Grandmothers: Mrs. Julian Heath with Some Emphasis Replies to Mr. George W. Perkins's Criticism of Housewives," *NYT*, February 28, 1915, sec. 5, p. 16.

Manufacturer support for food and drug law: Wood, "Strategic Use of Public Policy"; Robert H. Wiebe, *The Search for Order, 1877–1920* (New York: Hill & Wang, 1967), p. 191; Gabriel Kolko, *The Triumph of Conservatism: A Reinterpretation of American History, 1900–1916* (Chicago: Quadrangle Books, 1963), pp. 103, 108–9.

Historians on regulation: See esp. Kolko, *Triumph of Conservatism;* Wiebe, *Search for Order;* Martin J. Sklar, *The Corporate Reconstruction of American Capitalism, 1890–1916: The Market, the Law, and Politics* (Cambridge: Cambridge University Press, 1988); James Weinstein, *The Corporate Ideal in the Liberal State,*

1900–1918 (Boston: Beacon Press, 1968); Robert H. Wiebe, *Businessmen and Reform: A Study of the Progressive Movement* (Chicago: Quadrangle Books, 1962). **PAGE** 258   Conflicts over regulation: Thomas K. McCraw, *Prophets of Regulation: Charles Francis Adams, Louis D. Brandeis, James M. Landis, Alfred E. Kahn* (Cambridge: Harvard University Press, 1984), p. 67; Martin J. Sklar, "The Corporate Reconstruction of American Society, 1896–1914: The Market and the Law" (Ph.D. diss., University of Rochester, 1982), p. 23. "Indeed, such differences": Sklar, *Corporate Reconstruction,* p. 16.

Butter and margarine: Jack High and Clayton A. Coppin, "Wiley and the Whiskey Industry: Strategic Behavior in the Passage of the Pure Food Act," *Business History Review* 62 (Summer 1988): 289.

Manufacturer opposition: See Vivek Bammi, "Nutrition, the Historian, and Public Policy: A Case Study of U.S. Nutrition Policy in the 20th Century," *Journal of Social History* 14 (Summer 1981): 630.

National Association of Manufacturers: Wiebe, *Businessmen and Reform,* p. 49. **PAGE** 259   Manufacturer lobbying: See Sheldon Hochheiser, "The Evolution of U.S. Food Color Standards, 1913–1919," *Agricultural History* 55 (October 1981): 385–86.

Remsen Board: Anderson, *Health of a Nation,* 210ff., 257, 270; Weber, *Food, Drug, and Insecticide Administration,* pp. 18–19. **PAGE** 260   "He was hampered and restrained": "Dr. Wiley Enters Politics," *NYT,* October 4, 1912, p. 12.

"None will regret": "Dr. Harvey W. Wiley Resigns," *GR,* April 1912, p. 56.

Bulk vs. packaged foods: See Harvard Bureau of Business Research, *Management Problems,* pp. 31–32.

Acme Hominy: Ernest Cohn, "Reaching the Dealer over the Consumer's Shoulder," *PI,* March 27, 1913, pp. 3–6. "To create in the public's mind": p. 4. **PAGE** 262   Weights and measures exhibits: Samson, "Emergence of a Consumer Interest," pp. 107–9. **PAGE** 263   Chicago city official: Quoted in Samson, "Emergence," p. 105.

Philadelphia bureau officer: Quoted in Samson, "Emergence," p. 110. **PAGE** 264   Mayor's Committee on Food Supply: Samson, "Emergence," p. 126. On home economists, see Strasser, *Never Done,* pp. 256–57. **PAGE** 265   "BUY IN BULK—NOT IN PACKAGE": *PI,* January 28, 1915, reprinted in *FAB,* pp. 3–5.

Calkins, DeWeese, and Musher responses: *PI,* February 4, 1915, reprinted in *FAB,* pp. 500–501. **PAGE** 266   Housewives' League resolution: "Women for Package Food," *NYT,* February 2, 1915, p. 12. For league responses to Food Supply Committee, see also *PI,* February 11, 1915, reprinted in *FAB,* pp. 6–8; Marshall, "Modern Women vs. Grandmothers," pp. 16–18.

Mrs. Julian Heath: Samson, "Emergence of a Consumer Interest," p. 158. Samson analyzes the league's by relying on its own publications, pp. 158–78.

New York Times report: "Women Will Rout Crooked Tradesmen," *NYT,* December 18, 1911, p. 5.

Sunday *Times* Heath interview: Edward Marshall, "Women Can Force Cost of Living Down if They Wish," *NYT,* January 28, 1912, sec. 5, p. 2.

PAGE 267 *Ladies' Home Journal* article: Mrs. Julian Heath, "How Housewives Waste Money," *LHJ,* February 1913, p. 83.

Annals article: Mrs. Julian Heath, "Work of the Housewives' League," American Academy of Political and Social Science, *Annals* 48 (July 1913): 122.

"We housewives are learning": "750,000 Women Leagued for Better Housekeeping," *NYT,* November 8, 1914, sec. 5, p. 6.

PAGE 268 "I, too, talked scornfully": Marshall, "Modern Women vs. Grandmothers," p. 16.

Charges and hearings: Articles in *NYT:* "Housewives' League Near Serious Split," November 17, 1915, p. 11; "Housewives Agree to Hear Mrs. Heath," November 19, 1915, p. 7; "Lawyers in a Tilt in Housewives' Case," December 21, 1915, p. 4; "Counsel Won't Let Mrs. Heath Testify," December 28, 1915, p. 6; "Housewives Clash at End of Hearing," January 5, 1916, p. 10; "Mrs. Heath Victor in Housewives' Fight," May 9, 1916, p. 7; "Question Mrs. Heath," January 4, 1918, p. 9; "Mrs. Heath Won't Resign," June 28, 1918, p. 11; "Will Mrs. Heath Resign?" July 3, 1918, p. 9; "Mrs. Heath Refuses to Quit the League," July 16, 1918, p. 20.

"A dead organization": "O'Malley Suspects Day," *NYT,* December 13, 1919, p. 6; see also "Hirshfield Seeks Quinn Market Data," *NYT,* December 12, 1919, p. 14.

PAGE 269 Christine Frederick on household efficiency: See Strasser, *Never Done,* pp. 214–19, 246–50.

Frederick testimony: U.S., House of Representatives, Committee on the Judiciary, *Hearings on Trust Legislation,* 63rd Cong., 2nd sess., February 1914, pp. 725–33. "I am here as a consumer": p. 728. See also "Hits at Bargain Follies," *NYT,* February 19, 1914, p. 11.

PAGE 270 "I thought that the best way": *Hearings on Trust Legislation,* p. 731; "When a dealer offers me three cans": p. 727; "Staples like bread": p. 728.

PAGE 271 Paul Cherington: *ABF,* p. 404.

PAGE 272 Daniel Pope: Pope, *Making of Modern Advertising,* p. 104.

Kellogg testimony: *Hearings on Trust Legislation,"* pp. 544–45.

"The average grocer": Advertisement in *AG,* July 28, 1909, p. 14.

December announcement of terms: "Kellogg Toasted Corn Flake Co.," *AG,* December 8, 1909, p. 12.

PAGE 274 "Heat for a moment": See, for example, "The Sweet Heart of the Corn," CAH, Cereals.

"Because they work cheap": Porter and Livesay, *Merchants and Manufacturers,* p. 215. Company warehouses: p. 217.

"There is a strong feeling": Raymond W. Gage, "The Mix-Up, Centering About the Jobber," *PI,* September 22, 1910, p. 31.

Other companies' selling terms: Diamond Match and Babbitt Soap: Gage,

"Mix-Up," pp. 30–31. Post: See postcard listing terms, "From March 15, 1912, to April 30, 1912," CAH, Cereal. Fairbank: "The Fairbank Co. Selling Plans," *AG,* July 28, 1909, p. 14.

PAGE 277   List of company policies: "Table of Prices on Articles Sold with and Without Price Maintenance," *PI,* June 27, 1912, reprinted in *ABF,* pp. 386–90.

"Uncle Sam": A. Rowden King, "The License Plan of Price Protection on Patent Goods," *PI,* July 21, 1910, p. 3.

Gillette: King, "The License Plan," pp. 5–6. On licenses, see also Waldemar Kaempffert, "Necessity of Fixed Prices in National Selling, II," *PI,* January 30, 1913, pp. 114–19.

Blade resharpening; Kaempffert, "Necessity of Fixed Prices, II," p. 119.

PAGE 278   Dr. Miles decision: Quoted in *ABF,* pp. 410–11.

Printers' Ink on Dr. Miles: "The Fight for Protected Prices," *PI,* January 12, 1910, pp. 3–6. See also *ABF,* pp. 409–11, 415.

American Grocer on Kellogg and Dr. Miles: "Kellogg's Belief," *AG,* June 14, 1911, p. 19.

"Most ingenious of all": Waldemar Kaempffert, "Necessity of Fixed Prices in National Selling," *PI,* January 23, 1913, p. 124.

Notice on corn-flakes box: "Making Minimum Retail Prices Possible," *GM,* June 1912, p. 8; Kaempffert, "Necessity of Fixed Prices," pp. 124–25. On Dick case, see Kaempffert, "Necessity of Fixed Prices, II," pp. 112–14.

PAGE 280   "Deserving of warm praise": "For Protected Retail Prices," *GM,* October 1912, p. 7.

"The case is regarded": "Corn Flakes Trade Called a Monopoly," *NYT,* December 27, 1912, p. 12. See also the editorial "Price Fixing," *NYT,* December 27, 1912, p. 8.

"Said carton": "Petition in Equity," filed in Detroit, December 26, 1912, in District Court of the United States for the Eastern District of Michigan, Southern Division. The United States of America v. Kellogg Toasted Corn Flake Company, pp. 6–7.

"The things we aimed to accomplish" and George Batten vice-president: William H. Johns, "The Kellogg Side of the Government Suit," *PI,* January 2, 1913, p. 26.

PAGE 281   "Here we are confronted": "Kellogg Putting It Up to the Jobber," *PI,* January 23, 1913, p. 116. See also a similar appeal to jobbers a year later, in "Kellogg's Fight on Chain Stores," *PI,* September 17, 1914, p. 24.

Eastman: R. O. Eastman, "National Advertising on Trial in Kellogg Suit," *PI,* March 6, 1913, p. 28.

Thomas K. McCraw: McCraw, *Prophets of Regulation,* p. 102.

PAGE 282   Congressman Alben Barkley: Quoted in Pope, *Making of Modern Advertising,* pp. 103–4.

"We have been able to carry it so far": Quoted in Pope, *Modern Advertising,* p. 101.

Manufacturers' polls: Nystrom, *Economics of Retailing,* p. 262n. See also descriptions of the Kellogg and Kodak polls in articles reprinted from *PI* in *ABF*, pp. 396–98, 413–14.

Brandeis: Louis D. Brandeis, "Cutthroat Prices: The Competition That Kills," *Harper's Weekly*, November 15, 1913, p. 13. See also Brandeis, "On Maintaining Makers' Prices," *Harper's Weekly*, June 14, 1913, p. 6.

PAGE 283   Russell on tobacconist: Charles Edward Russell, "Lawless Wealth," in Swados, *Years of Conscience*, p. 99.

District court decision: Reprinted in "Dealers' Rights and the Manufacturers' Rights," *A&S*, August 1915, pp. 70–73.

Judge Lacombe: Quoted in Charles L. Miller, *Legal Status of the Maintenance of Uniform Resale Prices* (New York: American Fair Trade League, 1916), p. 18.

PAGE 284   "The history of the case": "Patents and Price Fixing," *NYT*, October 12, 1915, p. 10. See also "Can't Fix Resale Prices," *NYT*, April 16, 1915; "Answers Federal Suit," *NYT*, April 23, 1915, p. 14.

A Chicago patent lawyer: Rogers, *Good Will, Trade-Marks*, p. 260.

1988 Supreme Court decision: See Paula Dwyer, "A Red Flag for Red Tags," *Business Week*, May 16, 1988, p. 38.

CHAPTER 9. EPILOGUE

PAGE 286   Maytag and Maxwell House segmentation: Kathleen Deveny, "Maytag's New Girth Will Test Its Marketing Muscle," *Business Week*, February 16, 1987, pp. 68–72; Amy Dunkin, "Maxwell House Serves Up a Yuppie Brew," *Business Week*, March 2, 1987, p. 62.

Branded services: See Arlie Russell Hochschild, *The Managed Heart: Commercialization of Human Feeling* (Berkeley: University of California Press, 1983), pp. 90–98.

Branded produce: Thomas Whiteside, "C.E.O., TV," *New Yorker*, July 6, 1987, discusses Frank Perdue and his competitors; Richard W. Stevenson, "Bumper Crop of Brand Names," *NYT*, November 12, 1986, p. D1.

PAGE 287   Product image and development of needs: See William Leiss, "Needs, Exchanges, and the Fetishism of Objects," *Canadian Journal of Political and Social Theory* 2 (Fall 1978): 27–48; Stephen Kline and William Leiss, "Advertising, Needs, and 'Commodity Fetishism,' " *Canadian Journal of Political and Social Theory* 2 (Winter 1978); Jean Baudrillard, *For a Critique of the Political Economy of the Sign*, trans. Charles Levin (St. Louis: Telos Press, 1981); Kate Soper, *On Human Needs: Open and Closed Theories in a Marxist Perspective* (Atlantic Highlands, N.J.: Humanities Press, 1981); John Kenneth Galbraith, *The Affluent Society* (Boston: Houghton Mifflin, 1958); Daniel Horowitz, *The Morality of Spending: Attitudes Toward the Consumer Society in America, 1875–1940* (Baltimore: Johns Hopkins University Press, 1985); Stuart Ewen, *All Consuming Images: The Politics of Style in Contemporary Culture* (New York; Basic Books, 1988).

PAGE 288   Moral issues: Vance Packard, *The Hidden Persuaders* (New York: David McKay, 1957), p. 258.

Marketing influence and control: See Michael Schudson, *Advertising, the Un-*

easy Persuasion: Its Dubious Impact on American Society (New York: Basic Books, 1984).

PAGE 289   "Tangible cliques of producers": Harrison C. White, "Where Do Markets Come From?" *American Journal of Sociology* 87 (November 1981): 543–44.

PAGE 290   Paper products and cornflakes: I am indebted for this argument to an unpublished paper by Irwin Zuckerman, "A Suggestion for Needed Research on the Microeconomics of 'Excess Resource Consumption.'"

PICTURE CREDITS

IIⓒ3IIIIIIIIIIIⓒ3IIIIIIIIIIIⓒ3IIIIIIIIIIIⓒ3IIIIIIIIIIIⓒ3II

Baker Library, Harvard University: *pp. 47, 48, 49, 239.*
Chicago Tribune Company: *pp. 140, 141, 151, 152, 154.* ⓒ Copyrighted, Chicago Tribune Company, all rights reserved, used with permission.
Collection of Avertising History, Archives Center, National Museum of American History, Smithsonian Institution: *pp. 9, 13, 22, 31, 33, 34, 36, 39, 40, 41, 42, 46, 70, 71, 85, 90, 92, 98, 99, 100, 103, 104, 105, 106, 108, 110, 112, 114, 115, 116, 117, 118, 120, 122 top, 132, 135, 137, 142, 145, 162, 165, 166, 167, 169, 170, 172, 173, 174, 175, 179, 183, 185, 187, 188, 192, 197, 212, 218, 220, 223, 236, 237, 243, 244, 259, 261, 262, 275, 276.*
David R. Godine, Publisher: *pp. 24, 64, 65, 67, 94.* From *Prairie Fires and Paper Moons: The American Photographic Postcard, 1900–1920.* Copyright ⓒ 1981 by Hal Morgan and Andreas Brown. Reprinted by permission of David R. Godine, Publisher.
Historical Society of Seattle and King County: *p. 68.*
The Library of Congress: *pp. 7, 60, 62, 63, 76, 122 bottom, 130, 147, 177, 181, 182, 190, 209, 211, 216, 217, 234, 240, 245, 247, 250, 273, 279.*
Procter and Gamble Company: *p. 120.* Courtesy of The Procter & Gamble Company. Used with permission.
The Schlesinger Library, Radcliffe College: *pp. 4, 54, 96, 160.*
State Historical Society of Wisconsin: *pp. 16, 191, 214.*
University of Washington Libraries, Special Collections: *pp. 61* (photo by Asahel Curtis, neg. no. 16396), *66* (no photographer, neg. no. UW 5733), *127* (no photographer, neg. no. UW 9310), *205* (no photographer, neg. no. UW 5329), *264* (photo by James Lee, neg. no. 1117).
Wm. Wrigley Jr. Company: *pp. 142, 188.* Courtesy of the Wm. Wrigley Jr. Company.

INDEX

||||||||||C||||||||||

Page numbers in *italics* refer to illustrations.

ABOUT THE AUTHOR

Susan Strasser is the author of *Never Done: A History of American Housework* and co-author of *Washington: Images of a State's Heritage.* She has held fellowships from the Smithsonian Institution, the American Council of Learned Societies, the Bunting Institute at Radcliffe College, and the Harvard University School of Business Administration. For thirteen years she was a member of the faculty of The Evergreen State College. She has also taught at Princeton University and lectured at numerous colleges around the country. She lives in Washington, D.C.